Understanding Sybase ASE 15.7

Lionel Bolnet

Author
Lionel Bolnet

Printed with the help of
www.lulu.com

Table of contents

Preamble

The Author

Lionel Bolnet is a computer engineer who graduated from EFREI in 2007. He worked as a Sybase database administrator for 8 years in three major banks based in Paris. He is currently an employee of Capdata, a company belonging to the Osmozium group, a digital services company, specialized in IT infrastructure management.

Who is this book for?

This book is for people desperately looking for a source of information on **ASE 15.7**.

It may be suitable for both beginners in the database field and competing DBMS administrators who want to clarify the specifics of ASE in order to become a Sybase DBA. It also highlights what's new in version 15.7 compared to previous versions.

What this book will teach you

- The basic bricks of ASE.
- The innovations of version 15.7.
- How to create an ASE dataserver.
- Understand how ASE records its data.
- Get out of the usual incidents.
- Best practices to observe as a DBA.
- Know how to back up ASE efficiently.
- Enter the head of the optimizer.

- Use tools and procedures that are not formally documented.
- ASE's specificities on Windows and Unix.
- Indexes at ASE.
- The author's toolbox.
- Finally, a final quiz to test your knowledge.

Introduction to ASE

Sybase Adaptive Server Enterprise (ASE) is a database management system (DBMS) developed in the 1980s. It is one of the least documented and least "understood" of all DBMS systems.

This book is intended for people who want to learn more about how Sybase ASE works, whether they are beginners or experienced.

Very precise and overly technical syntax is deliberately omitted so that this book remains pleasant to read and light. For exact syntax, readers should refer to the official Sybase ASE documentation at `http://infocenter.sybase.com/help/index.jsp`. One of the most useful documents, the **Quick Reference Guide**, is available free of charge in PDF format.

The major release discussed in this book is **Sybase ASE 15.7** released in September 2011. It should be understood that there are several versions of ASE 15.7 and therefore some of the features detailed in this book may not apply to the 15.7 that the reader is used to working on.

Several versions 15.7

The following table lists the main variations of ASE 15.7:

Full name of the version	Release date
Adaptive Server Enterprise 15.7 SP130	August 2014
Adaptive Server Enterprise 15.7 SP121	April 2014

Adaptive Server Enterprise 15.7 SP100	July 2013
Adaptive Server Enterprise 15.7 SP60	December 2013
Adaptive Server Enterprise 15.7 SP50	July 2013
Adaptive Server Enterprise 15.7 ESD #3	June 2013
Adaptive Server Enterprise 15.7 ESD #2	July 2012
Adaptive Server Enterprise 15.7	September 2011

"ESD" stands for Electronic Software Distribution. "SP" stands for Service Pack. In both cases these are minor enhancements to version 15.7.

It is likely that other minor versions of ASE will be released after this book is written (July 2015).

What's new in ASE 15.7

Here are the new features included in ASE from the first version 15.7 (September 2011).

1. Two cores: "*threaded* mode" or "process mode".
2. Compression of data in tables.
3. Kerberos authentication.
4. Strong password encryption.
5. Login profiles.
6. Ability to reduce the size of the transaction log of a database.
7. Use of large objects in stored procedures.
8. Non-materialized columns on disk.
9. Ability to log `select into` operations.
10. `Merge` order.
11. Display statistics in XML.

12. `sybdiag` **tool**.
13. `Syberf` **tool**.
14. **Commands** `create login, alter login, drop login`.
15. **Commande** `alter thread pool`.

Glossary

Acronyms

DBA = Database Administrator.

ASE = Adaptive Server Enterprise.

O.S. = Operating System.

OLTP = Online Transactional Processing.

OLAP = Online analytical processing.

SQL = Structured Query Language.

DDL = Data Definition Language.

Error messages

Originally, Sybase ASE is american software, so error messages are always in English. For example, the error messages are always in English:

```
1> create tabble example (id int, name char(20))
2> go
Msg 155, Level 15, State 2:
Server 'TACTILOU', Line 1:
'tabble' is not a recognized CREATE option.
```

The objective of the original version of this book was to target French-speaking users and DBAs. In this logic, here is the procedure to install the library of error messages in French in an ASE dataserver:

On Windows:

```
langinst.exe -Usa -S<dataserver> -P<mdp_sa> french utf8
```

On Unix:

```
langinstall -Usa -S<dataserver> -P<mdp_sa> french utf8
```

Then, you have to specify that you want to enable French as the default language for the account you are using:

```
sp_modifylogin sa , deflanguage , french
```

And it's over. All error messages will now be in French.

```
1> create tabble example (id int, name char(20))
2> go
Msg 155, Level 15, State 2:
Server 'TACTILOU', Line 1:
'tabble' n'est pas une option CREATE reconnue.
```

System

Adaptive Server Enterprise or Sybase?

Adaptive Server Enterprise is software that is commonly referred to as "Sybase" because it is the name of the company that invented and marketed it for 23 years.

Also, the exact term used in official documents to describe this software once installed on a machine is "Adaptive Server". However, in the French-speaking DBA community, the two terms most often used are

- **Dataserver** (or spelled dataserver, or even shortened to "server" for short) to describe all the files and raw devices that make up a single Adaptive Server.
- **Instance** to describe a running Adaptive Server.

To put it simply, we can round out the angles by admitting that "ASE", "Adaptive Server", "Sybase", "Dataserver", "Instance" all mean vaguely the same thing.

To complicate matters, the ASE executable program does not have the same name when running under Windows and when running under Unix.

- Under Windows: you have to run `sqlsrvr.exe`.
- Under Unix: you have to run `dataserver`.

Like most computer systems, an ASE instance consists of executable binaries (commonly called "distribution") and files or raw devices containing inert (non-executable) data. This combination of binaries and files is very common.

Analogy. *We have to think of the couple that Microsoft Word forms with ".doc" files, Excel with ".xlsx" files or VLC with MP3 files.*

Simplified diagram

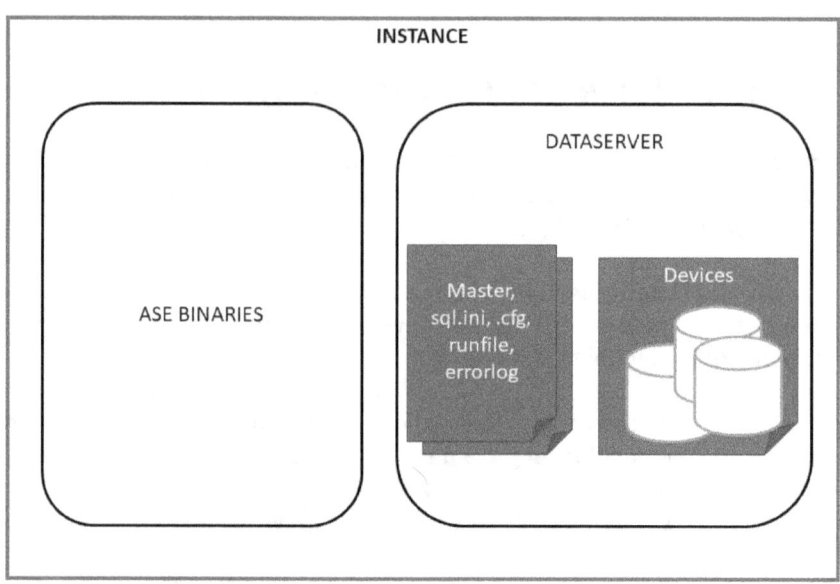

Figure 1 : Simplified diagram of ASE

Any user or administrator of Sybase Adaptive Server Enterprise understands that a dataserver is a database management system: it receives SQL queries and returns rows of data.

Client/server system

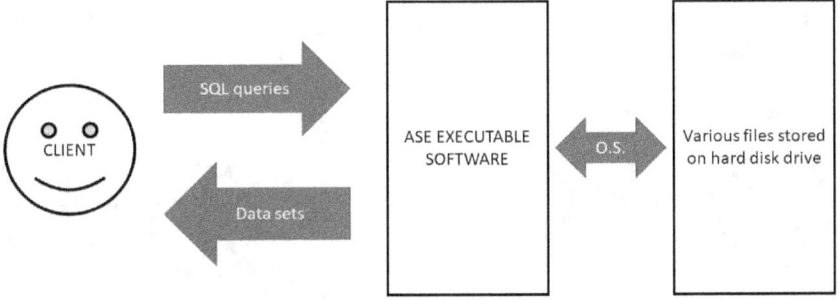

Figure 2 : Path between a client and the data files

Client/server symmetry

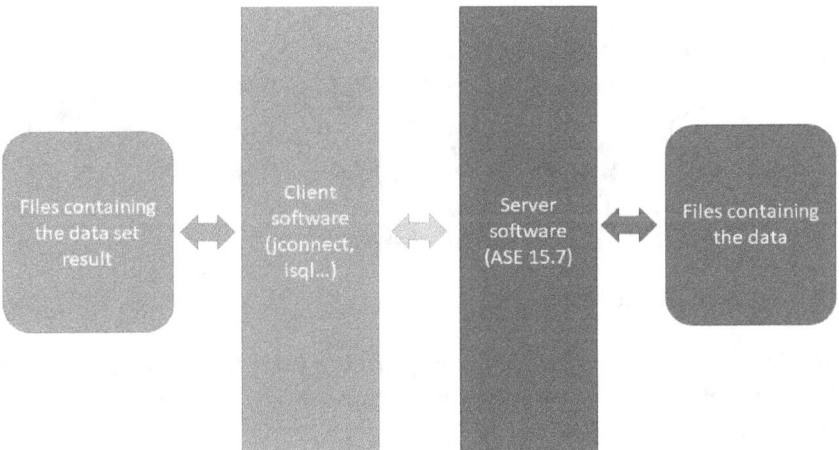

Figure 3 : Client/server symetry

The client software gives life to inert data (SQL queries are only strings and the results are only numeric or textual data).

The server software gives life to inert files too! Dataserver configuration files or database devices are just inert data.

Hardware architecture

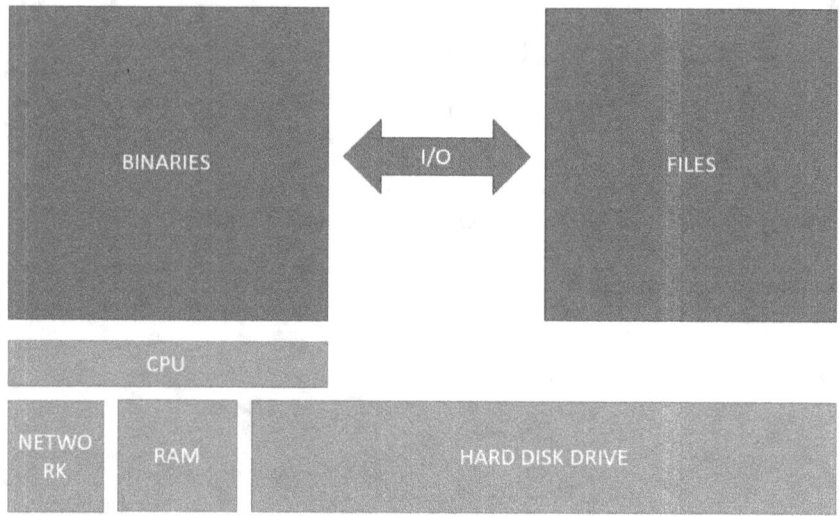

Figure 4 : Resources

Binaries orchestrate resources

The binaries have an active role: they are the ones that coordinate the 4 hardware elements that are the RAM, the hard disk, the network and the processor.

However, binaries are logical elements. Not material. Binaries are like a punch card: they contain a program designed by Sybase that acts as a partition. This program is called ASE.

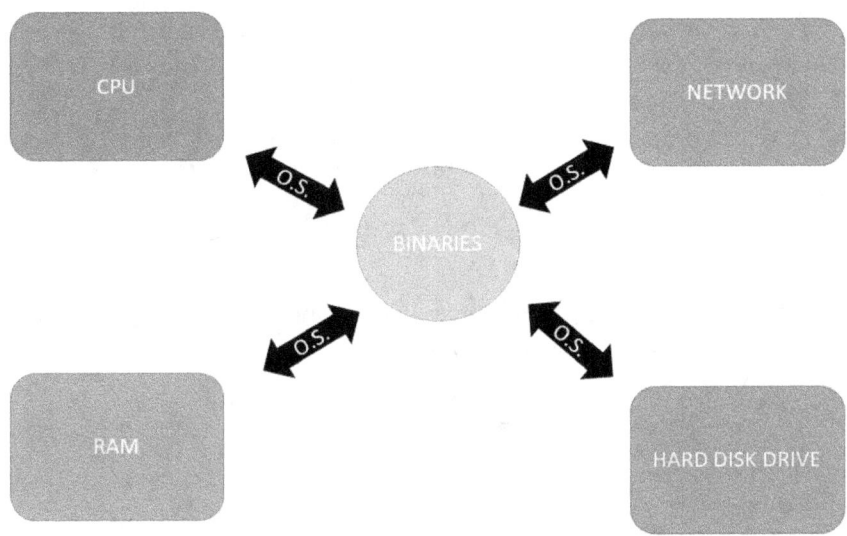

Figure 5 : Binaries orchestrating the resources

Analogy. An orchestra is a group of musical instruments, therefore material. The score is a logical element (recorded on a material support). This score harmoniously coordinates all the material.

Binary

dataserver

This is the ASE binary under Unix environments. By calling it with the "-v" option, you can find out the version:

```
dataserver -v
Adaptive Server Enterprise/15.7/EBF 23007 SMP SP130
/P/Sun_svr4/OS 5.10/ase157sp13x/3819/64-bit/FBO/Sat Aug 23
01:36:19 2014
```

sqlsrvr.exe

This is the ASE binary for Windows environments. By calling it with the "-v" option, you can find out the version:

```
sqlsrvr -v
Adaptive Server Enterprise/15.7/EBF 21339 SMP SP101
/P/X64/Windows Server/ase157sp101/3439/64-bit/OPT/Thu Jun 06
12:11:05 2013
```

bcksrvr.exe

This is the binary of the Backup Server under Windows. By calling it with the "-v" option, you can find out its version:

```
bcksrvr -v
Backup Server/15.7 SP101/EBF 21339/P/X64/Windows
Server/ase157sp101/4236/64-bit/OPT/Thu Jun 06 09:42:26 2013
```

backupserver

This is the binary of the Backup Server under Unix. By calling it with the "-v" option, you can find out its version:

```
backupserver -v
Backup Server/15.7 SP122/EBF 22774/P/Sun_svr4/OS
5.10/ase157sp12x/4489/32-bit/OPT/Fri Apr 18 23:04:22 2014
```

Files

There are at least 7 file types required to start an ASE instance. The arrows indicate the technical dependencies of each one: each file indicates where another one is located.

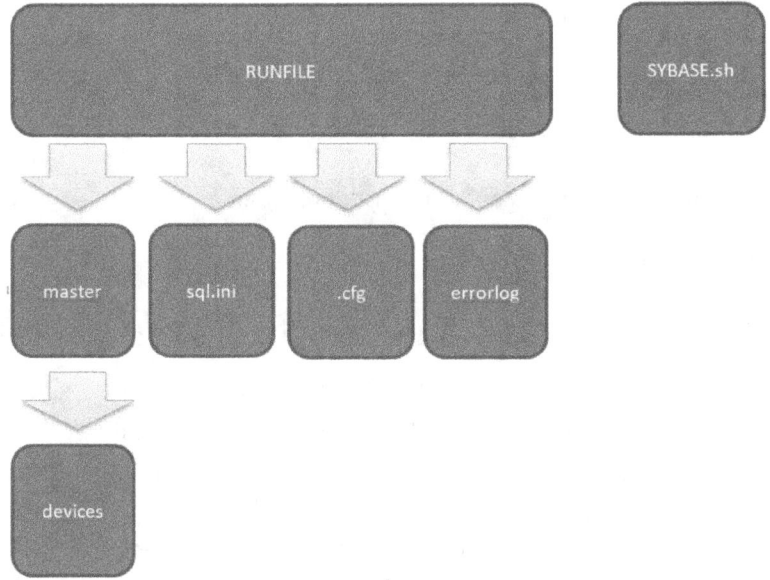

Figure 6 : Usual files required

Runfile

The runfile (= startup file) is an executable file referring to all the others: master, errorlog, config, sql.ini, etc... It is responsible for starting the instance. It is very likely that if one of the files referred to in the runfile is missing, the instance will not be able to start.

It is composed of a call to the binary followed by several options:

```
dataserver -d ... -e ... -c ... -c ...
```

-d = device master path

-e = errorlog path

-c = path to the configuration file

-s = name of the dataserver in the interfaces file

-T = list of traceflags

-m = starts the instance in "1 user only" mode.

And many other options.

Traceflags" are small indicators that change the behavior of the instance. For example:

- 208 = For each query, display the locking strategy.

- 342 = Prohibit nested loop joints.

- 4001 = Log all unsuccessful connection attempts.

- 3609 = Start without building the tempdb.

- 3610 = Divisions by zero do not make an error.

- 8101 = Disables saving connection dates and times in the lastlogindate column of `syslogins`, thus avoiding creating contention on the `syslogins`.

It can be useful to build a set of several runfiles depending on the situation. For example, "normal runfile", "diagnostic runfile", "weekend runfile", "lost password runfile"...

Example of a runfile for Windows:

```
rem
rem Adaptive Server Information:
rem name:                  TACTILOU
rem master device:         C:\Sybase\data\master.dbf
rem server page size:      2048
```

```
rem master device size:          200
rem errorlog:                    C:\Sybase\ASE-
15_0\install\TACTILOU.log
rem interfaces:                  C:\Sybase\ini
rem
"C:\Sybase\ASE-15_0\bin\sqlsrvr.exe" -
d"C:\Sybase\data\master.dbf" -sTACTILOU -e"C:\Sybase\ASE-
15_0\install\TACTILOU.log" -i"C:\Sybase\ini" -M"C:\Sybase\ASE-
15_0" -c"C:\Sybase\TACTILOU.cfg"
```

Example of runfile at Unix:

```
#!/bin/sh
#
# ASE page size (KB):     2048
# Master device path:     /dev/vx/rdsk/abricot/tpfr6-master
# Error log path:
/abricot/sgbd/TACTILOU/errorlog/TACTILOU.log
# Configuration file path: /abricot/sgbd/TACT...5_0/TACTILOU.cfg
# Directory for shared memory files:
/abricot/sgbd/TACTILOU/ASE157/ASE-15_0
# Adaptive Server name: TACTILOU
/abricot/sgbd/TACTILOU/ASE157/ASE-15_0/bin/dataserver \
-d/dev/vx/rdsk/abricot/tpfr6-master \
-e/abricot/sgbd/TACTILOU/errorlog/TACTILOU.log \
-c/abricot/sgbd/TACTILOU/ASE157/ASE-15_0/TACTILOU.cfg \
-M/abricot/sgbd/TACTILOU/ASE157/ASE-15_0 \
-sTACTILOU \
```

Sql.ini or interface

The interface files (on Unix) and sql.ini (on Windows) contain the list of ASE instances that can be reached over the network. Each instance is identified by a name and indicates the machine and port through which a client can reach them. It is not forbidden to specify several ports for the same instance.

Example of sql.ini file (on Windows):

```
[TACTILE]
master=NLWNSCK,apricot,5004
query=NLWNSCK,apricot,5004
master=NLWNSCK,apricot,5010
```

```
query=NLWNSCK,apricot,5010
```

Example of interface file (At Unix):

```
TACTILOU master tcp ether apricot 1051
        query tcp ether apricot 1051
        master tcp ether apricot 1050
        query tcp ether apricot 1050
```

Errorlog

It is the only file that lists problems or changes in the configuration of the instance. This file is extremely valuable because it is a form of a dataserver's medical file: all the problems that may have occurred are recorded in the errorlog. For example: error 1608 means "abrupt connection failure suffered by ASE, such as a network outage, client machine shutdown, saturated network traffic, etc.". Here is an excerpt from errorlog:

```
00:0006:00000:00001:2015/07/23 21:11:04.09 server Started
ANALYSIS pass for database
00:0006:00000:00001:2015/07/23 21:11:04.09 server Completed
ANALYSIS pass for databas
00:0006:00000:00001:2015/07/23 21:11:04.09 server Log contains
all committed transact
00:0006:00000:00001:2015/07/23 21:11:04.09 server Started REDO
pass for database 'dbc
00:0006:00000:00001:2015/07/23 21:11:04.11 server Completed REDO
pass for database 'd
00:0006:00000:00001:2015/07/23 21:11:04.11 server Timestamp for
database 'dbccdb' is
00:0006:00000:00001:2015/07/23 21:11:04.11 server Recovery of
database 'dbccdb' will
00:0006:00000:00001:2015/07/23 21:11:04.11 server Started
recovery checkpoint for dat
00:0006:00000:00001:2015/07/23 21:11:04.11 server Completed
recovery checkpoint for d
00:0006:00000:00001:2015/07/23 21:11:04.11 server Started
filling free space info for
00:0006:00000:00001:2015/07/23 21:11:04.20 server Completed
filling free space info f
00:0006:00000:00001:2015/07/23 21:11:04.20 server Started
cleaning up the default dat
```

```
00:0006:00000:00001:2015/07/23 21:11:04.20 server Completed
cleaning up the default d
00:0006:00000:00001:2015/07/23 21:11:04.20 server Checking
external objects.
00:0006:00000:00001:2015/07/23 21:11:04.23 server The
transaction log in the database
```

The columns of the errorlog are:

- Instance ID (in the case of a Sybase clustered ASE). It is often 00.
- Thread ID. In process mode, it is the number of the engine.
- Process family ID. It is often 00000.
- Spid = identifier of the process that generated the message.
- Date and time of the event.
- Indication that the message comes from the kernel or dataserver
- Error Message

xxxxxx.cfg

This is the configuration file of the instance. It contains just under 400 configuration parameters. It can be edited manually provided it is done on a stopped instance. For a started instance, it is rather advisable to change its parameters using the sp_configure procedure.

If this file is deleted in the operating system while the instance is open ... nothing serious happens. Simply, the next time you change a parameter with sp_configure, a new file will be generated.

It is also possible to generate them with the command sp_configure "configuration file",0,"restore" ,"C:/errorlog/conf.cfg".

SYBASE.sh (or Sybase.bat for Windows)

This is the file that contains all environment variable declarations.

Device master

It is the main device of a dataserver. It is the only device that contains the list of all other devices. It is a file that is not readable with a text editor. It is structured with 2 elements:

- An allocation table,
- Several pages.

This device contains:

- The page size of the dataserver,
- The path of all other devices,
- All passwords, including the one of sa,
- The list of all the bases,
- The last start date of the instance...

At each startup, the `sysdevices` table is updated with the location of the master device mentioned in the runfile. This means that the master device can be moved without disturbing the dataserver at startup as long as the runfile is updated.

Virtual devices

Virtual devices are the files or raw devices containing the data bases of a dataserver. They are therefore very precious.

Other files

A Sybase ASE dataserver consists of several files, but it also creates files repeatedly. ASE produces about 5 types of files: Dumps, Devices, Configuration, Errorlog and Manifest. The disk space occupied by these files must be monitored.

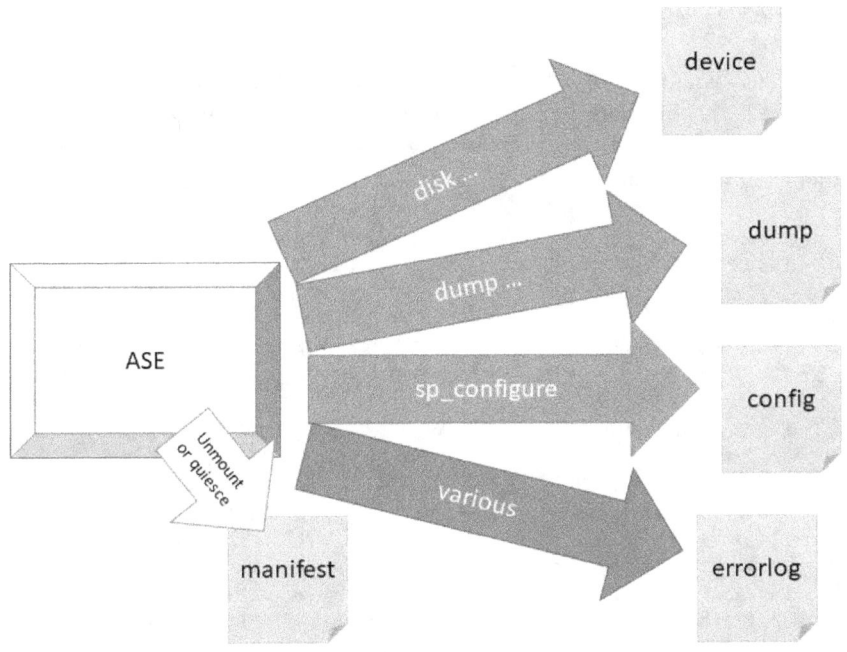

Figure 7 : Each type of file produced or edited by ASE is caused by a command

`disk`

All `disk` commands are able to create or enlarge a file on the filesystem: these files are devices. `disk init, disk mirror, disk resize....`

dump

All `dump xxx` commands are able to create one or more files on the filesystem: these files are backups. `dump database, dump transaction, cumulative dump, dump configuration.`

sp_configure

It always renames the old configuration file and generates a new one for each call. This mechanism makes it possible to log all configuration changes in a directory. sp_configure manages to write a file to the filesystem thanks to the undocumented config_admin() function.

```
24/06/2015 00:25              13,236 TACTILOU.001
02/07/2015 22:56              13,238 TACTILOU.002
05/07/2015 00:00              13 232 TACTILOU.003
05/07/2015 16:24              13,226 TACTILOU.004
05/07/2015 16:35              13,221 TACTILOU.005
05/07/2015 20:01              13 215 TACTILOU.006
12/07/2015 23:17              13 221 TACTILOU.007
12/07/2015 23:46              13,227 TACTILOU.008
13/07/2015 01:45              13 221 TACTILOU.009
13/07/2015 01:45              13 227 TACTILOU.010
13/07/2015 01:50              13 221 TACTILOU.011
15/07/2015 09:49              13 215 TACTILOU.012
07/15/2015 14:16              13 377 TACTILOU.013
15/07/2015 15:08              13,371 TACTILOU.014
18/07/2015 01:02              13,377 TACTILOU.015
18/07/2015 08:53              13,371 TACTILOU.016
18/07/2015 08:53              13,367 TACTILOU.017
23/07/2015 21:10              13,367 TACTILOU.bak
19/07/2015 14:48              13 367 TACTILOU.cfg
```

After 1000 configuration files, ASE will overwrite number 001 and start again.

Unmount or **quiesce**

These are commands that generate a file containing the options and the structure of a database. This file is called a manifest.

Errorlog

The only type of file that grows regularly without explicit action is the errorlog file. This file grows especially when there are errors, stacktraces, crashes, when someone disconnects from the instance, when using DBCC commands... Some production instances can generate an errorlog of 1.5 MB/day.

Installation

First step: the binaries

The first step of an ASE dataserver installation is to drop the binaries in a tree structure on a machine.

Usually, the whole is grouped in a folder with a meaningful name such as "ASE157" or "SYBASE".

Second step: the text files

Many of the files needed are simply text files that you simply copy from an existing ASE instance and then modify slightly in a text editor. They are

- SYBASE.sh
- RUNFILE
- Sql.ini or interfaces
- The configuration file (.cfg) is optional at this level.

Third step: create a device master

The master device is the first virtual device of an ASE dataserver. It is the only device that is not created with the `disk init` command. The method to create it is called **"zbsd"**. It consists in executing the binary (dataserver or sqlsrvr.exe) with 4 main parameters:

- -z < PAGE SIZE>
- -b <DIVISION OF THE DEVICE MASTER>
- -s < NAME OF DATASERVER>
- -d <PATH OF THE DEVICE MASTER'S FILE >

For example, under Windows to create a 500MB master device with a page size of 2k in order to have a dataserver named "SYDNEY":

```
sqlsrvr.exe -z 2k -b 500M -s SYDNEY -d
"C:\Sybase\device\master.dbf
```

Another example, under Solaris, to create a 1000MB master device with a page size of 4k in order to have a dataserver named "BUCAREST":

```
dataserver -z 4k -b 1000M -s BUCAREST -d
"/machine/sgbd/sybase/master.dat
```

This command will automatically generate 3:

- An errorlog
- A configuration file (.cfg file)
- A device master file

Fourth step: start the dataserver

The same binary that enabled the creation of the master device will now be used to start the dataserver. To start a dataserver, the main parameters are *"cesd"*:

- -c < PATH OF THE CONFIGURATION FILE>.
- -e < PATH OF THE ERRORLOG FILE >
- -s < NAME OF DATASERVER>
- -d <PATH OF THE DEVICE MASTER'S FILE >

For example, under Windows:

```
sqlsrvr.exe -d "C:\Sybase\data\master.dbf" -s TACTILOU -e
"C:\Sybase\ASE-15_0\install\TACTILOU.log" -c
"C:\Sybase\TACTILOU.cfg"
```

One can then connect for the first time to the instance. No "sp_" stored procedure exists (neither sp_helpdb, nor sp_who, etc...).

However, you can for example launch the following queries to glean some information:

```
print "LIST OF BASES".
go
select name from sysdatabases
go

print "PROCESS LIST".
go
select spid , cmd from sysprocesses
go

print "LIST OF DEVICES
go
select name , phyname from sysdevices
go

print "SERVICE LIST".
go
select srvstatus, srvname from sysservers
go

print "LIST OF HOUSES
go
select name from syslogins
go
```

The result will almost always be the same:

```
LIST OF BASES
 name
 ------------------------------
 master
 model
 sybsystemdb
 tempdb

LIST OF PROCESSES
 spid cmd
 ------ ------------------------------
      2 DEADLOCK TUNE
      3 KPP HANDLER
      4 ASTC HANDLER
      5 CHECKPOINT SLEEP
      6 HK WASH
      7 HK GC
      8 HK CHORES
      9 PORT MANAGER
     10 NETWORK HANDLER
     11 LICENSE HEARTBEAT
     13 SELECT
```

```
LIST OF DEVICES
  name phyname
  ---------------- ----------------------- -----------------
  master C:\Sybase\data\master.dbf
  tapedump1 /dev/rmt4
  tapedump2 /dev/rst0

LIST OF SERVERS
  srvstatus srvname
  --------- -----------------------------
          8 SYB_BACKUP

LIST OF LOGINS
  name
  -----------------------------
  sa
```

These are the first hours of "life" for this Adaptive Server. It is so young that it doesn't even know its name:

```
1> select @@servername
2> go

 -------------------------------
 NULL
```

On the other hand, it knows how many times it has been started:

```
1> select @@bootcount
2> go

 -----------
           2
```

And the version of the binaries that run it:

```
1> select @@version
2> go

 -------------------------------------------
 Adaptive Server Enterprise/15.7/EBF 21339 SMP SP101
 /P/X64/Windows Server
```

Step 5: Run the installation scripts

To complete this brand new and empty dataserver, you have to manually "furnish" it with the following steps: create the devices and the sybsytemprocs, dbccdb, sybsecurity, etc.... databases. The `disk init` and `create database` commands work but not `sp_dboption` or `sp_helpdevice`.

The following illustration shows where each base should be located:

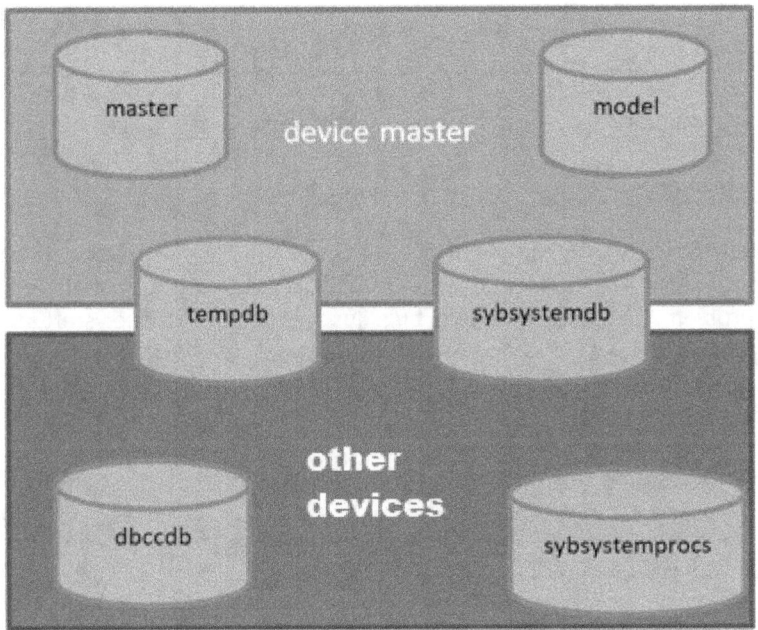

Figure 8 : Usual databases

Then, using the isql tool, you need to run the SQL script named `installmaster` which is delivered in the ASE distribution. Usually in the ASE-15_0/scripts directory. (It is called `instmstr` on Windows). In this same directory, there are other scripts. Among them, at least run `installmodel, instmsgs.ebf, installcommit, installsecurity`.

On Unix	On Windows
installdbccdb	installdbccdb
instmsgs.ebf	instmsgs.ebf
installmaster	instmstr
installsecurity	instsecu
installcommit	instcomm
installmodel	instmodl

There is no danger in running the `installmaster` script several times. In an older version of Sybase ASE, the `installmaster` often crashed on a *full log* problem. This was a known bug: just stop the instance, start it and restart the `installmaster`. This script does not overwrite any data in the tables. On the other hand, it crashes and recreates some system stored procedures.

Sixth step: customize the dataserver

Give an internal name to the dataserver. Usually the same name that is in the interfaces file.

```
sp_addserver TACTILOU, local, TACTILOU
```

Usually, you have to change the network path of the Backup Server because ASE names it as it pleases, but never as you want:

```
sp_dropserver SYB_BACKUP
go
sp_addserver SYB_BACKUP , ASEnterprise, TACTILOU_BS
go
```

Later in this book, the concept of Backup Server will be discussed in more detail.

This last step can be the one where the DBA adds its own stored procedures. See Appendices.

System basics

There are various databases in a dataserver: some are fundamental, some are mandatory and some are optional.

Fundamentals

`master`	This is the basis on which the entire dataserver is built. It is the only one that is not created with a "create database" command because it is the origin of the dataserver. Nothing exists before the master database.

Mandatory

`tempdb`	This is the base that will allow to store all temporary tables and work tables.
`model`	This is the model used to create all future bases.
`sybsystemprocs`	Contains most of the system procedures.
`sybsystemdb`	Used for distributed transactions.

Optional

dbccdb	Basis of work during consistency checks (DBCC)
sybsecurity	Basis of work of the audits.
maudb_audit	Contains the audit table.
tempdbsa	Temporary basis reserved for DBAs.

Four of these bases are unbearable:

```
1> drop database model
2> go
Msg 3708, Level 16, State 5:
Server 'DUBAI', Line 1:
Cannot drop the database 'model' because it is a system
database.

1> drop database master
2> go
Msg 3708, Level 16, State 4:
Server 'DUBAI', Line 1:
Cannot drop the database 'master' because it is a system
database.

1> drop database tempdb
2> go
Msg 3708, Level 16, State 6:
Server 'DUBAI', Line 1:
Cannot drop the database 'tempdb' because it is a system
database.
1> drop database sybsystemdb
2> go
Msg 3708, Level 16, State 7:
Server 'DUBAI', Line 1:
Cannot drop the database 'sybsystemdb' because it is a system
database.
```

System variables

System variables are dynamic values stored in variables that cannot be modified. They are recognized by their double-arobase. They are maintained only by the kernel of the instance. They give valuable information about the instance. To read them, just use the command `select` followed by their name:

`@@version` = Full name of the ASE version.
`@@errorlog` = Path to the errorlog file.
`@@boottime` = Date and time of the last start of the instance.
`@@servername` = Name of the instance.
`@@maxpagesize` = Dataserver page size.

Some of them only concern the user who invokes them:

`@@transtate` = Current status of the user's transaction.
`@@spid` = Process number of the session.
`@@rowcount` = Number of rows affected by the last query.

System tables

System tables are tables that allow the instance to manage itself. They are particularly sensitive and important. They can be consulted by the DBAs. Modifying them is not recommended but sometimes unavoidable to solve certain problems. Others simply cannot be modified because they do not exist in hardware: they are ghost tables that ASE generates in RAM only when they are called. By calling them with sp_help we can see that they have "0 row" and "0 page".

There are **57** system tables. The following list is not exhaustive.

`syslogins`

This is the table that contains the list of logins of the instance. A login is like a key to enter the dataserver. It is a name/password pair. You have to be very careful if you modify it because it is in join with many other tables: sysusermessages, sysremotelogins, sysloginroles, sysdatabases, sysalternates, sysusers, systhreshold, syssessions, sysprocesses and even syslogins itself.

The syslogins has evolved a lot between ASE 12.5.3 and ASE 15.7. There are 7 new columns.

sysdatabases

This is the list of the dataserver bases. It happens that modifying a row of this table can help in cases of base corruption. In particular, when a database refuses to be dropped, setting its status to the value 32 allows to get out of it: update sysdatabases set status = 300 where dbid = 80

sysstatistics and systabstats

These are the tables that contain the statistics of the objects in the database.

sysprocedures

As its name indicates, it is a table that contains the list of stored procedures of a database. But, surprisingly, it also contains the list of defaults, check constraints, triggers, views, rules. In the sysprocedures status column, 1026 means that the stored procedure can modify system tables, while the value 1154 means the opposite. When a stored procedure is created, if the parameter "allow updates to system tables" is set to 1, the procedure will always have the right to modify system tables. And vice versa.

sysindexes

As its name indicates, it is a table that contains a list of all the indexes in the database. However, it also contains the list of tables, and large objects (text, image ...).

- If indid = 0 it→ is a table
- If indid >= 1 it→ is an index itself
- If indid = 255→it is a "large object".

Opinion of the author. It seems absurd and unjustified to put tables and large objects in a table called ... `sysindexes`.

If status2 = 2 th→ index belongs to a single constraint or primary key.

sysconfigures

This table contains all the configuration parameters of the instance. But it also contains the sizes of the named caches.

sysstatistics

This is one of the two tables containing the statistics. Each row of this table concerns a column of a table or an index (sometimes several rows are necessary for the same column).

systabstats

This is one of the two tables containing the statistics. Each row in this table is related to a table or index.

sysdepends

This table lists all the dependencies between objects: i.e. the technical relations of the kind: views, trigger, foreign key, ...

`sysattributes`

Contains all the information of the options of the bases, tables, indexes, users, logins, as well as the links between objects. It is strongly advised not to modify it manually. In particular, it contains all the "bindings" (links between objects).

`sysservers`

Contains a list of several dataservers and Backup Servers including the name of the dataserver itself.

Others

There are still a lot of system tables. There are more and more with each version of ASE. Some of them have a name that doesn't even start with "sys". For example, "spt" tables are system tables that are not even officially documented. It is best to never touch them.

System views

System views are views created from system tables. There are 4 of them.

- `syscacheinfo`
- `syscachepoolinfo`
- `syspoolinfo`
- `sysquerymetrics`

System functions

A function is an object that performs a job and then returns a value after receiving others as a parameter. The following list is not exhaustive.

Some functions perform mathematical work:

- `avg()`
- `cos()`
- `floor()`
- `pi()`

Some functions perform temporal work:

- `current_time()` →gives the current time
- `getdate()` →gives the current date
- `newid()` →Returns a 36 character unique identifier

Some functions work on strings:

- `str_replace()` →allows you to replace characters
- `char()` →is a fake friend.
- `difference()` →evaluates the sound similarity between two words spoken in English.

Some functions give information related to the instance:

- `db_name()` →indicates the database in which we are located
- `asehostname()` →indicates the name of the machine that hosts the instance
- `row_count()` →indicates the number of pages in a table
- `is_quiesced()` →indicates if a base is in "quiesce".
- `datachange()` →function is not very reliable and has no effect on the indexes.
- `tran_dumpable_status()` →transaction log cannot be *dumped from* a database.

System stored procedures

A stored procedure is a set of instructions in SQL language. It is an executable object within an instance. You can call them as you want but there is a very practical rule: any stored procedure whose name starts with "sp_" or "xp_" and which is found in the sybsystemprocs or master databases can be invoked from any database.

Some procedures are written by users, others by DBAs. Most importantly, many stored procedures are written by the Sybase ASE vendor. There are **634 of** them. Here is a non-exhaustive list.

sp_post_xpload

Checks and rebuilds all non-clustered or clustered DOL indexes from a cross-platform load database. This procedure is very disk space consuming. If the free space is too small, the processing will fail due to lack of space in the data segments. The DBA can also drop and recreate the indexes manually but it is not faster.

sp_flushstats

Forces the statistics contained in memory to be written to the disk (in the systabstats table). This is particularly important before performing a dump database because in case of cross-platform load database, an error 3151 is to be feared if it is not done. Warning: this has nothing to do with DELETE STATISTICS.

sp_helpsort

Displays the character set and sort order of the instance.

sp_helpdb

Displays information about the databases: sizes, options, names, dbid, creation date, devices used, etc...

sp_helpsegment

Followed by the segment name (usually system, default or logging), this procedure indicates the number of occupied and free pages.

sp_spaceused

Size of a table and its indexes. It can be launched in two ways: sp_spaceused <table> or sp_spaceused <table> , 1.

sp_hidetext

This procedure acts brutally and irreversibly: it erases the text of all stored procedures, views, rules, default, check and trigger from the database. To be avoided.

sp_plan_dbccdb

Tool performing an estimation of the required dbccdb size in the dataserver.

sp_helpserver

Displays the list of servers known by this dataserver: other ASE servers, Sybase IQ instances or Backup Server. It also displays the name of the dataserver itself.

sp_helpuser

Displays the list of users of a database. If the name of a group is added next to it, it displays all the users of the group.

sp_lock

Displays the list of locks currently installed on the instance. There is always at least one row: it corresponds to the lock set during the result of the sp_lock procedure itself.

sp_helptext

Displays the textual content of stored procedures, views, defaults, functions, types, check, rules, access rules, and triggers. This text is stored in the `syscomments` table. For confidentiality reasons, it is possible to delete the text of a stored procedure, without altering its operation.

sp_objects_stats

Displays the restraint rate (locks) of a table for a defined period of time. Its result can lead to questioning the locking scheme of a table.

sp_showplan

Displays the execution plan of a session with a specified spid.

sp_helprotect

Displays the permissions of a user or object.

sp_add_resource_limit

This procedure is rarely used but it has an interest: it offers the possibility to limit the monopolization of the instance resources by imposing rules such as *killing a* login if its request returns too many rows.

sp_monitor

Displays a status report of the instance regarding its IO and CPU consumption. This should be the first procedure that is mentioned when you want to analyze the load of an instance.

sp_monitorconfig

Displays a statement about the metadata cache.

sp_help

Extremely used system procedure: it displays all the objects of a database: tables, rules, defaults, triggers, views, stored procedures, etc...

sp_pkeys

Display the foreign key of a table.

sp_helpconstraint

Display all constraints of a table.

sp_helpartition

Its name is a concatenation of the words help and partition except that Sybase has removed one of the "p's". It displays the partitions of a table, so you can see how many rows are in each one.

sp_deviceattr

Used to change the `dsync` and `directio` parameters of a device for the next boot.

sp_recompile

The name of this procedure is misleading. It is used to tell the optimizer that a new execution plan will have to be reconstructed the next time a query uses a table.

sp_sysmon

Diagnostic tool of the activity on the instance.

sp_changegroup

Procedure to change a user's membership group. To be taken into account, the user must log out and log back in.

sp_configure

This procedure is the dashboard of a dataserver: it allows you to view and modify the 382 parameters of Sybase 15.7. The configuration parameters of a dataserver each have a role of unequal importance. Over the course of his or her career, a DBA naturally learns to recognize which ones are the most important. An instance's settings are stored in a configuration file that ends with the ".cfg" extension. To find out which parameters are no longer the defaults, the syntax is `sp_configure nondefault`.

sp_sproc_columns

Displays the values received as inputs and returned as outputs for a given stored procedure.

sp_transactions

Displays the list of current transactions on the instance.

Do your own sp_

The flexibility of Sybase ASE is the ability to create an infinite number of other stored procedures using SQL commands, system functions, system variables, and system tables. Thus, anyone could develop:

sp_who2: which would be like `sp_who` but without displaying kernel sessions.

sp_helplogin: which would be a counterpart of sp_helpuser but with the logins.

sp_helpalias: to list all the aliases of a database.

sp_dump_all: to trigger a `dump database of` all the databases in succession.

sp_query: to display the text of a query without using `dbcc traceon`.

sp_kill_all: to kill all processes that use a base.

sp_list_indexes: to display all the indexes contained in a database.

The reader will find in the appendix and on the internet the complete code of the stored procedures proposed above, and many more.

Dataserver configuration

At ASE, almost all the configuration parameters can be consulted and modified with the stored procedure `sp_configure`.

If it is called without any argument, all parameters are displayed:

```
1>sp_configure
2>go

Group: Network Communication
```

```
 Parameter Name                      Default      Memory Used Config
Value Run Value      Unit                    Type
----------------------------- ----------- ----------- --------
---- ------------ -------------------- -------
 additional network memory               0                     0
0               0 bytes              dynamic
 allow remote access                     1                     0
1               1 switch             dynamic
 allow sendmsg                           0                     0
0               0 0 switch            dynamic
 default network packet size          2048                  #548
2048            2048 bytes             static
 early row send increment       2147483647                    0
2147483647    2147483647 rows              dynamic
 max network packet size              2048                     0
2048            2048 bytes             static
 max number network listeners            5                   851
5               5 number             dynamic
 network polling mode             threaded                     0
threaded        threaded name               static
 number of early send rows               0                     0
0               0 rows               dynamic
 number of network tasks                 1                     0
1               1 number             dynamic
```

If it is called with a parameter name, even a partial one, ASE displays all parameters that look like this word:

```
1> sp_configure 'number'.
2> go
Msg 17411, Level 16, State 1:
Server 'TACTILOU', Procedure 'sp_configure', Line 413:
Configuration option is not unique.

 Parameter Name                      Default      Memory Used Config
Value


                                 Unit                    Type
----------------------------- ----------- ----------- --------
----
-------------------------------------------------------------------
----
-------------------------------------------------------------------
----
----------------------------- -------------------- ----------
```

```
global cache partition number          1              0
1

                        number                  static
 max number network listeners          5             851
5

                        number                 dynamic
 number of Q engines at startup         0               0
0

                        number                  static
 number of alarms                      40              12
40

                        number                 dynamic
 number of aux scan descriptors       256            #420
256

                        number                 dynamic
 number of backup connections           0               0
0

                        number                 dynamic
 number of ccbs                         0             0 0
0

                        number                 dynamic
 number of devices                     10            #32
30

                        number                 dynamic
 number of disk tasks                   1               0
1
```

DBAs, in the course of their career, become familiar with the most common parameters. Here are a few of them:

Parameter	Role
disable disk mirroring	Enable or disable mirroring of virtural devices.
kernel mode	Choose ASE's core operating mode: by process (usually for small applications) or by thread (usually for large applications).
solaris async i/o mode	Important for instances running under SunOS
allow updates to system tables	Allow or disallow modification of system tables.
procedure cache size	Procedure cache size.
statement cache size	Query cache size.
number of open objects	Number of objects open at the same time.

There are **340** parameters in ASE 15.7 SP101. So, they are not all mentioned in this book.

DBCC

DBCC commands are commands that directly challenge the system kernel to perform tasks that are unusual and strictly reserved for a DBA audience. They are diagnostic and repair tools.

`dbcc traceon(3604)`

This is the first `dbcc` command that a DBA enters: it allows the next DBCC command outputs to be displayed on the screen. It only concerns the session of the person writing it.

`dbcc sqltext (<spid>)`

Allows you to display the text of a process query even if the query is finished.

> **Opinion of the author.** This syntax is not intuitive and requires a dbcc traceon beforehand. Do not hesitate to embed this syntax in a stored procedure. See Appendix "sp_query".

`dbcc traceoff(3604)`

Reverse of `dbcc traceoff`: stops the display of DBCC command outputs.

Note: it is possible to send the result of DBCC commands to a specific file. The syntax is then: `set tracefile "c:/my_trace.txt"`.

`dbcc traceon(3604,11201,11202,11203,11204,11205)`

Allows you to display a very verbose log of the instance activity which is described below (extract from the official documentation):

* *11201 - client connect, disconnect, and attention events.*

- *11202 - client language, cursor declare, dynamic prepare, and dynamic execute-immediate text.*

- *11203 - customer RPC events.*

- *11204 - messages routed to client.*

- *11205 - interaction with remote servers.*

- *11206 - logs file and directory processing steps.*

- *11207 - logs text and image processing.*

dbcc traceflags

Know which traces have been activated on an instance. There is also another method that consists of simply looking for the word "TRACEON" in the errorlog. This way you also know at what time each traceflag was activated. "Traceflag" is the name given to the indicators that are triggered with the numbers in brackets.

dbcc dbreboot

The following command is used to turn off a base station. It is a command to be used with great care. Generally, it is used by some confirmed DBAs to remove a very large base without it lasting too long. It is more a trick than a real procedure.

1. Run a `dbcc dbreboot('shutdown', MABASE)`
2. View the list of segments in the `sysusages` table
3. Carefully do a `delete` in this table to remove all the fragments from the database except the first data fragment and the first log fragment.
4. Make a `drop database`.

Demonstration:

60

```
1> dbcc dbreboot('shutdown', MABASE)
2> go
 ----------Shutting Down Database 'MABASE  ----------
 ----------Operation on Database ' MABASE ' Completed
Successfully  ----------

1> select dbid, lstart, segmap from sysusages where dbid = 4
order by 2
2> go
 dbid    lstart        segmap
 ------ ----------  -----------
      4          0            3
      4      25600            4
      4      40960            4
      4      56320            3
      4      56832            3
      4      57344            3
      4      57856            3

1> delete from sysusages where lstart > 25600 and dbid = 4
2> go
(5 rows affected)

1> drop database MABASE
2> go
```

dbcc dbrepair

When a base is really very corrupt, it can be difficult to drop. As a last resort, a DBCC command can unblock the situation and get the dropper. `dbcc dbrepair("databasename", "dropdb")`.

dbcc checkstorage

This is one of the two important commands for checking the consistency of a database's data. It checks the consistency of the database data pages. This operation can take an extremely long time. But there is a parry: creating a dedicated DBCC instance. All you have to do is reload a prod dump on this instance once a day and run the DBCCs on it. This way the real production is not impacted but the DBCCs will be done every day on its twin.

dbcc checkdb

61

This is one of the two important commands for checking the consistency of a database's data. This one performs a check of each table one by one.

dbcc checktable

It is a command that performs a complete diagnosis of a table. It can be used in several cases: disastrous performances, suspicion of fragmentation, table corruption problem.

Here is an example of execution. Highlighted parts indicate that the table is fragmented.

```
1> dbcc checktable( yellow)
2> go
Checking table 'jaune' (object ID 556525985): Logical page size
is 2048 bytes.
Checking partition 'jaune_556525985' (partition ID 556525985) of
table 'jaune'. The logical page size of this table is 2048
bytes.
The total number of data pages in partition 'jaune_556525985'
(partition ID 556525985) is 300.
Partition 'jaune_556525985' (partition ID 556525985) has 10000
data rows.
The total number of empty pages (with all deleted rows) in
partition 'jaune_556525985' (partition ID 556525985) is 0.
The total number of pages in partition 'jaune_556525985'
(partition ID 556525985) which could be garbage collected to
free up some space is 106
The total number of deleted rows in partition 'jaune_556525985'
(partition ID 556525985) is 0.
The total number of pages in partition 'jaune_556525985'
(partition ID 556525985) with more than 50 percent garbage is 0.
The total number of pages in partition 'jaune_556525985'
(partition ID 556525985) with more than 50 percent insert free
space is 0.

The total number of data pages in this table is 300.
The total number of pages which could be garbage collected to
free up some space is 106.
Table has 10000 data rows.
DBCC execution completed. If DBCC printed error messages,
contact a user with System Administrator (SA) role.
```

dbcc showrecovery

Displays a more indigestible report describing the *recovery of* each base.

```
dbcc serverlimits
```

Display all the limits of the ASE instance.

```
dbcc buffer
```

Displays the buffer cache header. Locate the word BUF_KEPT. Very verbose and unreadable: to be avoided!

```
dbcc dbcacheremove (<dbname>)
```

Allows you to remove a database from the cache. This command is useful in case an operation fails with the message "database in use" while no session is using the database in `sp_who`.

That being said, we must not forget that just because nobody "seems" to use a base when looking at `sp_who, it doesn't` mean that it is not really in use, because a person can use it with the syntax <BASE>.<OWNER>.<OBJECT> without even entering it with use.

```
1> sp_who
2> go
 fid spid status    loginame origname hostname blk_spid dbname       tempdbname cmd
 --- ---- --------- -------- -------- -------- -------- ----------- ---------- -----------------
   0    2 sleeping NULL     NULL     NULL            0 master       tempdb     DEADLOCK TUNE
   0    3 sleeping NULL     NULL     NULL            0 master       tempdb     SHUTDOWN HANDLER
   0    4 runnable NULL     NULL     NULL            0 master       tempdb     KPP HANDLER
   0    5 sleeping NULL     NULL     NULL            0 master       tempdb     ASTC HANDLER
   0    6 sleeping NULL     NULL     NULL            0 master       tempdb     CHECKPOINT SLEEP
   0    7 runnable NULL     NULL     NULL            0 master       tempdb     HK WASH
   0    8 sleeping NULL     NULL     NULL            0 master       tempdb     HK GC
   0    9 runnable NULL     NULL     NULL            0 master       tempdb     HK CHORES
   0   10 sleeping NULL     NULL     NULL            0 master       tempdb     DTC COMMIT SVC
   0   11 sleeping NULL     NULL     NULL            0 sybsecurity tempdb     AUDIT PROCESS
   0   12 sleeping NULL     NULL     NULL            0 master       tempdb     PORT MANAGER
   0   13 sleeping NULL     NULL     NULL            0 master       tempdb     NETWORK HANDLER
   0   14 sleeping NULL     NULL     NULL            0 master       tempdb     NETWORK HANDLER
   0   15 sleeping NULL     NULL     NULL            0 master       tempdb     NETWORK HANDLER
   0   16 sleeping NULL     NULL     NULL            0 master       tempdb     NETWORK HANDLER
   0   19 sleeping NULL     NULL     NULL            0 master       tempdb     LICENSE ...BEAT
   0   29 runnable sa       sa       TACTILOU        0 master       tempdb     DBCC
   0   30 runnable sa       sa       TACTILOU        0 master       tempdb     UPDATE
   0   31 running  sa       sa       TACTILOU        0 master       tempdb     INSERT

(19 rows affected)
(return status = 0)
1> drop database exemple
2> go
Msg 3702, Level 16, State 4:
Server 'TACTILOU', Line 1:
Cannot drop the database 'exemple' because it is currently in use.
```

So, before releasing the heavy artillery (dbcc dbcacheremove), it is advisable to check which are really the current users of a database, not with sp_who but with the syslocks table or the sp_lock procedure.

The following query, for example, displays all the names of users who have put a lock on a database:

```
1> select distinct a.spid, db_name(a.dbid) dbname ,
suser_name(b.suid) loginname from syslocks a, sysprocesses b
where a.spid=b.spid
2> go
 spid    dbname                           loginname
 ------  -------------------------------  --------------------------
 -----
     25 example                                  lbolnet
     55 park                        jnicholson
```

If a database refuses to drop just because users in other databases are locking it, dbcc dbcacheremove will be helpless but will still display a short diagnostic message and this will *kill* the troublesome process:

```
1> dbcc dbcacheremove("example")
2> go
Attempt to uncache the database 'exemple' with dbid 7.
The descriptors keep count is 1 and the system tasks keep count
is 0.
The descriptors hot count is 0 and the detached keep count is 0.
The per process keep count for spid 15 is 1.
The transaction '$ins' with xdes=0x1000f0201b0, state='Done
command-attached' was found active by spid 25.
The database 'exemple' could not be uncached.
```

Caches

Caches, or data caches, or named caches are areas of RAM memory whose role is to avoid reading and writing to disk. Indeed, a hard disk is a very slow hardware compared to RAM, so if you can avoid going there too often, you gain in performance. Moreover, caches can be consulted even when the disks are unavailable.

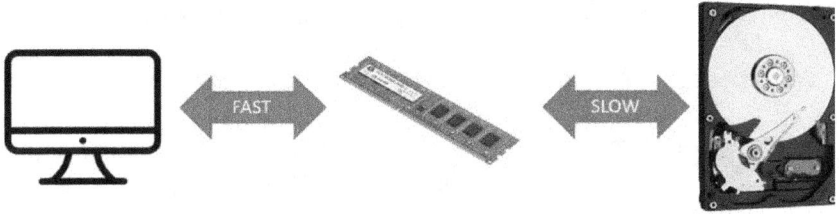

Figure 9 : The memory is always an intermediary between the client and the disk.

Whether it is select, insert, delete or update, all the basic commands submitted to an instance will cause one or more pages to rise in

RAM, in the caches. If the cache is large enough, the need to write to or read from the disk will be greatly reduced.

That's why the performance of a cache is measured in "cache hit ratio": it's the percentage of times the cache already had the page you needed and therefore saved you a round trip to the hard disk. To find out the origin of the pages in a query execution (disk origin = physical or memory cache origin = logical), a DBA can activate the `set statistics` option `io on and` then launch the query.

Let's take the example of a simple `SELECT` query. The first time I run it, none of the pages are already in the cache. The optimizer is forced to fetch 1000 pages from the disk.

The second time I run it, the optimizer will look for 800 pages on the disk and only 200 in the cache. This indicates that the cache is too small to hold the 1000 pages of the first run.

Cache hit ratio

100% means that all necessary pages are already present in the cache.

0% means that none of the required pages are already in the cache.

To get closer to 100%, there are two lines of improvement:

- enlarge the cover,
- link the cache to an object, a base or an index.

There can be several caches in a dataserver. The only one that is mandatory is called the default data cache. To create others, you must first make sure you have enough RAM available with the system commands (they depend on the O.S.). Then the command to execute is:

```
sp_cacheconfig newcache, "100M".
```

Then, it is possible to assign this cache to a specific object using the stored procedure `sp_bindcache`.

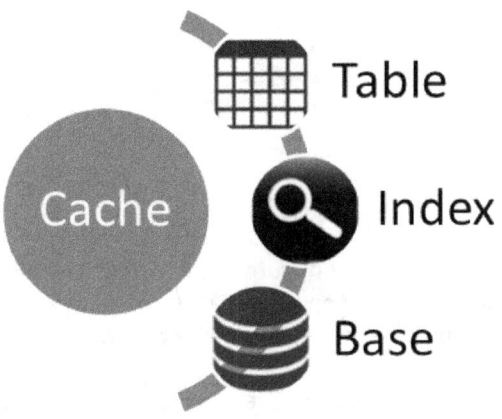

Figure 10 : A cache can be linked to a table, an index or a base.

To learn about the caches of an instance, there are a variety of tools:

- `sp_helpcache`
- `sp_cacheconfig`
- `sp_poolconfig`
- `select * from syscacheinfo`
- `select * from syscachepoolinfo`
- `select * from syspoolinfo`

👍 **System commands to know**

To find out how much RAM memory there is on a machine, type these commands:

- **Windows:** `systeminfo`
- **Linux:** `cat /proc/meminfo`
- **Solaris:** `prtconf | grep Mem`

Engines

Engines are concepts that allow Sybase ASE instances to be multitasking. If there is only one engine configured, the instance is single-tasked. Executing a request using multiple engines is called "parallelism". The parallel request will necessarily be faster than a normal request.

To find out how many engines are started on the instance it is necessary to do:

```
select * from master..sysengines
```

or

```
sp_helpthread
```

And to increase the number of engines:

```
sp_configure "max online engines" , 5
go
alter thread pool syb_default_pool with thread count = 5
go
```

This engine concept is therefore closely linked to the number of processors (CPUs).

 **System commands to know**

To find out how many processors there are on a machine, type these commands:

- Windows: `systeminfo`
- Linux: `lscpu`
- Solaris: `psrinfo`

Locking schemes

One of the mechanisms that ensures data consistency is called locking. Locking prevents the client from reading uncommitted data, i.e. uncertain data.

There are 3 locking schemes divided into two categories:

Category	Lock scheme
APL	`allpages`
	`datapages`
DOL	`datarows`

`Allpages`: All **index and data pages** affected by an update are locked until the transaction is completed.

`Datapages`: all **data pages** affected by an update are locked until the transaction is completed.

`Datarows`: all **rows affected** by an update are locked until the transaction is completed.

Opinion of the author. Allpages locking is archaic and not very efficient. It is better to set up a dataserver so that all future tables are created in a datapages locking scheme.

```
sp_configure "lock scheme", 0 , "datapages".
```

Whether it's a simple read (`select`) or a modification (`delete`, `update`), Sybase will always put a lock somewhere to ensure data consistency.

`Select` queries will tend to set shared locks. While `update` and `delete will tend to set` exclusive locks.

A shared lock is a mechanism that allows other sessions to use a page or row, but only if they also set shared locks. This can be compared to a handful of people reading a bulletin board. They share the reading of the panel.

An exclusive lock is a mechanism that only occurs if a page or row is not locked. In addition, they do not allow anyone else to come in and install a lock. This can be likened to someone who wants to change the poster of a panel but is waiting patiently for the readers (or other modifiers of the poster) to all be gone.

When an exclusive lock is waiting for all shared locks to be lifted or when a shared lock is waiting for an exclusive lock to be lifted, the request does not fall into error but is "blocked". That is, it will respond as soon as the situation clears up.

In `sp_who`, this kind of situation is easy to see:

```
spid status       loginame origname hostname blk_spid dbname
tempdbname cmd

----  ----------- -------- -------- -------- -------- ----------
---------- ------------------
```

```
21 recv sleep        sa        TACTILOU        0 disneyland
tempdb        AWAITING COMMAND

23 lock sleep        sa        TACTILOU       21 disneyland
tempdb        SELECT
```

We can see on the example above that session 23 is in "lock sleep" (= sleeping while waiting for a lock to be lifted) because of session 21. Whereas session 21 is in "`recv sleep`" (= sleeping while waiting for the client to give another order).

There are several outcomes to this case:

- Either customer number 21 completes its transaction by writing commit or rollback,

- Either client number 23 abandons its session.

- Either customer number 21 abandons its session.

- Either the DBA kills session 21 to let session 23 continue on its way.

Notion of lock

It is a value (about 240 bytes), represented figuratively by a padlock, which "lands" on a row or a page. Row locks only exist in DOL. When a table receives too many row locks on the rows of a page, ASE may have to merge all of them into a single page lock. And when too many pages are locked, ASE may decide to merge all of them into one object lock. This is called a "lock promotion".

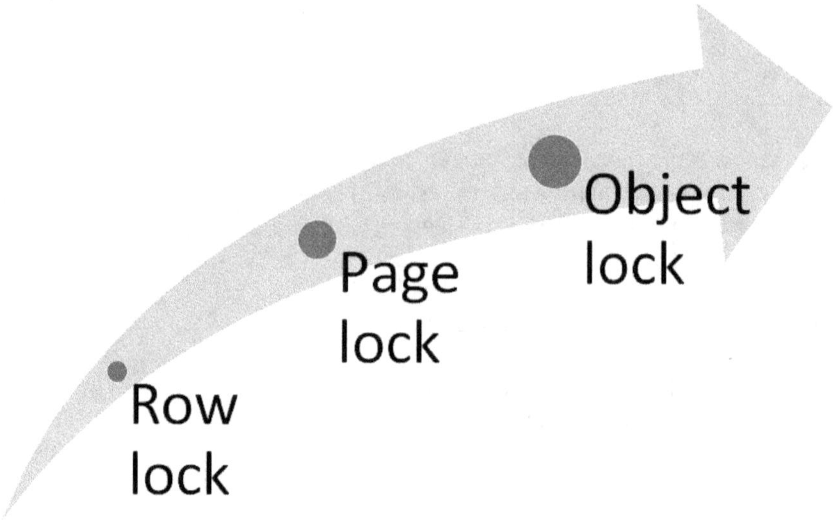

Figure 11 : Three scopes of locks

Locks can be viewed in the `syslocks` table or the system stored procedure `sp_lock`. For example:

```
1> select * from syslocks
2> go
 id           dbid   page        type   spid   class
fid       context row        loid        partitionid nodeid
 ----------- ------ ----------- ------ ------ --------------------
 ----------- ------ ------- ------ ----------- ----------- ------
    460525643         4            0         4        30 No Cursor Lock
0         0        0          60         0     NULL
    524525871         4        19309         5        31 No Cursor Lock
0         0        0          62         0     NULL
    524525871         4        17261         5        31 No Cursor Lock
0         0        0          62         0     NULL
    524525871         4        15213         5        31 No Cursor Lock
0         0        0          62         0     NULL
    524525871         4        11117         5        31 No Cursor Lock
0         0        0          62         0     NULL
```

	524525871		4		9069	5		31 No Cursor Lock
0	0	0			62		0	NULL
	524525871		4		2925	5		31 No Cursor Lock
0	0	0			62		0	NULL
	524525871		4		877	5		31 No Cursor Lock
0	0	0			62		0	NULL

(16916 rows affected)

Choose a locking scheme

There are several ways to choose the table locking scheme of a dataserver. The easiest way is to specify it when creating the table:

```
create table credits (id int, taux float) lock datarows
```

The other method is to choose a default locking scheme at the dataserver level. This will be the locking scheme chosen at each table creation if it is not specified:

```
sp_configure "lock scheme" , 0 , datapages
```

Finally, it is possible to change the locking scheme of a table at any time, but this can be tedious for very large tables. Indeed, switching from DOL to APL schema or the other way around requires a complete copy of the table data because DOL tables contain a small secret column (that neither the user nor the DBA can see) in which the identifier of each row is located. It is this identifier that will make it possible to lock only one row of a table and not all of them. But APL tables don't have this kind of column: their rows have no secret identifier. In order to be able to remove or add this column, switching from APL to DOL or DOL to APL requires a copy of the whole table in SELECT INTO, with all the disadvantages that this entails.

The syntax is:

```
alter table credits lock datarows

alter table credits lock datapages
```

```
alter table credits lock allpages
```

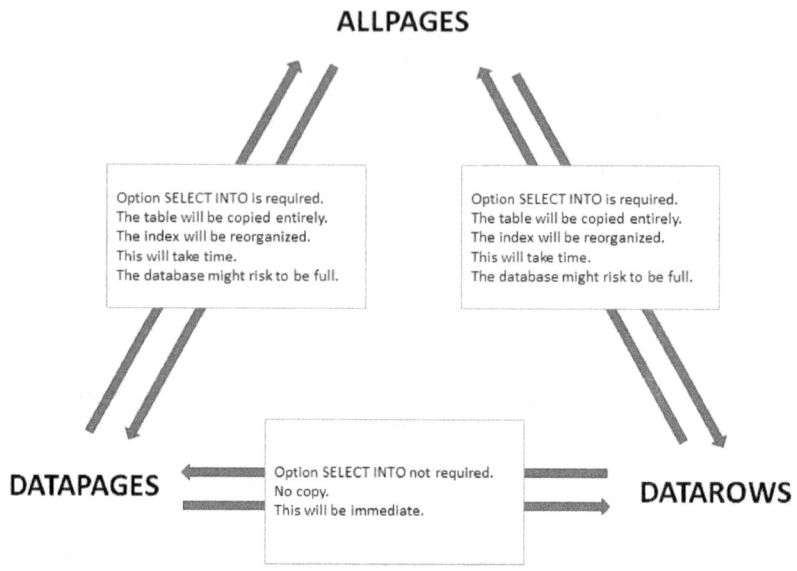

Figure 12 : The transition process between schemes

Sometimes, when changing the locking scheme, there may be messages about the maximum row size ("*row size could exceed row size limit*") or triggers ("*drop and recreate each trigger on this table*"). These messages are only precautionary warnings. There is nothing special to do.

Knowing the locking scheme of a table

To know the locking scheme of a table, you can

- either run `sp_help <elatablename>`
- either use the `lockscheme` function (`"<nameoftable>"`)
- or consult the `sysstats2` field of the `sysobjects` table.

Comparative Experience #1

"Locking diagrams".

Let's create two tables RED and YELLOW, without index.

- Red is in APL locking scheme.

- Yellow is in the DOL locking scheme.

Let's insert the same number of rows in both tables.

Let's compare table sizes:

	Red Table	**Yellow Table**
Nb of rows	100 000	100 000
Scheme of verr.	`allpages`	`datarows`
Volume (in pages)	2223	2440

DOL locks take up more space than APL locks. In this example, the difference is almost 10%. The extra space is due to the column containing the row identifier for the lock.

APL locked table	DOL locked table	
63d503cce7134315afb1efd4e238	325	63d503cce7134315afb1efd4e238
51630da0d1a241be9053efd4e238	326	51630da0d1a241be9053efd4e238
7fb555e0c0d042398732efd4e238	327	7fb555e0c0d042398732efd4e238
2baae84cd63a4d94b71aefd4e238	328	2baae84cd63a4d94b71aefd4e238
4806baf6067844a09ee5efd4e238	329	4806baf6067844a09ee5efd4e238
016424e51ef8450eb5f8efd4e238	330	016424e51ef8450eb5f8efd4e238
afc13a27e8c14312b84fefd4e238	331	afc13a27e8c14312b84fefd4e238
771c159217fd43d78136efd4e238	332	771c159217fd43d78136efd4e238
5fee80abea434f3e9ef0efd4e238	333	5fee80abea434f3e9ef0efd4e238
b28bae9e9eef42c683ccefd4e238	334	b28bae9e9eef42c683ccefd4e238
d7abe02b2b0f4a8f897defd4e238	335	d7abe02b2b0f4a8f897defd4e238
15ad22e9e4ae47d09bb4efd4e238	336	15ad22e9e4ae47d09bb4efd4e238
d3539459e981463fbf4cefd4e238	337	d3539459e981463fbf4cefd4e238
500bc89a93464439a082efd4e238	338	500bc89a93464439a082efd4e238
eff847c043534babbc11efd4e238	339	eff847c043534babbc11efd4e238
935b3e1732254a0baa32efd4e238	340	935b3e1732254a0baa32efd4e238
8d12d5dd3ef34de794c8efd4e238	341	8d12d5dd3ef34de794c8efd4e238
2748cf37c78e4fca9341efd4e238	342	2748cf37c78e4fca9341efd4e238
f27d51700c174d9297f3efd4e238	343	f27d51700c174d9297f3efd4e238

Figure 13 : DOL tables have a hidden colum in order to attribute a unique number to each row

Isolation

In the field of databases, isolation is the concept that ensures that two users of the same database don't see what the other is doing until they complete their transaction. It is therefore a subject close to the locking discussed above. There are 4 levels of isolation at ASE.

Isolation level 1: read committed

This is the default insulation level.

If user A runs a 1-million-row update, user B should not see some rows as they were before the update and some rows as they are after the update.

Because an operation must always be atomic: this means that it exists as a single indivisible entity. In reality, updating a million rows takes time. So, ASE decides that the select won't respond until the update is completely finished.

Example 1:

At 00:00, user Marc launches an update on a table.

```
update SCHOOLS set type = 1
```

At 00:01, the user Jean launches a select on the same table.

```
select type from SCHOOLS
```

This select does not run. It is suspended. John has no way of knowing, but he is blocked by Marc's update. A DBA can see it thanks to sp_who.

```
1> sp_who
2> go
 fid spid status        loginame origname hostname blk_spid dbname
tempdbname cmd
 --- ----  ----------  --------  --------  --------  --------  ------
----- ---------- --------
   0   28 running    marc             TACTILOU          0
example2     tempdb      UPDATE
   0   29 lock sleep jean      jean      TACTILOU         28
example2     tempdb      SELECT
```

At 00:05, Marc's update is finished. He sees a message confirming this. Only then does John's select really start.

```
(1000000 rows affected)
```

At 00:07, John's select is completed: He finds that all rows have a column type = 1.

Example 2a:

12:00, Marc opens a transaction

```
begin tran
```

12:01, Marc inserts a row in a table

```
insert into schools values (20, "Ecole Victor Hugo")
```

12:02, Jean does a select on this table

```
select * from schools
```

→The query remains suspended until Marc has written "commit" or "rollback". This can take seconds, minutes, hours or even days! By the way, it is interesting to see how many users call the DBAs for help shouting "*the base is slow!* "while their select is simply locked by the transaction of their colleague who has gone on vacation without committing.

Isolation level 0: read uncommitted

As its name indicates it is the total absence of insulation. This level allows anyone to look at data while it is not committed or rolled back or while its modification is not finished! The syntax of this select is:

```
select * from nameoftable at isolation read uncommitted
```

The interest of this syntax is to ignore any isolation to at least be sure to get a quick and immediate response! Speed rather that data reliability.

Example 2b:

12:00, Marc opens a transaction

```
begin tran
```

12:01, Marc inserts a row in a table

```
insert into schools values (20, "Ecole Victor Hugo")
```

12:02, Jean does a select on this table

```
select * from schools at isolation read uncommitted
```

→The request answers immediately despite one of the rows is not
committed!

```
id           name
----------- ----------------------
          11 Nelson Montfort School
          12 Lycée les Tulipes
          13 Rosa Parks School
          14 Nabilla College
          15 Steven Spielberg High School
          20 Victor Hugo School
```

Isolation level 2: serializable

This level locks objects even more aggressively. The "serializable" isolation
means that in the same transaction, a select will always return the same
result. It therefore strictly prohibits anyone from reading, deleting, updating
or inserting into a given table. So, it is no longer just a lock set by the person
who modifies the table, but a lock set by the person who reads it!

The syntax is:

```
select * from nameoftable at isolation serializable
```

Isolation level 3: repeatable read

This is an even more severe variant of "serializable". The reader is invited to
turn to the official documentation for more information. This level of
isolation is used very rarely.

The syntax is:

```
select * from nameoftable at isolation repeatable read
```

Session Settings

ASE is a software that can be configured at the instance level. But it is also possible to set up its own session. Session settings have no impact on other connections even if they use the same login.

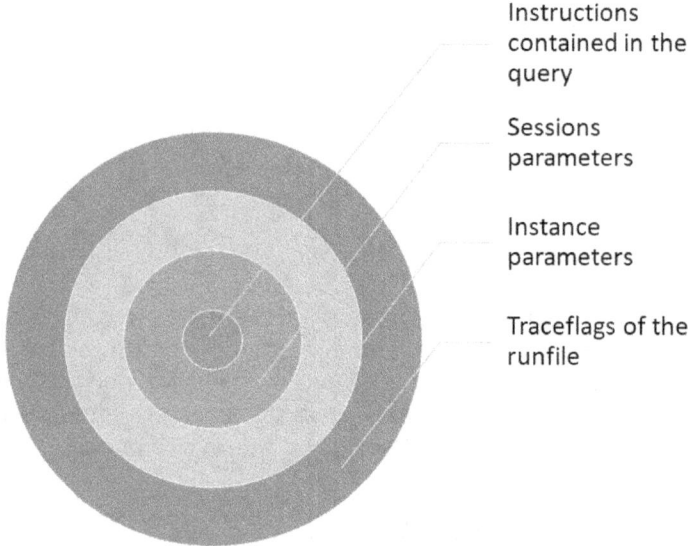

Instructions contained in the query

Sessions parameters

Instance parameters

Traceflags of the runfile

Figure 14 : Session parameters take precedence over instance parameters and traceflags, but not over the instructions contained in requests.

The best known is `set showplan on` which allows to display the execution plan of each query before the results.

```
1> set showplan on
2> go
1>
2> select top 5 * from sysindexes
3> go
```

80

```
QUERY PLAN FOR STATEMENT 1 (at line 2).
Optimized using Serial Mode
     STEP 1
          The type of query is SELECT.

          2 operator(s) under root

          |ROOT:EMIT Operator (VA = 2)
          |
          |  |TOP      Operator (VA = 1)
          |  |    Top Limit: 5
          |  |
          |  |SCAN        Operator (VA = 0)
          |  |     |    FROM TABLE
          |  |     |    sysindexes
          |  |     |    Table Scan.
          |  |     |    Forward Scan.
          |  |     |    Positioning at start of table.
          |  |     |    Using I/O Size 2 Kbytes for data pages.
          |     |    | With LRU Buffer Replacement Strategy for data pages.
```

There is a very long list of "set" commands that can change the parameters of a session. For example, there is a very long list of "set" commands that can change the parameters of a session:

set rowcount 6→limits the number of assigned rows to a maximum of 6 whether select, update or delete.

set transaction isolation level serializable→applies "serializable" isolation to all subsequent queries.

set nocount on→Do not display the number of affected rows at the end of the queries.

set statistics io on→Estimate the io of each query played

set statistics plancost on→Estimate the io and plan of each query played.

Component Integration Services

Component Integration Services (CIS) is a platform for remote connection between different instances. Thanks to CIS, one instance can communicate with another in order to emulate remote tables, remote databases, etc...

Figure 15 : CIS makes ASE communicating over the network

CIS makes transparent and homogeneous what may not seem transparent at first glance: communications between Oracle and ASE, access to tables miles apart, data transfer from Sybase IQ to Sybase ASE, table emulation of a text file, etc...

CIS uses a very precise syntax to define the data sources:

```
< INSTANCE>. < DATABASE>. < OWNER>. < OBJECT>
```

- If the base is omitted, it is equivalent to master.
- If the owner is omitted, it is equivalent to dbo.

CIS is extremely dependent on interface and sql.ini files. Because, in order to reach a remote instance, it is crucial to know its network coordinates.

Audit

The audit is a mechanism for recording certain activities taking place on an ASE instance. It may be the responsibility of a DBA to know everything that has happened on an instance and to detect intrusions, data theft or malicious acts.

Set up the audit

1. Create the sybsecurity database
2. Run the installsybsecurity (or instsecu) script
3. Restart the instance
4. `sp_configure "auditing", 1`

To set up certain monitoring systems

```
-- Audit the 'select' orders launched on the remuneration table
sp_audit 'select', 'all', 'remunerations', 'on'.
go

-- Audit the lbolnet login
sp_audit 'all',lbolnet,'all','on'.
go
```

See the surveillance set up

```
sp_displayaudit
```

Go read the audit report

```
1> use sybsecurity
2> go
1> select * from sysaudits_01
2> go
```

Or, for a more readable result:

```
select eventtime, audit_event_name(event), loginname, objname from
sysaudits_01 order by 1

eventtime                                  loginname objname
------------------- ------------------- --------- -------------
Jul 13 2015 1:50AM Auditing Enabled     sa        NULL
Jul 13 2015 2:01AM Non Fatal Error      lbolnet   NULL
Jul 13 2015 2:01AM Login                lbolnet   NULL
Jul 13 2015 2:01AM Non Fatal Error      lbolnet   NULL
Jul 13 2015 2:01AM Login                lbolnet   NULL
Jul 13 2015 2:01AM Login                lbolnet   NULL
Jul 13 2015 2:01AM Non Fatal Error      lbolnet   NULL
Jul 13 2015 2:01AM Access to Database    lbolnet  NULL
Jul 13 2015 2:04AM Logout               lbolnet   NULL
Jul 13 2015 2:04AM Select Table         JDurand   remunerations
```

Reserved words

When a word is reserved by the system, it must be put in square brackets to avoid ASE misunderstandings:

Example with the word "compressed

```
create table toto (id int, compressed char(40))
go
Msg 156, Level 15, State 2:
Server 'TACTILOU', Line 2:
Incorrect syntax near the keyword 'compressed'.
```

To set this:

```
create table toto (id int, [compressed] char(40))
go
```

Licenses

ASE's licensing policy is:

3 editions:

- ASE Developer Edition
- ASE Small Business Edition
- ASE Enterprise Edition

5 operating systems supported:

- HP-UX
- IBM AIX
- LINUX
- SunOS
- Windows

And a multitude of optional licenses unlocking special features:

- ASE_CORE
- ASE_PARTITIONS
- ASE_COMPRESSION
- ASE_ENCRYPTION
- ASE_HA
- ASE_JAVA
- ASE_ASM

...

The license file is usually found in $SYBASE/SYSAM-2_0/licenses and has the extension ".lic".

In addition, there is a properties file in $SYBASE/ase-15_0/sysam.

Check the license

To check the license of an instance, there are 3 methods:

1. Read the beginning of the errorlog of the instance just after starting it

85

```
SySAM: Using licenses from: C:\Sybase\\\SYSAM-
2_0\licenses\SYBASE_ASE_DE.lic;C:\Sybase\\\SYSAM-
2_0\licenses\SySAMLicenseServer.lic
SySAM: Checked out license for 2 ASE_CORE
(2015.1231/permanent/12FE BE55 1B69 AE84).
This product is licensed to: ASE Developer Edition - For
Development and Test use only
Checked out license ASE_CORE
Adaptive Server Enterprise (Developer Edition)
```

2. Use the stored procedure sp_lmconfig

```
1> sp_lmconfig
2> go

 Parameter Name      Config Value
 ---------------- ------------
 edition             DE
 license type        DT
 smtp host           null
 email recipients null
 email severity      null
 smtp port           null
 email sender        null


 License Name     Version     Quantity Status        Expiry Date
 Server Name
 --------------- ---------- -------- ------------ ---------------
 ------ -------------------
 ASE_HA           null        0        not used     null
null
 ASE_ASM          null        0        not used     null
null
 ASE_EJB          null        0        not used     null
null
 ASE_EFTS         null        0        not used     null
null
 ASE_DIRS         null        0        not used     null
null
 ASE_XRAY         null        0        not used     null
null
 ASE_ENCRYPTION null          0        not used     null
null
 ASE_CORE         2015.1231 2          OK           Permanent
null
 ASE_PARTITIONS 2015.1231 2            OK           Permanent
null
```

```
ASE_RLAC          null        0           not used      null
null
ASE_MESSAGING_TIBJMS null     0           not used      null
ASE_MESSAGING_IBMMQ null      0           not used      null
ASE_MESSAGING_EASJMS null     0           not used      null
ASE_TSM           null        0           not used      null
null

   Property Name Property Value
   ------------- --------------
   PE            DE
   LT            DT
   ME            1
   MC            25
   MS            null
   MM            null
   CP            0
   AS            A

Read the table master..monLicense
1> select * from master..monLicense
2> go
 InstanceID Quantity    Name                                  Edition
Type
Version        Status                        LicenseExpiry
GraceExpiry                  LicenseID
Filter         Attributes
 ---------- ----------- ------------------------------ ---------
-------------------- -----------------------------------------
-------------------- ---------------- -----------------------
------ --------------------------- -----------------------
------ -----------------------------------------------------
-----------------------------------------------------------
-------------------------- ------------- ------------------
----------------------------------------------
          0            8 ASE_CORE
Enterprise Edition              CPU license
2013.09290       OK
NULL                         1659 E60A 02AB 29A0 6D52 A371
5866 418A 3AEB D65D E7B8 CE31 B425 69F5 CC0F 1966 8643
PE=EE;LT=CP     CO=Sybase, Inc.;V=15.0;AS=A;MP=730;CP=0;EGO=
          0            8 ASE_ASM
Enterprise Edition              CPU license
2013.09290       OK
NULL                         1297 E549 5965 798D F028 5B3B
3234 CC3A 76B2 495D 3972 1465 335B B40C 1DF6 028E C089
PE=EE;AS=A     CO=Sybase, Inc.;V=15.0;AS=A;MP=730;CP=0;EGO=
```

Other features

A software often has less known or less appreciated features. Those of ASE will not be detailed in this book, but here is a list of them. It is important to remember that the official ASE website offers documents - in English - dealing with these subjects.

Here is a list of these features:

- Runtime classes.
- Les Extended Stored Procedures.
- Web Services.
- The Application Context Facility.
- Sybase Failover.
- Table encryption.
- Distributed transactions.

Starting and stopping ASE

DBAs always use the terms "start" or "stop" a dataserver when in fact, the real terms should be "open" or "close" because a dataserver is just a collection of files.

Yet with Word, Excel or Powerpoint, for example, it is generally said that you "open" a file. To conform to the usage of French-speaking DBAs, this book will use the terms "start" and "stop".

Start

Starting an ASE instance or starting a dataserver means running Sybase ASE binaries with the files on a dataserver.

To achieve this, the first step is obviously to connect to the machine that hosts ASE. It is impossible to start an instance without being locally connected on the machine.

Once connected, the environment variables must be mounted by running the SYBASE.sh file (or SYBASE.env or SYBASE.bat).

On Windows

There are two methods: either restart the service or run the runfile.bat.

Under Unix

You have to run `startserver -f < runfile>`.

Stop

Unlike starting, ASE can be stopped remotely because it is a simple SQL command. For security, few people can trigger this command.

For example:

```
1> shutdown
2> go
Msg 10353, Level 14, State 13:
Server 'TACTILOU', Line 3:
You must have any of the following role(s) to execute this
command/procedure: 'sa_role'
```

Stopping an instance can take a long time if there is intense activity. As long as ongoing requests are not committed or rolled back, the halt will be suspended.

To go faster, the DBA can therefore use the `shutdown with nowait` command, which as its name suggests, will stop the instance abruptly and immediately.

Diagnosing ASE

The most basic task of an ASE DBA is to diagnose the current state of an ASE instance. Following an alert, an on-call, a user request, a call from the system team, or after a machine crash, a DBA is often asked if an instance is doing well or poorly.

Remote diagnosis

The first diagnosis can be quite simple: connect from any client (e.g. isql) to the instance and see if it responds. But this remote diagnosis depends on the reliability of several elements: it is necessary to have an unlocked login and a valid password. The instance must be filled in the interface file (or sql.ini) of the client. The network must allow the connection (instance not in

DMZ, network not down). It is also necessary to privilege a client of a version adapted to the version of the diagnosed dataserver.

Local diagnosis

This time you have to be connected to the machine on which the instance is running and connect in isql.

The simple question

Once logged in, the instance must be queried. The two most common queries used by DBAs are `sp_who` and `sp_helpdb`. To ensure that the hard drives are working properly, the DBA should also attempt a `checkpoint all`. This command brings all cached data pages down to disk. You can also think of `select @@boottime` which gives the date and time of the last start of the instance.

General condition

ASE does not offer any tools that provide the overall health of an instance. As a DBA, it is essential to have a small stored procedure installed on all instances in the park, capable of displaying a report on the health of the dataserver to which one is connected. This procedure can be written by a DBA or found on the Internet.

In the appendix of this book is the source code of `sp_status`. By calling it, this procedure provides a report displaying **23** immediate indicators. For example:

```
1> sp_status
2> go
 YOU
 -------------------   ------------------------------------------
 -----------------
 Login/User/Spid        sa / dbo / 18

 INSTANCE
```

91

```
------------------- -----------------------------------
-----------------
Name                DUBAI
Version             Adaptive Server Enterprise/15.7/EBF 21339
SMP SP101 /P/X64/W
Errorlog            C:\Sybase\ASE-15_0\install\DUBAI.log
Page size           2048
Kernel              threaded mode

EVENTS
------------------- -----------------------------------
-----------------
Creation            Oct 29 2013 12:31AM
Upgrade             Oct 29 2013 12:32AM
Start               Jul 19 2015 9:52AM

CONFIGURATION
------------------- -----------------------------------
-----------------
Max memory          120000 (234 MB)
Number of engines   1

SESSIONS
------------------- -----------------------------------
-----------------
Total               21
Users               5
Blocks              0
Log suspend         0
Transactions        0

LISTEN TO
------------------- -----------------------------------
-----------------
Listener            Tactilou 5004

DATABASES
------------------- -----------------------------------
-----------------
                    dbccdb
Offline             example1
                    example2
You are in          master
                    model
                    sybsecurity
                    sybsystemdb
                    sybsystemprocs
                    tempdb
```

```
DUMP_OR_LOAD
------------------   -----------------------------------------
-------------------
LOAD  DATABASE        example1
DUMP  DATABASE        example2
```

Errorlog

The errorlog is a valuable history. It is a text file that contains the entire "medical file" of a dataserver since the day of its creation. Remember that its path can be obtained with the `select @@errorlog` query.

To consult it, starting from the end of the file, then seems obvious when diagnosing an instance. Beware, the errorlog file may not show anything special ... if the instance has been stopped abruptly.

System process

Several tools can be used to find out if an instance is running on a machine.

On Windows, you have to consult the task manager or services.

On Unix, you can run the `showserver` command or do a `ps -ef`.

Instance ok but database in trouble

Sometimes, especially after startups, an instance may be in great shape but one of the bases is not available when users try to connect to it. This is normal: it is still recovering. The progress of the recovery is not very verbose in the errorlog, so the DBAs sometimes doubt that it is working. You just have to be patient. The recovery can be seen in `sp_who`. To learn more, there is the `dbcc showrecovery` command.

Typical Problems

- The most serious problem we can encounter is of course the abrupt shutdown of the instance: this is when ASE stops completely without a DBA issuing the `shutdown` command. It can then issue a **STACK TRACE,** i.e. a long description of the failure in the errorlog.
- **LOG FULL** is when a database can no longer absorb transactions or complete those that have started due to lack of space in the transaction log.
- The **TEMPDB FULL is** when the temporary base is filled.
- The **OUT OF LOCKS** is a lack of locks. (see `sp_configure`)
- We can also detect **problems that are not problems,** such as a database that is unusable because it is reloading, or a blocking session that just needs to be *killed*.

Databases

General

At ASE, a database (often abbreviated to "db") is a logical container containing SQL objects. There are several databases in a dataserver.

To list all the bases of a dataserver, there are 3 methods:

- `select name from master..sysdatabases`
- `sp_helpdb`
- `sp_databases`

A database has a **name, number, creation date, owner, durability, size** and **options**. To access it, use the `use` command followed by its name. The other way to use its objects without "entering" them is to prefix the name of the objects. For example:

```
select * from family.dbo.people
```

In terms of storage, a database necessarily needs at least one device fragment to write its data.

It is not mandatory to specify either the size or the device when creating a database:

```
create database example
```

It is then created with the same size as the base model, log and data are mixed and one of the default devices is chosen. Usually this is the device master. If the dataserver has no "default" device, the command is wrong and the database cannot be created.

The best practice is to create at least 2 virtual devices before creating a base on it. One for the data and one for the transaction log:

```
disk init name='example_dat',
physname='c:/sybase/data/example_dat.dbf', size='50M'
go
disk init name='example_log',
physname='c:/sybase/data/example_log.dbf', size='10M'
go
create database example on example_dat = 40 log on
example_log = 10
go
```

At this stage, nothing is fixed: it is possible to enlarge a virtual device by adding space:

```
disk resize name='example_dat', size='30M
go
```

It is possible to enlarge a base. (Size is in mega).

```
alter database example on example_dat = 15
go
```

Specifying the size of the enlargement is not mandatory. ASE will choose a default value (between 1Mb and 4Mb depending on the page size of the instance):

```
alter database example on example_dat
go
```

Specifying the device is optional. If not specified, ASE will choose a "default" device, usually the master device and a default size. Nevertheless, it is better to avoid this simplistic syntax.

```
alter database example
go
```

Long awaited by Sybase DBAs worldwide, since version 15.7, it is possible to shrink the LOG part of a:

```
alter database example log off example_log = 5
go
```

And since version 15.7 SP100, it is also possible to shrink the DATA part of a database:

```
alter database example off example_dat = 15
go
```

Enlargement and reduction of the bases are thus carried out by stacking or unstacking fragments of devices of various sizes.

ASE does not recommend creating a data and log segment on the same device. It is possible but with an additional option:

```
1> create database EXAMPLE on mondevice = 50 log on mondevice =
10
2> go
CREATE DATABASE: allocating 15360 logical pages (30.0 megabytes)
on disk 'mondevice' (25600 logical pages requested).
Msg 1820, Level 16, State 1:
Server 'TACTILOU', Line 1:
This command adds log space to disk 'mondevice', which
previously contained only data. You must specify WITH OVERRIDE
to force this allocation.

1> create database EXEMPLE on mondevice = 50 log on mondevice =
10 with override
2> go
CREATE DATABASE: allocating 25600 logical pages (50.0 megabytes)
on disk 'mondevice' (25600 logical pages requested).
CREATE DATABASE: allocating 5120 logical pages (10.0 megabytes)
on disk 'mondevice' (5120 logical pages requested).
Caution: You have set up this database to include space on disk
11 for both data and the transaction log. This can make recovery
impossible if that disk fails.
Database 'EXEMPLE' is now online.
```

The disk init, create database, drop database and alter database operations are long-lasting operations because all data pages are formatted one by one. They must be launched with full knowledge of the facts.

However, there are accelerated syntaxes.

The syntax create database ... for load is a syntax that allows to create a database in almost a second! It does not initialize any page and of course the database is then totally unusable. It is essential to reload it with the load database command. So, you should always think about the occasions when a database must be created with the normal command or the for load command. Above all, it is essential to communicate well with your colleagues: a database in "for load", in production for example, looks like a corrupted or suspicious database. The "for load" command can even trigger an alert or an on-call!

To go faster on disk init and create databases, some DBAs pass all their devices in dsync=false and then reboot the instance. Indeed, the dsync=false option saves time because ASE does not wait for the actual writing to the disks and is satisfied with the operating system write buffer. However, let's recall that dsync=false is not recommended in the long term on all bases except tempdb. Reminder of the syntax:

```
sp_deviceattr mondevice , dsync , false
```

Finally, there is a syntax to create devices faster. It's like a normal disk init except that ASE doesn't waste time initializing all pages with zeros.

```
disk init ... skip_alloc = true
```

This option does not work on Windows:

```
1> disk init name = 'test', skip_alloc=true, size='30M',
physname = 'C:/test.dev'.
2> go
```

```
Warning: Ignoring the 'skip_alloc' option for device
'C:/test.dev' as it is not applicable to the special devices.
```

On the other hand, it works on Unix:

```
1> disk init name='device_tactilou_data55', size='100M',
physname='/abricot/sgbd/TACTILOU/devices/tactilou-data55',
skip_alloc = true
2> go
Warning: The 'skip_alloc' option of disk init/disk resize
command is turned on, and does not ensure allocation of the
specified number of pages. Please make sure file system has
enough space for future operations.
```

A small warning message states that using the `skip_alloc` option prevents ASE from really allocating disk space, so we must use this option carefully and make sure that we really have the disk space we are asking for.

In this example, taken on Unix, we can see that a 100 mega device occupies only 132 kb because the skip_alloc option has been used:

```
from -sh /abricot/sgbd/TACTILOU/devices/tactilou-data55
  132K     /abricot/sgbd/TACTILOU/devices/tactilou-data55
```

sp_helpdb

This is one of the most widely used stored procedures used by Sybase DBAs. When we call the procedure `sp_helpdb` followed by the name of a database, we have access to a lot of information such as its size, creation date, options, owner, identifier. But there is also a long list of "device_fragments", i.e. the constituent parts of the database. To the right of this table, there is a "created" field which indicates the date when a fragment joined the database. When all the fragments have the same date, it is generally the date when the database was last refreshed (or *loaded*, the anglicism used by some DBAs). Because there is an exception: when a database is *loaded* with a dump coming from itself (auto-load), the dates of the fragments do not represent the last load.

Example: base reloaded on December [1,] 2014

```
1> sp_helpdb disneyland
2> go
 name         db_size        owner dbid created        durability
lobcomplvl inrowlen status
  ---------- ------------- ---------  ------------ ---------- --
-------- -------- -------
 disneyland       150.0 MB sa         4 Dec 01, 2014 full
0      NULL select

(1 row affected)
 device_fragments                size            usage
created
 ------------------------------ ------------- ------------------
-- ---------------------
 disneyland_dat01                      10.0 MB data only
Dec 1 2014 11:43PM
 disneyland_log01                      10.0 MB log only
Dec 1 2014 11:43PM
 disneyland_dat01                      40.0 MB data only
Dec 1 2014 11:43PM
 disneyland_dat02                      30.0 MB data only
Dec 1 2014 11:43PM
 disneyland_dat03                      30.0 MB data only
Dec 1 2014 11:43PM
 disneyland_dat04                      30.0 MB data only
Dec 1 2014 11:43PM
```

Conversely, when a base has fragments of different dates, it means that it has never been *loaded* and that each fragment has been added over the years to enlarge the base. This is what happens in production for example.

Example: base created in January 2013 and regularly enlarged:

```
1> sp_helpdb disneyland
2> go
 name         db_size        owner dbid created        durability
lobcomplvl inrowlen status
  ---------- ------------- ---------  ------------ ---------- --
-------- -------- -------
 disneyland       150.0 MB sa         4 Jan 01, 2013 full
0      NULL select
```

```
(1 row affected)
device_fragments                     size            usage           created
----------------------------------   -------------   -------------   ------------------------
disneyland_dat01                     10.0 MB data only               Jan  1 2013 11:43PM
disneyland_log01                     10.0 MB log only                Jan  1 2013 11:43PM
disneyland_dat01                     40.0 MB data only               Feb  2 2013 10:29PM
disneyland_dat02                     30.0 MB data only               Apr  5 2013 14:53PM
disneyland_dat03                     30.0 MB data only               May  8 2014 10:41AM
disneyland_dat04                     30.0 MB data only               Mar  9 2015 01:43AM
```

master

The master base is the first base of a dataserver. It is fundamental. It is not intended to contain user data.

Its status is so particular that it is obviously forbidden to drop it or change its options.

The master base must absolutely remain on the master device. It can only be enlarged on fragments of the master device.

The master database contains system tables that are not present in the other databases. For example, syslogins or sysdatabases.

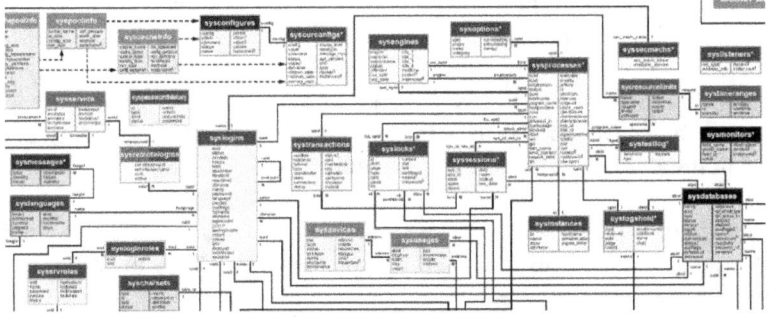

Figure 16 : Extract of ASE system tables

It is rare to have to reload it, but it is possible with a special procedure. It is advisable to save it regularly with the "dump database" command but also

101

to do regular "dump transaction master with truncate_only" since it cannot have the "trunc log on checkpoint" option.

Temporary bases

The most common temporary base is tempdb. It is a base like any other except that it is emptied each time the ASE instance is started. The tempdb is created by the *"zbsd"* dataserver creation script.

To create new ones, the syntax is simple:

```
create temporary database tempdb2 on tempdevice = 50
```

Its role is to store:

- The work tables necessary for operators DISTINCT, ORDER BY, GROUP BY, etc...
- Tables whose names begin with "#" are commonly called temporary tables or sharps tables. All users can create them. They are always contained in the tempdb. Each table is only visible to the session that created it. They disappear when the session is logged out.

Temporary bases are work areas that are not intended to record permanent data. Yet they have a crucial role to play. In case of 100% fill, the lack of disk space in the tempdb is a factor of incident.

It is possible and desirable in some cases to link a user to its own temporary database. This mechanism is used to isolate the requests of this user and therefore protects the integrity and performance of other processing. In a production environment, assigning a temporary database to certain users will avoid many production hazards and incidents. The syntax is as follows:

```
sp_tempdb 'bind', 'lg', 'users', 'DB', 'tempdb_users'.

go
```

This link between login and temporary base only takes effect after the user in question has logged out.

Example: before reconnection.

```
spid status      loginame     origname     hostname blk_spid
dbname tempdbname
----  ---------- ------------ ------------ -------- -------- ---
--- ----------
 32 recv sleep users TACTILOU users          0 master tempdb
```

Example: after reconnection.

```
spid status      loginame     origname     hostname blk_spid
dbname tempdbname
----  ---------- ------------ ------------ -------- -------- ---
--- -------------------
 31 recv sleep users TACTILOU           0 master tempdb_users
```

Nothing prevents us from doing the opposite, i.e. creating a temporary base strictly reserved for DBAs. In case of full tempdb, only the DBAs will be able to access the instance to intervene.

Tempdb size reduction

The possibility to reduce databases since 15.7 still does not apply to the tempdb database. But anyway, most DBAs had already cobbled together a solution long before 15.7.

```
1> alter database tempdb off tempdbdev2 = 150
2> go
Msg 5045, Level 16, State 1:
Server 'DUBAI', Line 4:
You cannot shrink database 'tempdb' because the database either
has reduced durability or is being used as a template.
```

The method is as follows. Warning: this procedure is not official.

1. Go to the master database
   ```
   use master
   ```

103

2. List all fragments of the tempdb
```
select * from sysusages where dbid = 2 order by
lstart
```
3. Activate the modification of system tables
```
sp_configure "allow update , 1
```
4. Delete the last fragment only. Be careful, at least one of the remaining fragments must have a segmap different from 0 otherwise the instance will never restart. Moreover, you must never remove the first fragment.
```
delete from sysusages where dbid = 2 and lstart =
206848
```
5. Abruptly stop the instance
```
shutdown with nowait
```

On reboot, the tempdb will have shrunk by one fragment. The operation can be repeated. This kind of brutal procedure has no effect on the tempdb because it is completely new at each boot. This is not true for a normal base.

Tempdb full

The tempdb database is used by almost all users of an instance. It can fill up when a user has performed a greedy operation (for example a sort of several million pages, a select into in a # table).

At this point, we are in a serious incident. The authority does almost nothing anymore:

- `select * from sysprocesses` no longer responds because it is not really a table. It is a snapshot view that ASE makes in the tempdb at the moment it is called.
- `select * from systransactions` no longer responds (for the same reason as sysprocesses).
- `sp_who` does not respond.
- `sp_helpdb` does not respond.
- `sp_tempdb` does not respond.
- `dump tran tempdb with truncate_only` ne répond pas.

Here is the only procedure that will work:

1. Go read in the errorlog the spid number of the process that fills the tempdb. This is the fourth column of the line "space available in the log".
2. Two possibilities:
   a. End this SPID only:
      ```
      select lct_admin('abort',<spid>)
      ```
   b. End all SPIDs that use the tempdb:
      ```
      select lct_admin('abort',0,2)
      ```
3. Decide if you also want to kill the spid responsible for the filling (`kill <spid>`)
4. Decide whether to increase the tempdb to prevent this from happening again.

Orphan tables

Sometimes the tempdb may contain "#" tables that no longer belong to anyone. Indeed, the session that created them may have been *killed without* its tables disappearing. To really delete them, there are 2 solutions:

```
dbcc orphantables('drop')
```

Or

```
shutdown
```

In-memory databases

An in-memory database is a database that never writes its pages to disk.

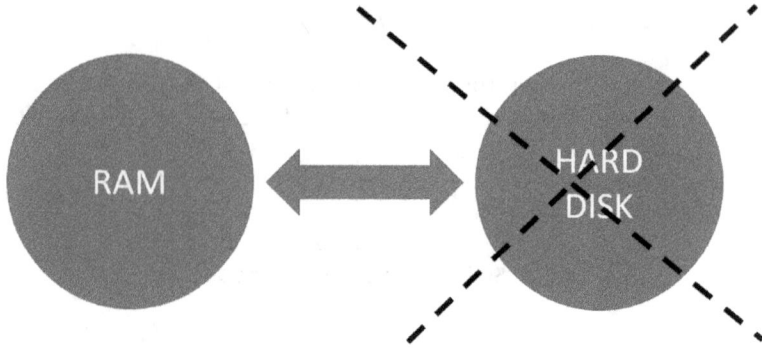

Figure 17 : An in-memory base does not need a hard disk.

The advantage of these bases is their great **working speed**. On the other hand, they have an indubitable constraint: at each instance stop, all their content is **lost**. They can therefore only be used in a context that lends itself to it. For example, as temporary databases or in the case of fast real-time applications such as online gaming, etc...

To create them, there are 3 steps:

1. Create an in-memory **cache**
2. Create an in-memory **device**
3. Create an in-memory **database**

For example:

```
sp_cacheconfig cache_games , '5M' , inmemory_storage
go
disk init name='jeux_device', physname='jeux_cache', size='5M',
type='inmemory'
go
create inmemory database jeux on jeux_device = 5 with durability
= no_recovery
go
```

sp_dboption

This is the stored procedure for changing database options. Each option can be active (true) or inactive (false).

In version 15.7 SP130, there are **30 options**. This number has been steadily increasing.

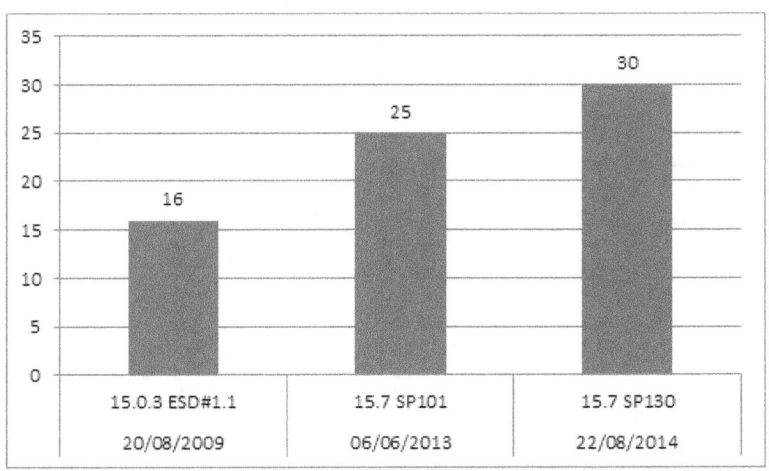

Figure 18 : Number of options

1. abort tran on log full

2. allow incremental dumps

3. allow nulls by default

4. allow page signing

5. allow wide dol rows

6. async log service

7. auto identity

8. dbo use only

9. ddl in tran

10. deallocate first text page

11. defer_index_recovery auto

12. defer_index_recovery manual

13. defer_index_recovery none

14. defer_index_recovery parallel

15. deferred table allocation

16. delayed commit

17. enforce dump tran sequence

18. full logging for all

19. full logging for alter table

20. full logging for reorg rebuild

21. full logging for select into

22. identity in nonunique index

23. no chkpt on recovery

24. no free space acctg

25. read only

26. scratch database

27. select into/bulkcopy/pllsort

28. single user

29. trunc log on chkpt

30. unique auto_identity index

Most of them have an explicit name, others are less intuitive.

The syntax of sp_dboption is:

```
sp_dboption <base> , "<option>". , <true or false>
```

The easiest way to find out which options are set on a base is to run `sp_helpdb`. But there are two important things to keep in mind:

For one thing, not everything `sp_helpdb` displays is an option. It can be an observation. For example, the following terms are not options:

- offline

- mixed log and data

- suspect

- no options set

- don't recover

- proxy

- in-memory

- scratch

- archive

On the other hand, with the multiplication of the number of options on the bases, it seems that the ASE editor has sometimes forgotten to integrate them in the `sp_helpdb` procedure. For example, the "allow page signing" option does not appear in `sp_helpdb` even if it is set to "true".

Option: Select into/bulkcopy/pllsort

This option is one of the best known by people who work with Sybase ASE. It is an option that allows or disallows copies of **unlogged** data.

When performing an `insert, update, delete` or even `create table` or `create index,` the operation is described in the transaction log so that it can be re-run in case of "database recovery".

But some operations cannot be replayed because they cause bulk data refactoring without describing the precise manipulation in the transaction log. These operations are said to be "weakly logged". Are concerned...

- Select into
- Bcp in fast bcp mode
- Switching from DOL to APL or vice versa
- Deleting a column
- Reorg rebuild

This option therefore authorizes operations that will end the completion of the transaction log. That is to say that to restart on a complete and coherent transaction log, it is necessary to systematically perform a `dump database` after these types of operations.

Option: No checkpoint on recovery

This option, when set to "true", indicates that you should not finalize the recovery of the database after its load. The goal is to be able to continue to apply `load tran` even when the base is open.

The danger of this option is in case of a stay of proceedings. When it is restarted, the recovery of the database will take centuries because all transactions that took place between the last load and the stop of the instance will have to be replayed.

Option: Full logging for select into

This option is a real revolution in the world of ASE. Since version 15.7, it is possible to log the select into in the transaction log.

This means that it is now possible to perform select into or alter table operations without interrupting the tran dump.

However, the obvious drawback is the future problems of full logging (filling the transaction log) that will be generated by this option. Because it is precisely because the data manipulated by the select into commands were voluminous that the transaction log did not record them.

Example:

SELECT INTO is logged	Nb of rows	Width of the rows	Size of the data	Nb of pages used for the data	Nb of pages used for logging
Oui	5000	54 bytes	270 000 bytes	148	72
Non	5000	54 bytes	270 000 bytes	148	8

Durability

Durability is a concept introduced in a previous version of ASE. This concept deals with the effort that ASE must make to maintain the data in a database after a case has been discontinued.

There are 3 levels of sustainability:

1. **Full**: the contents of the database must reappear the next time the instance is started. This is the most common durability.
2. **At_shutdown**: the contents of the database should reappear **at** the next start provided that the instance has been stopped properly with the shutdown command. In case of a sudden shutdown, nothing is kept and the database is in a "suspicious" state.
3. **No_recovery**: the content of the database is permanently lost at each stop, whether clean or brutal. Like the tempdb for example.

Quiesce database

The `quiesce database` command is used to suspend all writes to disk. Reading is still possible but nothing can be inserted, deleted or modified. By definition, this feature should be used with moderation. There can be several reasons to use it:

- Basic Duplication
- Instance cloning
- Dump/Load cross-platform

Users are then suspended with the following error message

« *Your query is blocked because it tried to write and database 'disneyland' is in quiesce state. Your query will proceed after the DBA performs QUIESCE DATABASE RELEASE ".*

To quiesce a database, the syntax is:

```
quiesce database <label> hold <delabase name>
```

To cancel the quiesce, the syntax is:

```
quiesce database <label> release
```

Be careful, you must know the name of the tag that was used to install the `quiesce database` to be able to remove it afterwards. If you don't remember it, don't panic, just run this

```
dbcc traceon(3604)
go
dbcc resource
go
dbcc traceoff(3604)
go
```

Then, in the generated report, look for this:

```
QUIESCEDB_INFO:
Quiesce Point #1:
        Tag Name = disneyland
        Process id = 23
        Databases quiesced by this process:
        disneyland
END OF QUIESCEDB_INFO
```

Tip: the simplest is to name the quiesce label with the same name as the base as in the example above.

Duplicating a base

The quiesce command is very useful when you want to move or duplicate a database.

First of all, you have to interrupt the writting on the source database:

```
quiesce database disneyland hold disneyland for external
dump to "C:/sybase/manifest_disneyland.bin"
```

Then, you have to copy all the device files from the database.

Nom	Modifié le	Type	Taille
disneyland_dat1 - Copie.dbf	28/11/2013 22:59	Fichier DBF	102 400 Ko
disneyland_dat1.dbf	28/11/2013 22:59	Fichier DBF	102 400 Ko
disneyland_dat2 - Copie.dbf	28/11/2013 22:49	Fichier DBF	102 400 Ko
disneyland_dat2.dbf	28/11/2013 22:49	Fichier DBF	102 400 Ko
disneyland_log1 - Copie.dbf	28/11/2013 22:49	Fichier DBF	10 240 Ko
disneyland_log1.dbf	28/11/2013 22:49	Fichier DBF	10 240 Ko
disneyland_log2 - Copie.dbf	28/11/2013 22:59	Fichier DBF	51 200 Ko
disneyland_log2.dbf	28/11/2013 22:59	Fichier DBF	51 200 Ko

When the copy is finished, you can release the quiesce from the source database.

```
quiesce database disneyland release
```

The manifest is a file that accompanies the devices. It is an extract from the master that will be useful in the next step. To read it, we can use this syntax:

```
mount database all  from
"C:/sybase/manifest_disneyland.bin" with listonly
```

You can now create a new database with the manifest and the copied devices:

```
mount database disneyland as disneyland2
from "C:/sybase/manifest_disneyland.bin"
```

```
using
disneyland_dat1 as "C:\Sybase\data\disneyland_dat1 - Copy.dbf",
disneyland_dat2 as "C:\Sybase\data\disneyland_dat2 - Copy.dbf",
disneyland_log1 as "C:\Sybase\data\disneyland_log1 - Copy.dbf",
disneyland_log2 as "C:\Sybase\data\disneyland_log2 - Copy.dbf"
```

And finally, you have to put it online

```
online database disneyland2
```

From that moment on, the manifest is no longer of any use and can be deleted. We can then see that the database is well created and has devices whose names have been chosen by ASE.

```
sp_helpdb disneyland2
```

name	db_size	owner	dbid	created	durability	lobcomplvl	inrowlen	status
disneyland2	260.0 MB	sa	5	Nov 25, 2013	full	0	0	select into/bulkcopy/pllsort, trunc log on chkpt

(1 row affected)

device_fragments	size	usage	created	free kbytes
AAAI#disneyland_dat1	100.0 MB	data only	Nov 29 2013 12:22AM	100200
AAAJ#disneyland_dat2	100.0 MB	data only	Nov 29 2013 12:22AM	102000
AAAK#disneyland_log1	10.0 MB	log only	Nov 29 2013 12:22AM	not applicable
AAAL#disneyland_log2	50.0 MB	log only	Nov 29 2013 12:22AM	not applicable

Devices names have been automatically generated

Unmount

The command unmount is used to "detach" a database from its dataserver. The base and its devices are completely removed from the dataserver. It is reversible. A manifest file allows you to reintegrate the database and its devices in the dataserver if you wish. This command works

115

only if mirroring is disabled: `sp_configure 'disable disk mirroring', 1.`

This feature is used to easily move a database from one dataserver to another.

But above all it has a diverted use: it allows to drop a very large base without waiting. When a base is very large, the dropper with `drop database` can take several hours!

For example, on a small scale, to remove a 5000 MB base:

drop database grosse_base	unmount database grosse_base to '/tmp/toto'.
49 seconds and 157 ms	2 seconds and 563 ms

Constraints:

1. The instance has to be in a disabled mirroring configuration.
2. The base must be the only one to use its devices.

Data storage

Transaction log

Obviously, a database is expected to contain data. But in a transactional environment like ASE offers, databases contain something else: **a transaction log**. It contains a lot of diverse information, but in the eyes of DBAs, it takes the form of a simple two-column table called `syslogs` that is stored exclusively in the `logsegment`. Even if it's a table, consulting it doesn't bring much to the naked eye. The syslogs table contains only 2 columns: a transaction identifier and an operation identifier.

```
1> select top 10 * from syslogs
2> go
 xactid            op
 ------------------
 0xc05000000600 63
 0xc05000000600 71
 0xc05000000600 30
 0xc150000300      0
 0xc150000300     72
 0xc15000000300 66
 0xc150000300     72
 0xc15000000300 66
 0xc150000300     67
 0xc150000300     63
```

One can make a `distinct` to know how many transactions are present in the transaction log:

```
select count(distinct xactid) from syslogs
```

Or a `group by` to know how many modified rows each transaction has generated:

```
select xactid, count(op) from syslogs group by xactid
order by count(op)
```

It should be noted that in the "op" column, rows deletions are generally numbered 66, additions are made with 3 operations: 63+30+0 and modifications are numbered 65.

There is also a DBCC command to view the transaction log (very verbose).

```
1> dbcc traceon(3604)
2> go
1>
2> dbcc log
3> go
```

As its name implies, the transaction log is a history of all transactions that take place on the base. The role of this history is to ensure the consistency of the database in all circumstances. It allows:

- To ensure that a transaction is totally committed or totally cancelled (commit or rollback).
- To allow a base to be restored after an abrupt stay of proceedings.
- Reload the database to return the data as it was at a specific date and time.

In sybase linguo, the data is called "DATA" and the transaction log is called "LOG". Data and transaction log cohabit in a database. Sybase DBAs typically propose that a transaction log occupies 10% of the database space.

It is not possible to view the contents of the transaction log, but you have to imagine a chronological list of changes. The transaction log can be used to cancel an operation as well as to reproduce it.

Illustration with a table of 5000 rows:

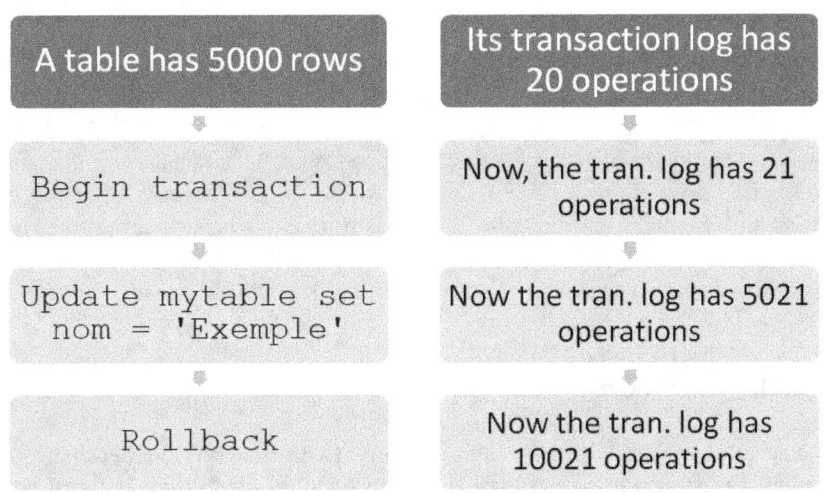

Figure 19 : Example of chronology of a transaction log

On the above chronogram, we can see that each row modified in the data systematically gives rise to a new entry in the transaction log. And rollback, i.e. the reversal of a transaction is made possible because all changes have been mentioned in the transaction log. In fact, the log stores the values before and after the change.

It is therefore normal to see 10,000 rows in a transaction log following a 5000-rows update which is then rolled back (5,000 reversal operations). The larger a database is and the more extensive the modification operations will be, the larger the LOG part must always be increased in proportion to the increase in its DATA part.

The LOG part of a base could grow forever but this is not desirable. So, to bring down the level of this history, there are 3 solutions.

Truncate only

The first is to purge the transaction log of all completed transactions. For example, in the case presented above, the 5000 updated rows are then rolled back. The result is a transaction log of 10,000 rows. Since the transaction is now complete, these 10,000 rows can be deleted. To do so, the command `dump transaction mabase with truncate_only` must be run. Good to know: the possible absence of Backup Server does not prevent to do a `dump tran with truncate only`. Moreover, whatever the value of `tran_dumpable_status()`, you can always do a `dump tran with truncate only`. The oldest transaction still present in a transaction log is the one that prevents to dump the log. It is visible by `selecting * from master..syslogshold`.

Trunc log on checkpoint

The second method consists of activating an option on the database to explain that as soon as the data is saved on disk, all the contents of the transaction log that concerns completed transactions must be automatically erased. This option is `trunc log on chkpt`. It is therefore a very automatic mode of operation.

Dump transaction to ...

This method consists of purging the transaction log while copying it to an external file. By doing so, a complete history of the database is maintained outside the instance in a backup filesystem. This method is not automatic unless a threshold is triggered and a stored procedure `sp_thresholdaction is set up`.

From logical to physical

If there is one aspect on which all DBMS editors diverge, it is the architecture of data storage on disk.

At Sybase, there are the notions of files, device, fragment, base, segment, partition, page...

A **file** is a traditional concept in computing: it is a contiguous succession of bytes recorded on a medium in the form of an entity designated by an alphanumeric name. It is one of the most palpable notions of computing because in everyday life most of us use files (MP3, DOC, PDF, TXT...).

A **device** is a concept introduced by Sybase to refer to a file that is part of the database server, whether or not it is in use. It then becomes permanently attached to the dataserver and does not need to be manually deleted.

A **database** is a container of objects and tables. In order to be stored somewhere, a database must rely on one or more devices. Each time a database uses a device, it is called a fragment.

A **fragment is** therefore both a piece of database and a piece of device. A fragment must therefore be delimited so that the fragments are clearly separated. This is where Sybase introduces the notion of **page**.

A **page** is an elementary brick that is always the same size. Generally, 2048 bytes. Each fragment thus has a first and a last page. A database has the right to use only the pages included in its fragments. When the data reaches the last page, it must move on to the next fragment.

Then there is the notion of **segment**. It's a soft zone: it doesn't have a specific size allocated to it, it's just a kind of label that we give to several fragments. Knowing that each fragment can have several labels. So, it's really a very virtual notion.

Finally, there are **partitions**: these are groups of pages belonging either to a table or to an index. So, a partition contains only real data, not empty space. A partition is composed of several pages not necessarily contiguous. Partitions know which pages belong to them thanks to the OAM (Object Allocation Map).

We are therefore faced with a mille-feuille of computer concepts. The most down-to-earth being the file and the most virtual being the table or index.

Relationships:

- There are several rows on a partition.
- There are several partitions on a segment.
- There are several segments on a fragment.
- There is only one virtual device in a fragment.
- There is only one file attached to a virtual device (or two in case of mirroring).

Here are two graphs describing the successive layers of data storage, from the most virtual to the most material (logical to physical):

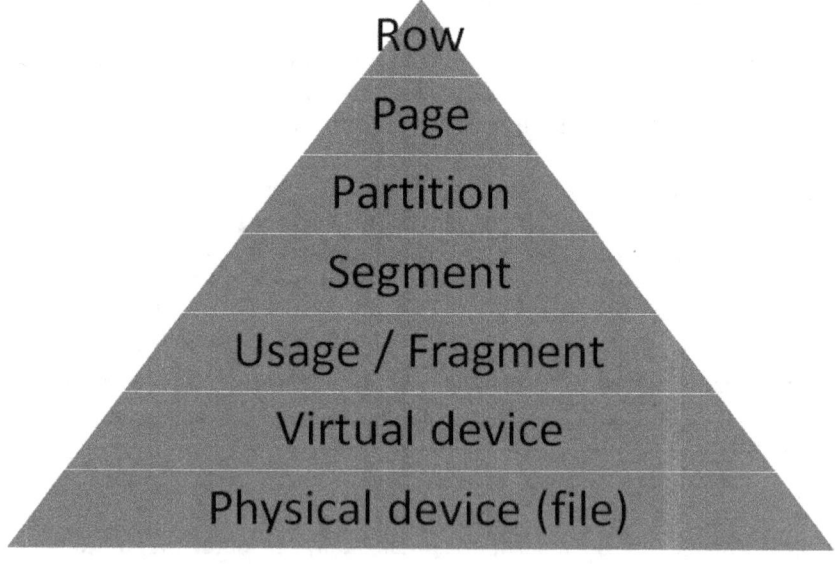

Figure 20 : Pyramid of data concepts (1)

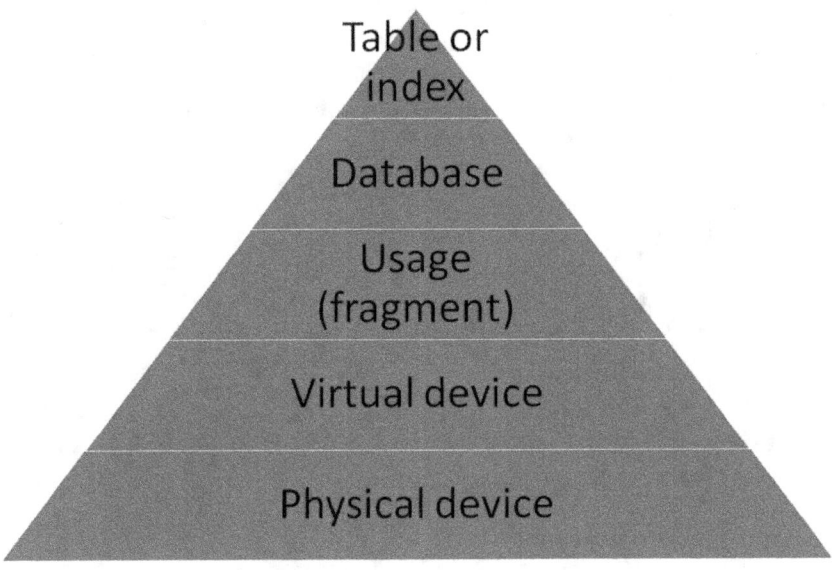

Figure 21 : Pyramid of data concepts (2)

Page

The page is the name Sybase gives to blocks of the same size that make up a dataserver. It is the smallest unit of measure for disk space at Sybase ASE. Sybase considers a database to be like a book, consisting of a succession of pages of the same size. The size of the pages must be chosen when the dataserver is created. Thereafter, it will be impossible to change this.

The possible page sizes are 2kb, 4kb, 8kb or 16kb. To choose the right page size you have to think about two aspects:

- A base can only be reloaded with a dump from a dataserver of equivalent size.
- The 2k size is preferable for OLTP and 16k for OLAP.

The page is the cornerstone of Sybase ASE. Whether it's `SELECT`, `UPDATE`, `DELETE` or `INSERT`, Sybase needs to "move" pages up and down. Moving a page up means reading it from the hard drive, inside the file, and putting it into a variable in RAM. Conversely, moving a page down means writing the contents of a variable to the hard disk, inside the file.

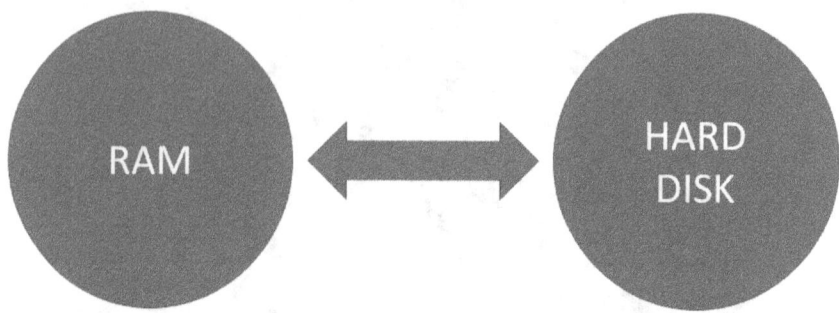

Figure 22 : Data constantly flow between RAM and hard drive

The notion of page avoids cluttering up RAM with data that is not needed. Sometimes, ASE performs Asynchronous Prefetch: it collects on the disk, pages of data that it does not need but that are close to the ones it needs. This is to save time.

Analogy. *You have to imagine that the hard disk is like a cellar and the memory is like an apartment: nobody wants to dump all the contents of his cellar in his living room just to look for a pair of winter gloves.*

The pages are all numbered and yet they are not numbered! They are not numbered because since they are contiguous and of identical size, it is easy to pick the one you want.

And that's where Sybase introduces two new storage devices: **scope** and **UA.**

1 extent = 8 pages

1 U.A. (Allocation unit) = 32 extents = 256 pages.

They are used to manage the many DML operations UPDATE, DELETE and INSERT. Indeed, in a database, there are frequently a large number of modifications: additions, deletions which concern several different tables. The database server must be able to store all these modifications without mixing everything up. The tables must each "know" where their rows are and not get mixed up with each other.

For this, each object (table or index) has one or more partitions. Each partition points to what is called an OAM (Object Allocation Map). It is a table that contains the list of UAs that make up the partition. The address of a UA is simply the address of the first page of the UA. This page is called "Allocation Page". It too is a table that contains the list of extents that are occupied by data.

Finally, there is one last notion at Sybase: chaining. Each page of an extent is double-chained to the others thanks to two pointers: the pointer to the next page and the pointer to the previous page.

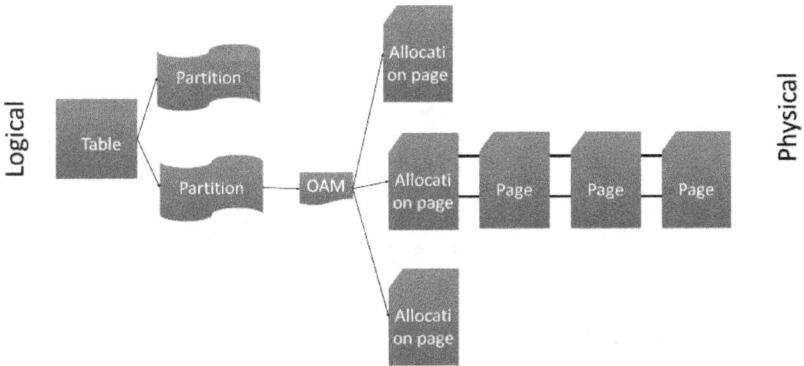

Figure 23 : From logical concept to physical concept

To sum up: Sybase ASE's data storage is like a maze or a plate of spaghetti. Data and indexes from multiple tables are intermingled and adjoined

125

without mixing thanks to complex but rigorous concepts: pages, OAMs, Page Allocations.

The downside is that the loss or corruption of a single Sybase ASE file would result in the irretrievable loss of data from several different tables and indexes.

Table

The table is the elementary particle in a database. A table is an object that has a structure (columns) in which rows are stored.

Attributes

- Name

- Locking diagram

- Owner

- Creation date

Sub-objects

- Columns

- Data rows

- Primary keys

- Foreign keys

- Permissions

- Constraints of uniqueness

- Check constraints

- Index

- Triggers

- Partitions

Links

- Defects

- Rules

- Caches

- Database

Creation syntax

```
create table millefeuilles
(id int identity , name char(35))
lock datarows partition by roundrobin 8
```

The syntax of the CREATE TABLE is composed of 3 parts.

Before the parenthesis

This part is only dedicated to the name of the table.

In parenthesis

This part is the most important: it is dedicated to the logical structure of future records but also to the integrity constraints.

- Column types,

- Column names,

- Default,

- Constraints check,

- Null or Not null,

- Identity,

- Primary keys,

- Foreign keys

After the parenthesis

This is the most optional. It is dedicated to the physical storage of future table data.

- Locking diagram

- Segment

- Partitioning

- Max_rows_per_page

- Exp_row_size

- Reservepagegap

- Compression

Width

The structure of a table is composed of one or more columns. There is no limit to the number of columns, however, the sum of bytes in a record is limited by the page size. This is called the "table width".

The table width limit varies according to the size of the dataserver pages. Indeed, ASE still refuses to store a single record on several pages. This limit varies from 1962 bytes for 2K APL tables to 16300 bytes for 16K DOL tables.

When a table has a structure that can cause a record to overflow on several pages, a warning message appears.

```
2> create table test (id int, name char(500), first name
varchar(300), incentive varchar(600), address
varchar(800))

3> go

Warning: Row size (2218 bytes) could exceed row size
limit, which is 1964 bytes.
```

And when a record actually reaches this limit, it is aborted, rolled back and an error message appears.

```
Msg 511, Level 16, State 2:
Server 'TACTILOU', Line 2:
Attempt to update or insert row failed because resultant
row of size 2108 bytes is larger than the maximum size
(1962 bytes) allowed for this table.
Command has been aborted.
(0 rows affected)
```

To reduce the width of a table that exceeds its limit, there are only 3 axes of intervention:

1. Dropping some columns.
2. Reduce the length of some fields.
3. Stop abusing the varchar type and use char instead.

The DBA may have to accompany the EOM in the vertical cutting of its table. A view containing a joint on two tables will replace the old table.

PERSONNE

ID	PRENOM	NOM	ADRESSE	VILLE
25	JACK	FILON	78 Rue de l'enstanbouille	MEUDON
89	RAYMOND	HERB	14 Rue du chat poisseux	TOULOUSE
153	PHILIPPE	BYOG	1 avenue des serpantins	BORDEAUX
217	LAETICIA	FAUCHAND	3 chemin Pierre de Ronsard	PARIS

PERSONNE_IDENT

ID	PRENOM	NOM
25	JACK	FILON
89	RAYMOND	HERB
153	PHILIPPE	BYOG
217	LAETICIA	FAUCHAND

PERSONNE_ADR

ID	ADRESSE	VILLE
25	78 Rue de l'enstanbouille	MEUDON
89	14 Rue du chat poisseux	TOULOUSE
153	1 avenue des serpantins	BORDEAUX
217	3 chemin Pierre de Ronsard	PARIS

```
create view PERSONNE as select A.*, B.ADRESSE, B.VILLE
from PERSONNE_IDENT A, PERSONNE_ADR B where A.ID = B.ID
```

Deleting a column and its impacts

It is not possible to delete a column if an index is created on it. You must first delete the index.

In general, ASE "likes" to rebuild tables. This is what happens especially when you want to delete a column: the command `alter table ...` `drop` behaves like a `select into`. That is to say, the table is entirely duplicated without the undesired column and then the old table is deleted. This duplication necessarily leads to a sudden increase in the disk space occupation.

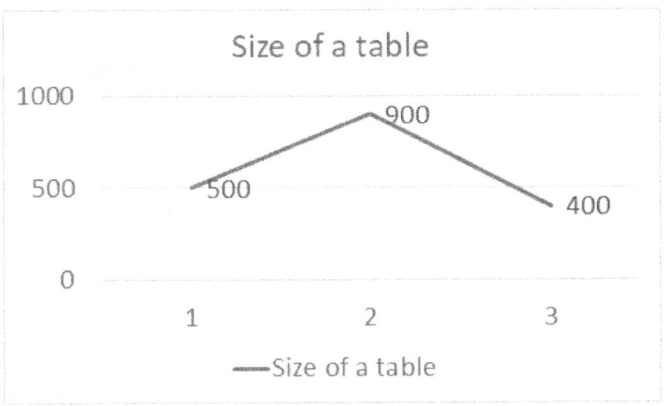

Figure 24 : Initially the table has a size of 500 MB. In order to drop a column, Sybase copies it (step 2) which occupies 900 MB. Then it drops the previous table. The new table occupies only 400 MB.

Therefore, if the `select into` option is not enabled on the database, deleting a table column fails:

```
Msg 11052, Level 16, State 1:
Server 'TACTILOU', Line 2:
The 'select into' database option is not enabled for
database 'disneyland'. ALTER TABLE with data copy cannot
be done. Set the 'select into' database option and re-
run.
```

Fortunately, since version 15.7 ESD #2, the syntax `ALTER TABLE ... DROP ... WITH NO DATACOPY` allows to delete columns without copying the data. Thus, the advantages are: speed of execution, optional select into option, no lock and stable disk space.

In the following example, two identical tables will respectively undergo a classic `alter table drop` and an `alter drop with no datacopy`:

	TABLE_A	**TABLE_B**
Number of rows	36000	36000
Number of pages	1125	1125
Request	`alter table TABLE_A drop name`	`alter table TABLE_B drop nom with no datacopy`
Duration	233 milliseconds	47 milliseconds
Number of pages after	327	1235
Select into required	Yes	No
Indexes recreated	Yes	No

It's amazing: the new "`with no datacopy`" feature in ASE 15.7 tends to increase the size of tables that have lost a column! Conversely, it is considerably faster than the other one: this new syntax just hides the old column. The dropped column is therefore still present on the disk but invisible.

Both syntaxes have virtues and disadvantages. It is advisable to choose intelligently the one that corresponds to the needs of each one.

Best practice: it is so expensive to delete a column, that it is better to use the same command for several column deletions to save time.

For example:

```
alter table toto drop name, first name
go
```

instead of

```
alter table toto drop nom
go
alter table toto drop prenom
go
```

Modification of column type

The syntax for changing the type of a column is as follows:

```
alter table EXAMPLE modify MACOLONNE varchar(50)
```

But beware, it is not allowed for anything and everything:

```
1> alter table EXAMPLE modify name text
2> go
Msg 13907, Level 16, State 1:
Server 'TACTILOU', Line 1:
ALTER TABLE 'EXEMPLE' failed. You cannot modify column 'nom' to
TEXT/IMAGE/UNITEXT type.
```

For all strings, depending on the old type and the new type of the column, ASE will either copy the table by `select into` or act immediately or refuse the request. It is also possible to change the length of the same type: for example, from varchar(10) to varchar(30).

Old type	New type	ASE's action
Varchar	Char	Select into
Varchar	Varchar (larger)	Immediate consideration

Varchar	Varchar (smaller)	Select into
Varchar	Text	Prohibited
Char	Char	Select into
Char	Varchar	Select into
Char	Text	Prohibited
Text	Char	Select into
Text	Varchar	Select into

Best practice: it is so expensive to modify some columns, that it is better to use the same command for several column modifications to save time. For example:

```
alter table toto modify nom char(30), prenom char(30)
go
```

Instead of

```
alter table toto modify nom char(10)
go
alter table toto modify prenom char(20)
go
```

Adding a column

The syntax for adding a column to a table is:

```
alter table < labelname> add < columnname> type
```

ASE adopts two different behaviors depending on the type of column added. If the added column admits null values and has no default value, then adding the column is a simple formality. It is **immediate**. Indeed, the system does not need to dwell on adding a completely empty column.

On the other hand, if the column does not admit a null value and has a default value, ASE must copy the whole table by `select into` method in order to add this new column. DBAs are used to the consequences: risk of overflow of the data segment space, long duration, and unlogged operation requiring to make a dump database afterwards.

Summary table of column addition:

Null or not null	Default or no default	ASE method
NOT NULL	DEFAULT	Select into
NOT NULL	No DEFAULT	FORBIDDEN
NULL	DEFAULT	Immediate addition
NULL	No DEFAULT	Immediate addition

Best practice: it is so expensive to add some columns, that it is better to use the same command for several column additions to save time. For example:

```
alter table toto add
nom char(10) default 'Durand' not null,
prenom char(20) default 'Jean' not null
go
```

Instead of

```
alter table toto add nom char(10) default 'Durand' not null
go
alter table toto add prenom char(20) default 'Jean' not null
go
```

Prevent fragmentation with exp_row_size

ASE has an option which stands for "Expected row size".

Comparative Experience #2

The "exp_row_size" option

Let's compare a table with this option and a table without it:

```
create red table (id int, name varchar(40))
with exp_row_size = 36
go
create yellow table (id int, name varchar(40))
go
```

Next, let's insert 10000 rows measuring much less than 36 bytes and then let's note their sizes:

- red has 244 pages
- yellow has 106 pages

Unsurprisingly, the table that was asked to provide 36-byte rows consumes more space.

Now, let's modify all the rows of these two tables in order to really consume 36 bytes

```
update red set name = newid()
update yellow set name = newid()
go
```

Comment:

- red has 266 pages
- yellow has 300 pages

Explanation: the "red" table provides disk space in case a 36-byte wide row is inserted. On the other hand, the "yellow" table wrote all its first data consecutively, leaving little room for future larger data. When the "yellow" table is updated, it is unable to save the new 36-byte records into its current smaller records. ASE then decides to make pointers to less contiguous spaces. This takes up a lot of disk space.

The `exp_row_size` parameter therefore avoids future fragmentation. It is more economical in terms of disk space in the long term.

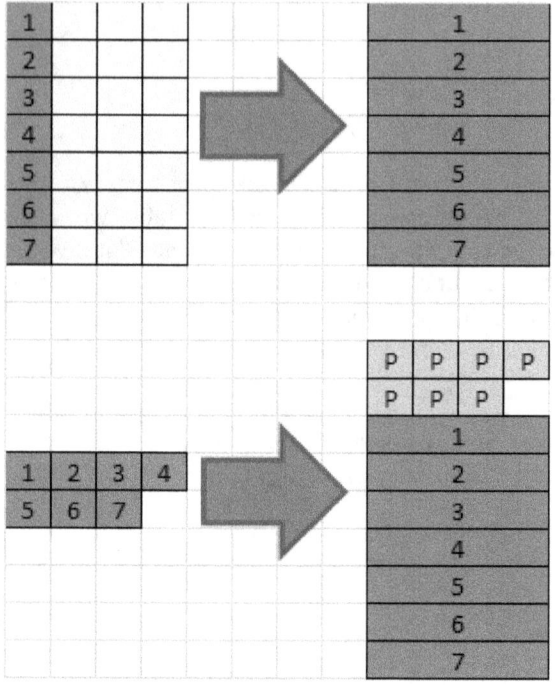

Figure 25 : Exp_row_size vs no exp_row_size

Size of a table

There is a very useful function to know the volume of a table: data_pages(). It has 3 syntaxes:

```
-- Size of the table + its indexes
select data_pages(<id of the base>, <id of the table>)

-- Table size only
select data_pages(<id of the base>, <id of the table>, 0)

-- Size of the index whose id is n
select data_pages(<id of the base>, <id of the table>, <n>)
```

138

It is usually coupled with two other very useful functions: db_id() and object_id():

```
-- Returns the ID of a table
select object_id("matable")
-- Returns the ID of a database
select db_id("matable")
-- Returns the ID of the current database
select db_id()
```

Sybase also offers two stored procedures that can announce the size of a table in kilobytes:

```
1> sp_spaceused CITIES , 1
2> go
 index_name size      reserved unused
 ---------- -------  -------- ------
 IDX1         598 KB 624 KB    26 KB
 IDX2        3872 KB 3888 KB 16 KB

(1 row affected)
 name     rowtotal reserved data     index_size unused
 ------  -------- -------- -------  ---------- ------
 CITIES 98000     11780 KB 7260 KB 4470 KB
```

and

```
1> sp_spaceusage "display summary", "table" , VILLES
2> go
Warning: Some output column values in the result set may be
incorrect. Runnin
All the page counts in the result set are in the unit 'KB'.
 OwnerName TableName Type UsedPages RsvdPages ExpRsvdPages
PctBloatRsvdPages
 --------- -------- ----- -------- -------- ----------- ----
-------------
 dbo       CITIES   DATA    7262.0   7268.0      7056.0
3.00
 dbo                INDEX  CITIES 4474.0   4512.0      4464.0
1.06
```

Temporary table with #

ASE users all have the possibility to create temporary tables. These are tables whose name starts with #. Their access is limited to the session that created them. Other sessions are unable to see them. And their lifetime does not exceed the lifetime of the session that created them. Their creation syntax is classical:

```
create table #temporary (id int, name char(20))
```

They are stored in the tempdb. It is possible to view them with sp_help.

```
1> use tempdb
2> go
1>
2>
3> sp_help
4> go
 Name                                    Owner Object_type
 --------------------------------------- ----- ------------
 sysquerymetrics                         dbo      view
 #sphelp1rs01000300010380416 dbo      user table
 #temporary00000280010373540 guest user table
```

Their full name contains a succession of numbers: these are the identifiers that will allow you to have several temporary tables with the same name but each belonging to a different session.

Even the DBAs can't consult them!

```
1> select * from #temporary00000280010373540
2> go
Msg 208, Level 16, State 1:
Server 'TACTILOU', Line 1:
#temporary00000280010373540 not found.
```

But if you're really motivated, there's an unofficial trick:

1. Dump database tempdb ...
2. Create a base of the same size
3. *Loader* this base with the dump

4. Enter this database
5. Make a `sp_configure "allow up", 1`
6. Modify the `sysobject` table to remove the famous "#" in the table names
7. Now making a `select` on the tables will work.

Example:

```
1> dump database tempdb to "c:/tempdb.dbf".
2> go
Backup Server: 4.171.1.1: The current value of 'reserved pages
threshold' is 85%.
Backup Server: 4.171.1.2: The current value of 'allocated pages
threshold' is 40%.
Backup Server: 4.171.1.5: The current value of 'parallel scan'
is 2.
Backup Server session id is: 25. Use this value when executing
the 'sp_volchanged' system stored procedure after fulfilling any
volume change request from the Backup Server.
Backup Server: 4.41.1.1: Creating new disk file c:/tempdb.dbf.
Backup Server: 6.28.1.1: Dumpfile name 'tempdb15196088EB '
section number 1 mounted on disk file 'c:/tempdb.dbf'
Backup Server: 4.188.1.1: Database tempdb: 882 kilobytes (2%)
DUMPED.
Backup Server: 4.188.1.1: Database tempdb: 1068 kilobytes (12%)
DUMPED.
Backup Server: 4.188.1.1: Database tempdb: 1238 kilobytes (22%)
DUMPED.
Backup Server: 4.188.1.1: Database tempdb: 1408 kilobytes (33%)
DUMPED.
Backup Server: 4.188.1.1: Database tempdb: 2088 kilobytes (74%)
DUMPED.
Backup Server: 4.188.1.1: Database tempdb: 2258 kilobytes (85%)
DUMPED.
Backup Server: 4.188.1.1: Database tempdb: 2428 kilobytes (95%)
DUMPED.
Backup Server: 4.188.1.1: Database tempdb: 2516 kilobytes (100%)
DUMPED.
Backup Server: 3.43.1.1: Dump phase number 1 completed.
Backup Server: 3.43.1.1: Dump phase number 2 completed.
Backup Server: 3.43.1.1: Dump phase number 3 completed.
Backup Server: 4.188.1.1: Database tempdb: 2524 kilobytes (100%)
DUMPED.
Backup Server: 3.42.1.1: DUMP is complete (database tempdb).
```

```
1> disk init name = 'tempdb2', size='404M',
physname='c:/tempdb2'.
2> go
1> create database tempdb2 on tempdb2 = 404
2> go
CREATE DATABASE: allocating 206848 logical pages (404.0
megabytes) on disk 'tempdb2' (206848 logical pages requested).
Database 'tempdb2' is now online.
1> load database tempdb2 from "c:/tempdb.dbf".
2> go
Backup Server session id is: 28. Use this value when executing
the 'sp_volchanged' system stored procedure after fulfilling any
volume change request from the Backup Server.
Backup Server: 6.28.1.1: Dumpfile name 'tempdb15196088EB '
section number 1 mounted on disk file 'c:/tempdb.dbf'
Backup Server: 4.188.1.1: Database tempdb2: 5124 kilobytes (1%)
LOADED.
Backup Server: 4.188.1.1: Database tempdb2: 47622 kilobytes
(11%) LOADED.
Backup Server: 4.188.1.1: Database tempdb2: 90632 kilobytes
(21%) LOADED.
Backup Server: 4.188.1.1: Database tempdb2: 133642 kilobytes
(32%) LOADED.
Backup Server: 4.188.1.1: Database tempdb2: 176652 kilobytes
(42%) LOADED.
Backup Server: 4.188.1.1: Database tempdb2: 219662 kilobytes
(53%) LOADED.
Backup Server: 4.188.1.1: Database tempdb2: 262672 kilobytes
(63%) LOADED.
Backup Server: 4.188.1.1: Database tempdb2: 305682 kilobytes
(73%) LOADED.
Backup Server: 4.188.1.1: Database tempdb2: 348692 kilobytes
(84%) LOADED.
Backup Server: 4.188.1.1: Database tempdb2: 391702 kilobytes
(94%) LOADED.
Backup Server: 4.188.1.1: Database tempdb2: 413720 kilobytes
(100%) LOADED.
Backup Server: 4.188.1.1: Database tempdb2: 413728 kilobytes
(100%) LOADED.
Backup Server: 3.42.1.1: LOAD is complete (database tempdb2).
Started estimating recovery log boundaries for database
'tempdb2'.
Database 'tempdb2', checkpoint=(3344, 4), first=(3344, 4),
last=(3344, 4).
Completed estimating recovery log boundaries for database
'tempdb2'.
Started ANALYSIS pass for database 'tempdb2'.
Completed ANALYSIS pass for database 'tempdb2'.
```

```
Started REDO pass for database 'tempdb2'. The total number of
log records to process is 1.
Completed REDO pass for database 'tempdb2'.
Use the ONLINE DATABASE command to bring this database online;
ASE will not bring it online automatically.
1> online database tempdb2
2> go
Started estimating recovery log boundaries for database
'tempdb2'.
Database 'tempdb2', checkpoint=(3344, 4), first=(3344, 4),
last=(3344, 4).
Completed estimating recovery log boundaries for database
'tempdb2'.
Started ANALYSIS pass for database 'tempdb2'.
Completed ANALYSIS pass for database 'tempdb2'.
Recovery of database 'tempdb2' will undo incomplete nested top
actions.
Database 'tempdb2' is now online.
1> use tempdb2
2> go
1> sp_configure "allow up", 1
2> go
 Parameter Name                       Default     Memory Used Config
Value

Run Value

                              Unit              Type
------------------------------ ----------- -----------
------------------------------ -------------------- ----------------
-----
 allow updates to system tables          0                0
1

1

                             switch              dynamic

(1 row affected)
Configuration option changed. ASE need not be rebooted since the
option is dynamic.
Changing the value of 'allow updates to system tables' does not
increase the amount of memory Adaptive Server uses.
(return status = 0)
1> update sysobjects set name='TOTO' where
name='#temporaire00000280010373540'
2> go
(1 row affected)
```

```
1>
2> select * from TOTO
3> go
 id            name
 ----------- --------------------------------------------------------
             1 lost confidentiality!
```

Partition

A partition is a block of data belonging to a table or an index. All the rows of a table must be in at least one partition. It is a kind of bag containing records.

Partitioning therefore consists of a logical division of tables without any impact on the syntax of SELECT, DELETE, INSERT and UPDATE queries. The operation is perfectly transparent for writing queries.

Each partition is a sub-object of the table and contains some of its data rows.

Partitions are not searchable: no SQL query allows to see which rows are in a partition.

If nothing special is specified in the CREATE TABLE command, ASE creates the table with a single partition to which it gives an alphanumeric name.

Example:

```
create table company (id int, name char(20))
go
sp_helpartition company
go
```

As this table has only one partition, all the rows that will be inserted will go inside this single partition.

```
 partition_name           partition_id pages    row_count segment
 create_date
 -------------------- ------------- ------- --------- ------- --
 ----------------
```

```
company_1792006384      1792006384           1           20 default
Jun 26 2015 8:42AM
```

At any time, it is possible to add partitions ("Round-robin" type):

```
alter table enterprise partition 4
```

But no existing rows are moved when creating new partitions.

```
partition_name          partition_id pages row_count segment
create_date
  --
company_1792006384      1792006384      1           20 default
Jun 26 2015 8:42AM
company_1808006441      1808006441      1            0 default
Jun 26 2015 8:48AM
company_1824006498      1824006498      1            0 default
Jun 26 2015 8:48AM
company_1840006555      1840006555      1            0 default
Jun 26 2015 8:48AM
```

The simplest and most widespread partitioning is **"round robin"** partitioning. It does not require a special license. It is a cyclic fair distribution algorithm: each new record inserted will start on a next partition. So, there are no criteria describing the content of each partition other than chance.

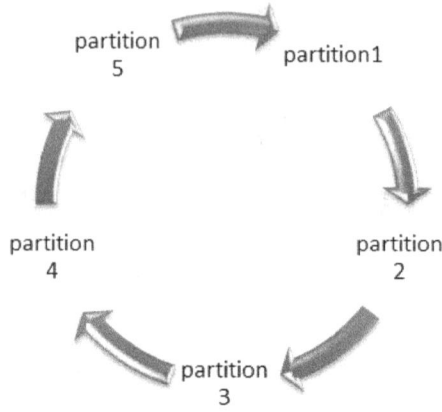

Figure 26 : Round-robin distributes the data equally in the partitions

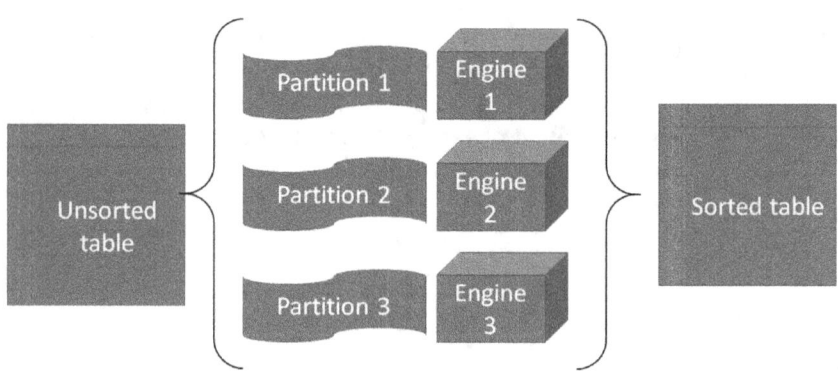

Figure 27 : A table being sorted by 3 engines

The interest of this cyclic partitioning lies in the fact that the tables are divided into several blocks and then worked on in **parallel**. For example, sorting the table will be faster because several engines will be able to sort the table simultaneously.

Moreover, to create a clustered index on a partitioned table, the prerequisites are more numerous. For example, partitioning complicates clustered indexes.

```
1> create clustered index indexo on entreprise (id)
2> go
Msg 1538, Level 17, State 1:
Server 'TACTILOU', Line 5:
max utility parallel degree 3 is less than the required 'max
utility parallel degree' 5 to create clustered index on
partition table. Change the parallel degree to required parallel
degree and retry.
```

Semantic Partitioning

There are 3 other ways to partition a table. But unlike round-robin partitioning, which simply distributes the data on partitions while completely ignoring the data content, the three other partitioning modes divide the data of a table according to semantic criteria. All 3 semantic partitioning modes require the ASE_PARTITION license.

There are 3 types of semantic partitioning:

- **Hash**: you can choose the column on which ASE will base a hash. It is not possible to know this hash rule: ASE chooses it best to distribute the rows evenly over all partitions. It is important to choose a very meaningful column to get the most out of this hash.
- **List**: segregation of the table rows according to specific values in a decisive column.
- **Range**: Segregation of the table rows according to ranges of values in a decisive column.

Partitioning by range is very efficient on tables containing a lot of rows, especially if some rows are rarely consulted.

At the time of partitioning, it is judicious to cut its table in 3 or 4 pieces. Let's take the example of an application specialized in meteorology: it stores all the daily weather data of all the cities in the world. The table in question will progressively contain many rows. However, most of the read requests that will reach it will be limited to the most recent dates: today's, yesterday's and the day before yesterday's weather. The table is therefore cluttered by its history.

Among all the data contained in the table, in order to facilitate the reading of recent dates, it is possible to associate range partitioning and segmentation.

Indeed, it may be wise to create 3 segments in the base: each one connected to a different device. The devices themselves can be allocated on physical media of different performance and cost:

- A device for "old" data, e.g. an inexpensive hard disk offering basic performance but huge storage space.
- A device for "recent" data, for example, a more powerful hard disk, much more expensive.
- A device for "current" data, for example, an SSD medium known to be particularly fast but too expensive to have huge capacities.

Note that it is not mandatory to have disks of unequal performance. You can very well have 3 equally fast disks. It's just more expensive financially but it's not a technical limit.

From then on, with a breakdown by date, data older than a month will be found on the first device, data older than a month but older than a week will be found on the second disk and finally, data older than a week will be accessible at an unequalled speed thanks to the SSD of the third device. Thanks to the "partition pruning" (= elimination of partitions), during its tablescan, the optimizer will ignore certain partitions if it is 100% sure that the data it is looking for is not there.

```
The type of query is SELECT.
ROOT:EMIT Operator
```

```
| SCAN
Operator| FROM
TABLE|
temperatures| [ Eliminated Partitions: 1 2 ]
| Table Scan.
| Forward Scan.
| Positioning at start of table.
| Using I/O Size 2 Kbytes for data pages.
| With LRU Buffer Replacement Strategy for data pages.
```

During off-peak periods, for example at night or on weekends, the table will have to be systematically rebuilt to refresh this partitioning. Partitions that have not changed (typically the one containing the oldest data) will not be rebuilt.

The limitation of this system is the way the data is searched afterwards: only date-based searches in the chronological sense will benefit from this implementation. For any search such as "weather from all January 1st from 1970 to nowadays" or "all weather data from New York City from 1970 to nowadays", the partitioning will have no effect and will be even worse than before because all 3 disks will be used, including the slowest one. To overcome these cases, "denormalization" can be used.

The advantage of the system is its complete transparency for the application: nothing needs to be redeveloped on the application side.

Let's get down to business. We must first allow semantic partitioning (by-hash, by-list or by-range) by passing the command

```
sp_configure 'enable semantic partitioning', 1
```

Then you have to create the *n* devices corresponding to the *n* storage media:

```
disk init name='device_lent',
physname='D:/sybase/meteo_data', size='1000M'
disk init name='device_medium',
physname='E:/sybase/meteo_data', size='100M'
```

```
disk init name='device_rapide',
physname='F:/sybase/meteo_data', size='50M'
```

Then, the database must be attached to the n devices:

```
create database meteo
ondevice_lent=1000,
device_medium=100,
device_rapide=50
```

Then you have to create the n corresponding segments:

```
sp_addsegment segment_slow, meteo,
device_lentsp_addsegment
segment_medium, meteo, device_mediumsp_addsegment
segment_rapid, meteo,
device_rapid
```

Finally, the table is cut out by dividing it over the n segments:

```
alter table temperatures partition by range
(date)
(
partition_ancienne values <= ('2013-01-01') on
segment_lent,
partition_recente values <= ('2013-02-15') on
segment_medium,
partition_actuel values <= (MAX) on segment_rapide)
```

This kind of alter has an immediate effect on data movement and index recreation: long duration and problems with locks and disk space are to be expected!

You can also find this kind of mount with by-list partitioning for other applications. For example, we can imagine a table containing data that can be consulted and data that has been "deleted" in the application sense. In a way, visible data and hidden data but which remain in the table for historical preservation reasons.

As before, we will partition to keep the hidden data on an inexpensive and therefore low-performance physical disk and the visible data on a high-performance disk.

But there is a big disadvantage with list partitioning: when the column responsible for partitioning contains an unexpected value, the INSERT falls into error. The application is therefore required to correctly manage the content of the decisive column.

Example of implementation:

```
alter table contracts partition by list (visibility)
(
 partition_cachee values (0) on segment_cachee,
 partition_visible values (1) on segment_visible
)
```

When a semantic partitioning changes because of an ALTER request, the data is immediately moved to comply with the new partitioning rule.

View the contents of the partitions

To find out how many rows are in each partition of a table, run the system procedure sp_help or sp_helppartition:

```
partition_name     partition_id compression_level pages
row_count
------------------ ------------ ------------------ ----- --------
old_partition      896003192 none                   464    14846
recent_partition   912003249 none                    81     2581
current_partition  928003306 none                    81     2573
```

151

There is also a `row_count()` function that can indicate the number of rows of a partition with the following syntax:

```
select row_count(<dbid>, <tableid>, <partitionid>)
```

But to really see the rows of a partition, there is no SQL syntax.

Only method: use the BCP tool. For example:

```
bcp example..table1 table1 partition recent_partition out
partition.txt -U sa -S TACTILOU -P lionel -c
Starting copy...
1000 rows successfully bulk-copied to host-file.
2000 rows successfully bulk-copied to host-file.
2581 rows copied.
Clock Time (ms.): total = 15 Avg = 0 (172066.67 rows per sec.)
```

Segment

In an unmixed database, i.e. a database in which the data and the transaction log are separated, there are at least 3 segments:

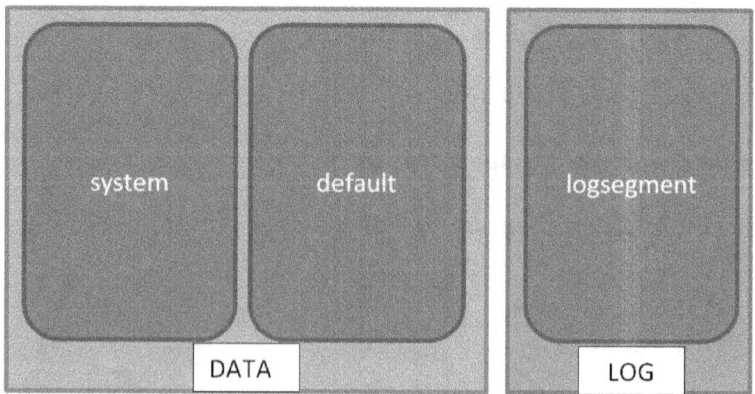

The system tables will invest the "system" segment. The user tables will invest the "default" segment and the log will be recorded in the

152

"logsegment" segment. Warning: a segment has no defined size. It is a soft zone. By default, the segments are spread over all devices of the same usage (all DATA devices or all LOG devices). This means that the "default" segment and the "system" segment are competitors in data devices.

But it is possible to prevent a segment from spreading on a particular device with the following syntax:

```
sp_dropsegment <segname>, <dbname>, <device>
```

Thanks to the segment concept, it is possible to successfully register a table on a specific device. To do this, you need:

1. Create a segment on a device

```
sp_addsegment history_seg , visits , history_dev
```

2. Create a table on this segment

```
create table history_table (id int ...) on history_seg
```

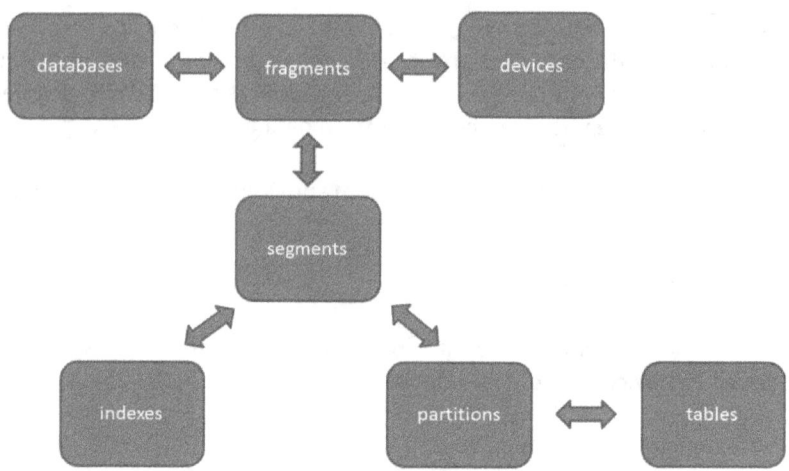

Figure 28 : From a relational point of view, segments are the relationship between indexes, partitions and fragments.

There is a link between segments and fragments. This link is manifested by a join between the `syssegments` and `sysusages` tables. The join condition is a bit convoluted and deserves some attention: Sybase opts for a bitmask join.

In the `syssegments` table, each segment has an integer identifier. In the `master..sysusages` table, each fragment has a numerical value called **segmap**. This number is the sum of the powers of 2 corresponding to the segments attached to this fragment.

Example A:

If a fragment is attached to segments 0 and 1, the segmap = $2^0 + 2^1 = 3$.

Example B:

If a fragment is attached to segments 2 and 5, the segmap = $2^2 + 2^5 = 36$.

This raises the problem of the legibility of such a method. The join needed to decode this is the following:

```
select * from syssegments, master..
sysusageswhere segmap & power(2,segment) =
power(2,segment)
```

The small "&" is a binary logical operator AND.

To find out which objects are on a particular segment, run the stored procedure sp_helpsegment followed by the segment name.

For example, on a brand-new base, we can see this:

```
1> "default" sp_helpsegment
2> go
 segment name      status
 -------  -------  ------
         1 default         1
 device size free_pages
 ------  -----  ----------
 master 7.0MB         2670
Objects on segment 'default':
 table_name        index_name           indid partition_name
 ---------------  -----------------  ----- --------------------

 syscomments       syscomments          0 syscomments_6
 syscomments       csyscomments         2 csyscomments_6
 sysreferences     sysreferences        0 sysreferences_16
 sysreferences     ncsysreferences      2 ncsysreferences_16
 sysreferences     nc2sysreferences     3 nc2sysreferences_16
 sysreferences     csysreferences       4 csysreferences_16
 sysusermessages csysusermessages       1 csysusermessages_15
 sysusermessages ncsysusermessages      2 ncsysusermessages_15

Objects currently bound to segment 'default':

 table_name        index_name           indid
 ---------------  -----------------  -----

 syscomments       syscomments          0
 syscomments       csyscomments         2
 sysreferences     sysreferences        0
 sysreferences     ncsysreferences      2
 sysreferences     nc2sysreferences     3
 sysreferences     csysreferences       4
 csysusermessages           csysusermessages 1
 sysusermessages ncsysusermessages      2

 total_size         total_pages        free_pages        used_pages
 -----------------  ---------------  ---------------  ----------------
```

155

```
7.0MB                  3584              2670              914
(return status = 0)
```

This example shows that some system tables are however stored on the default segment.

Remove the tempdb from the master device

When a dataserver is created, the tempdb base is automatically created on the master device with a 4MB fragment:

```
 device_fragments                    size           usage
created
 ----------------------------- ------------- ------------------
-- ------------------
 master                               4.0 MB data and log
Jul 19 2015 10:33AM
```

On the one hand, it is advisable to enlarge it on a new device:

```
 device_fragments                    size           usage
created
 ----------------------------- ------------- ------------------
-- ------------------
 master                               4.0 MB data and log
Jul 19 2015 10:33AM
 tempdb_device                      100.0 MB data and log
Jul 19 2015 10:42AM
```

And on the other hand, to disable the fragment present on the master device:

```
1> sp_dropsegment "default", tempdb , master
2> go
DBCC execution completed. If DBCC printed error messages,
contact a user with System Administrator (SA) role.
Segment reference to device dropped.
(return status = 0)

1> sp_dropsegment "logsegment", tempdb , master
2> go
DBCC execution completed. If DBCC printed error messages,
contact a user with System Administrator (SA) role.
DBCC execution completed. If DBCC printed error messages,
contact a user with System Administrator (SA) role.
```

```
The last-chance threshold for database tempdb is now 16 pages.
Segment reference to device dropped.
(return status = 0)

1> sp_dropsegment "system", tempdb , master
2> go
DBCC execution completed. If DBCC printed error messages,
contact a user with System Administrator (SA) role.
Segment reference to device dropped.
WARNING: There are no longer any segments referencing device
'master'. This device will no longer be used for space
allocation.
(return status = 0)
```

Fragment

Sybase officially uses the term "fragment" to describe the concept of a piece of database on a piece of virtual device.

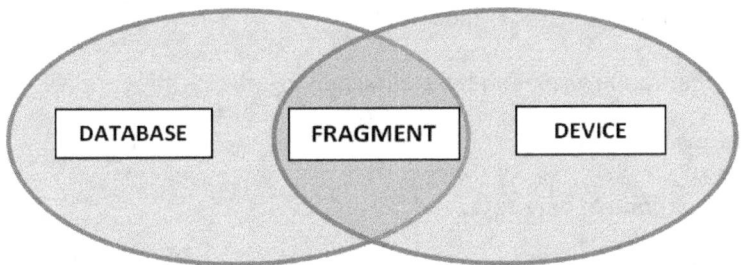

Figure 29 : A fragment is a piece of data belonging to a database and also to a device

sysdatabases is the table that contains the list of databases.

sysdevices is the table that contains the list of virtual devices.

sysusages is the table that contains the relationship between the bases and the devices, i.e. the fragments. We can also call them "usages".

157

The join between these 3 tables is:

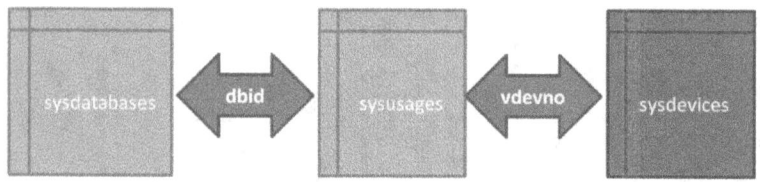

Figure 30 : The table sysusages is the join between sysdatabases and sysdevices

In `sysusages`, the lstart column marks the address of the fragment in the base while vstart marks the address of the fragment in the device. Size is the size of the fragment in number of pages.

There are 4 types of fragments. Their differences can be seen in the segmap column of the `sysusages` table.

Those that can **only** contain **the** transaction **log:**

```
segmap = 4
```

Those that contain **only data:**

```
(segmap & 4) = 0
```

Those that can contain **transaction log and data** (LOG and DATA mixed):

```
segmap <> 4 and (segmap & 4) = 4
```

The ones that should not contain **any transaction logs or data**. This is a very special case when you remove all the segments present on a device in a database. This is only done to separate the tempdb from the master device. By convention, we consider this empty fragment as "data".

```
segmap = 0
```

Virtual device

A virtual device is both a logical and a physical element. It is an entity referring to a file or raw device governed by the operating system. These are the devices that carry all the contents of the dataserver on hard disk.

The list of devices can be viewed with `sp_helpdevice` or in the `sysdevices` table. The 4 main characteristics of a device are:

1. Its name
2. Its physical file
3. Its size
4. Its IO mechanism

The primary key of a device is the vdevno. It is an integer. Actually, the name of a device has no functional value: it's just a convenience for DBAs. You can completely rename a device (even the master device!) without any danger. There is no official procedure but you just have to `update sysdevices set name = ...` where `vdevno = ...` . Just be careful not to lock the sysdevices too long.

On the other hand, the physical name is the path to the file on the disk. It is therefore fundamental.

Instructions for handling the devices

```
-- Create a device
disk init name='<device_name>', size='<size in mega>',
physname='<path>'
-- Enlarge a device
disk resize name='<device_name>', size='<megabyte size to
be added>'.
```

Mechanism io

The io mechanism is the way ASE has to manage the entries on the filesystem. There are 3 of them:

- Dync off and Directio off: The OS writes but does not check the quality.
- Dsync true: The OS ensures the quality of the writings.
- Directio true: ASE supports the hard drive directly.

The IO mechanism is only taken into account at the start of the instance and only for filesystems. But it is possible to change the parameter for the next start with `sp_deviceattr`.

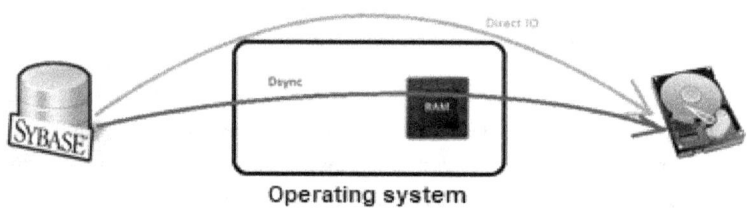

Operating system

Figure 31 : Difference between dsync and directio

In **directio = false**, the ASE instance will send its data to the operating system to be written to the hard disk. In reality, for a moment, the data will be located in a buffer before landing on the disk.

This is where the notion of dsync (disk synchronization) comes in. If **dync = true**, ASE will wait until it receives the acknowledgement from the hard disk before considering that the data is well written. Of course, the data is well protected, but this slows down performance during each write.

While in **dsync = false, once the** data is sent to the operating system, ASE considers (wrongly) that the data is in a safe place and does not ask for a disk acknowledgement. In fact, the data is temporarily in RAM.

directio = true bypasses the operating system completely: ASE will write directly to the hard disk. The only drawback: not always allowed by operating systems.

Setting both options dsync and directio to false, is risking a loss of data in case of a power failure, because in full writing, some data will be in RAM and therefore will disappear during the absence of electricity. ASE always warns the DBAs with an alert message:

```
1> sp_deviceattr dbccdb_dat1 , dsync, false
2> go
Warning: 'C:\Sybase\data\dbccdb_dat1.dbf', is a file
system device. A system failure may cause data loss if
the dsync option is set to false.
```

There are 2 cases where you can set directio and dync to false without fear:

- The devices of the **tempdb.**
- **Raw** devices.

The tempdb is totally erased and recreated each time the instance is started. So even if a writing problem occurred during the shutdown, it will be of no consequence. Moreover, it is a very busy database so setting it to dsync = false increases the writing speed and therefore improves the performance of the whole dataserver.

And the raw devices are already hard disks used directly by the ASE instance so the dsync and directio parameters are indeed on them.

Here is a decision schema that summarizes the I/O mechanisms to be preferred for file system devices.

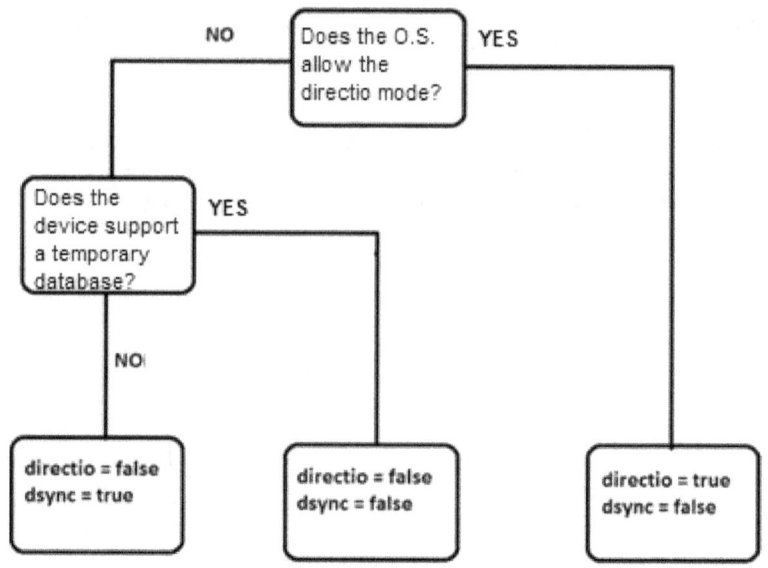

Figure 32 : Decision tree for directio and dsync

Physically moving devices by stopping the instance

This is a simple yet totally unofficial manipulation. To move the devices of an instance, you must first activate the right to write in the system tables: `sp_configure 'allow update', 1`

Then, one can carefully make `updates` in the `sysdevices` table. For example:

```
update sysdevices
set phyname = 'D:/Sybase/data/toto_dat01.dbf'
where vdevno = 7
```

Warning: this update does not cause anything at the time of writing. It is only at the next start up that it will make sense. So, you have to stop the instance with the `shutdown` command. Then really move the:

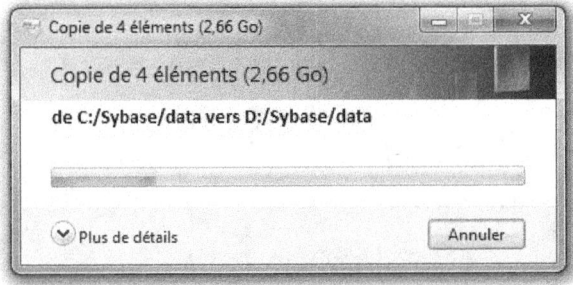

Figure 33 : Windows copy

And finally, restart the instance.

To move the master device, it is even simpler: just stop the instance, modify the runfile ("-d" parameter) and restart the instance.

Physically moving devices without stopping the instance

For one reason or another, a DBA may need to move a device file without stopping the instance. The only way to do this is to take advantage of the device mirroring feature. Mirroring (pairing) involves assigning two files to the same device so that one is the backup file in case the other fails. It is a precautionary measure that is rarely used in companies. Firstly, because it slows down performance and secondly because, nowadays, hard disks in SAN arrays are reliable and redundant (in RAID, etc...).

However, there is still a useful application for mirroring: moving devices. The following procedure requires the following configuration to be in place: `sp_configure "disable disk mirroring" , 0` and then a restart of the instance to be taken into account.

Opinion of the author. By default, mirroring is disabled on ASE. A good habit is to restore this feature as soon as possible after a dataserver installation.

1. Mirror the device

```
disk mirror name='MABASE_dat1' ,
mirror='C:\Sybase\devices\mb_dat1.dbf'
```

2. Unmirroring the device

```
disk unmirror name='MABASE_dat1' , side='primary' ,
mode='remove'
```

5. Physically delete the old file in the OS.

```
rm D:\Sybase\devices\mb_dat99.dbf
```

Missing device

At the start of an instance, a virtual device may be missing for several reasons (someone has inadvertently moved, renamed or deleted it). The instance will still start but the databases created on the device will be completely inaccessible. Even dropping the database will be impossible. Missing devices are visible with sp_helpdevice.

```
1> sp_helpdevice
2> go
 device_name        physical_name
description
vdevno vpn_low vpn_high
 --------------- ------------------------------------ ---------
-------------------
 ------ ------- --------
 dbccdb_dat1        C:\Sybase\dubai\dbccdb_dat1.dbf         file
system device, special
      8        0     15359
```

```
dbccdb_log1        C:\Sybase\dubai\dbccdb_log1.dbf        file
system device, special
      9          0      5119
disneyland_dat01 C:\Sybase\dubai\disneyland_dat01.dbf file
system device, special
      4          0      25599
disneyland_dat02 C:\Sybase\dubai\disneyland_dat02.dbf unknown
device type, specia
      5          0      15359
disneyland_dat03 C:\Sybase\dubai\disneyland_dat03.dbf file
system device, special
      6          0      15359
disneyland_dat04 C:\Sybase\dubai\disneyland_dat04.dbf file
system device, special
```

Default device

It is possible to define "default devices" (default disk). They are devices like any other except that they can be chosen by ASE if you request a basic creation or upgrade without specifying a device.

The syntax is:

```
sp_diskdefault <devicename> , <defaulton or defaultoff>
```

This default disk posture is not mandatory for any device, not even the master device.

Conversely, it is possible to set all data devices of the instance to "defaulton". The management of the dataserver space is greatly facilitated: there is no need to name the devices during create database or alter database nor to know the size of each device. Instead, just specify "on default = ...".

```
create database example on default = 100
go
alter database example on default = 200
go
alter database example on default = 120
go
```

Filling

One of the tasks of a DBA is to avoid or solve filling problems. At Sybase ASE, the only storage entity that can "fill 100%" is the segment. In a production environment, fills often result in application incidents of varying severity for the enterprise. They are almost as serious as downtime.

Figure 34 : Unlike a washbasin, a base cannot overflow.

As a reminder: a segment is a zone without a defined size that extends over several device fragments. Generally, there are 3 segments per base: "default", "system" and "logsegment". When one of the segments doesn't find any more space to save any row, we have a segment full.

For example:

```
1>insert into bleu values (100, 'Test')
2>go
Msg 1105, Level 17, State 2:
Server 'TACTILOU', Line 1:
Can't allocate space for object 'bleu' in database
'exemple2' because 'default' segment is full/has no free
extents.
```

166

It was possible to detect this problem before insertion:

```
1> sp_helpdb exemple2
2> go
 name       db_size        owner dbid created        durability lobcomplvl inrowlen status
 --------   ------------   ----- ---- --------------  ---------- ---------- -------- ---------------

 exemple2      119.0 MB sa        7 Jul 11, 2015 full               0       NULL select
into/bulkcopy/pllsort,

(1 row affected)
 device_fragments      size usage                   created                   free kbytes
 ----------------      ---- ---------------------    -----------------------   -----------
 master             50.0 MB data only               Jul 11 2015 11:54PM                    0
 master             60.0 MB log only                Jul 11 2015 11:54PM       not applicable
```

The command sp_helpsegment can also display a clear vision of each segment.

```
1> use exemple2
2> go
1> sp_helpsegment "default"
2> go
...
total_size       total_pages      free_pages      used_pages
---------------  ---------------  ------------    --------------
  58.0MB            29696             0              29696
```

The solutions in case of data segment filling are quite obvious:

- **Purge** some tables.
- **Compress** some tables.
- **Reorganize** some tables.
- **Enlarge** the database.

But it is also possible to fill in the transaction log segment. In this case, the error message is as follows:

```
1> update blue set name = newid()
2> go
Space available in the log segment has fallen critically
low in database 'exemple2'. All future modifications to
```

this database will be suspended until the log is
successfully dump
ed and space becomes available.
The transaction log in database exemple2 is almost full.
Your transaction is being suspended until space is made
available in the log.

This time, the request is not aborted. It is on hold and will do nothing until the situation is clarified. It can be seen in the stored procedure sp_who:

fid	spid	status	loginame	origname	hostname	blk_spid	dbname	tempdbname	cmd
0	2	sleeping	NULL	NULL		NULL	NULL	0	
				master	tempdb		DEADLOCK TUNE		
0	3	sleeping	NULL	NULL		NULL		0	
				master	tempdb		MIRROR HANDLER		
0	4	sleeping	NULL		NULL	NULL	NULL	0	
				master	tempdb		SHUTDOWN HANDLER		
0	5	sleeping	NULL	NULL		NULL	NULL	0	
				master	tempdb		KPP HANDLER		
0	6	sleeping	NULL		NULL	NULL	NULL	0	
				master	tempdb		ASTC HANDLER		
0	7	sleeping	NULL		NULL	NULL	NULL	0	
				master	tempdb		CHECKPOINT SLEEP		
0	8	sleeping	NULL	NULL		NULL	NULL	0	
				master	tempdb		HK WASH		
0	9	sleeping	NULL	NULL		NULL	NULL	0	
				master	tempdb		HK GC		
0	10	sleeping	NULL	NULL		NULL	NULL	0	
				master	tempdb		HK CHORES		
0	11	sleeping	NULL	NULL		NULL	NULL	0	
				master	tempdb		DTC COMMIT SVC		
0	12	sleeping	NULL		NULL NULL		NULL	0	
				master	tempdb		PORT MANAGER		
0	13	sleeping	NULL	NULL		NULL		0	
				master	tempdb		NETWORK HANDLER		
0	14	sleeping	NULL	NULL		NULL	NULL	0	
				master	tempdb		NETWORK HANDLER		
0	15	sleeping	NULL	NULL		NULL	NULL	0	
				master	tempdb		NETWORK HANDLER		
0	16	sleeping	NULL	NULL		NULL	NULL	0	
				master	tempdb		NETWORK HANDLER		
0	19	sleeping	NULL	NULL		NULL	NULL	0	
				master	tempdb		LICENSE HEARTBEAT		

168

0	30 sleeping sa	sa	TACTILOU	0
example2	tempdb	LOG SUSPEND		
0	32 running sa	sa	TACTILOU	0
master	tempdb	INSERT		

Can't allocate space for object 'syslogs' " messages are sent in the errorlog by the HK WASH system session. Then, every minute, the CHECKPOINT SLEEP session announces in the errorlog the number of sessions suspended due to lack of disk space: "*n tasks are sleeping waiting for space*".

ASE has a semi-automatic mechanism to manage full logsegment problems: thresholds.

A few pages before full fill, ASE triggers a stored procedure called sp_thresholdaction. The only problem ... is that it does not exist by default. The DBA has to create it and decide de facto what it should do in case of a fill. Typically, DBAs choose this:

```
-- Empty the transaction log when the threshold is triggered
use sybsystemprocs
go

drop procedure sp_thresholdaction
go

create procedure sp_thresholdaction
as
        declare @order varchar(200)
        select @commande = "dump tran " + db_name() + " with
truncate_only"
        exec(@order)
go
```

The above procedure will delete all the transactions already committed in the transaction log (principle of the dump transaction with truncate_only command). But this procedure does not guarantee that enough space will be freed for the request to resume its work: if the request modifies too many rows, it will be impossible to process it without enlarging the logsegment.

The other method consists in *dumpering* the transaction log on disk but this method requires to specify the hard disk filesystem in the procedure:

```
use sybsystemprocs
go

drop procedure sp_thresholdaction
go

create procedure sp_thresholdaction
as
        declare @order varchar(200)
        select @command = "dump transaction " + db_name() + " to
'/machine/sgbd/backups/dump.tran'""
        exec(@order)
go
```

To find out how many pages of the fill is set as the threshold of a logsegment, you have to perform:

```
1> sp_helpthreshold
2> go
 segment name     free pages     last chance?     threshold procedure
 -------------    ------------   --------------    ---------------------
 logsegment                     2200                      1 sp_thresholdaction
```

If, however, one of the sessions that generated the logsegment fill should still be deleted, ASE provides a command to abort the transaction without disconnecting its process:

```
select lct_admin("abort", <spid>)
```

Example:

```
1> sp_who
2> go
 fid spid status     loginame origname hostname blk_spid dbname
tempdbname cmd
 --- ----  --------  -------- -------- -------- -------- --------
 --- ---------- ----------------
     0    17 running sa             sa          TACTILOU              0
master        tempdb        INSERT
     0    32 sleeping lbolnet lbolnet TACTILOU             0 example
tempdb       LOG SUSPEND
```

170

```
(19 rows affected)
(return status = 0)
1> select lct_admin('abort',32)
2> go
lct_admin(abort): Process 32 waiting on log-suspend state on
database 'exemple is being aborted


----------
          1

(1 row affected)
1> sp_who
2> go
 fid spid status     loginame origname hostname blk_spid dbname
tempdbname cmd
--- ---- -------- -------- -------- -------- -------- --------
--- ---------- ----------------
    0    17 running sa         sa       TACTILOU          0
master      tempdb     INSERT
    0    32 sleeping lbolnet lbolnet TACTILOU          0 example
tempdb      ROLLBACK
```

171

Performance

Factors

Factors that can affect the performance of a Sybase ASE instance include:

- The size of the bases,

- The way requests are written,

- The data model,

- The freshness of statistics,

- The disk, filesystem, raw devices,

- The configuration of the instance,

- The hardware,

- The network.

On Windows, the performance analysis tools are `perfmon` and `taskmgr`.

At Unix, the performance analysis tools are `top`, `vmstat`, `netstat`, `iostat`.

Most importantly, a DBA must use Sybase's performance diagnostics tools:

- `sp_sysmon`

- `sp_object_stats`
- `sp_monitor`
- `sp_monitorconfig`
- `sp_audit`
- Monitoring tables
- Historical Server
- Monitor Server
- `optdiag`
- ASEMon
- The traceflags

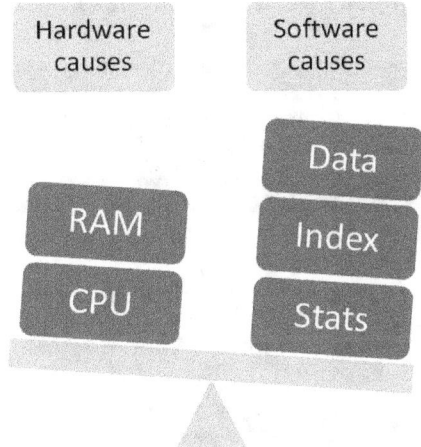

Figure 35 : Even a powerful infrastructure can give poor performance if the problem is in the dataserver.

From query to result

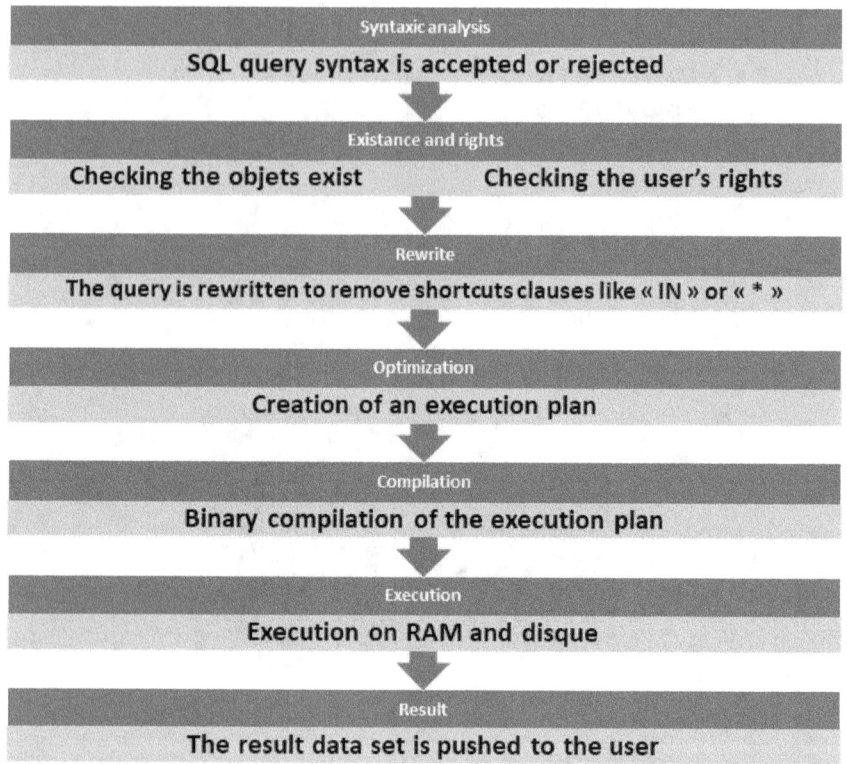

sp_sysmon

The sysmon is the easiest to use and most intuitive diagnostic tool. The `sp_sysmon` procedure must be followed by a study duration, i.e. a period of time during which the activity of the instance will be scrutinized and analyzed. 10 minutes is enough if you are in a hurry, but you can also run it for a whole night. It depends on the company's policy.

The information returned will be valuable:

- Time spent on CPU, disk IO or nothing (idle)
- Network problems
- Number of "dirty" pages (= modified)
- Number of locks installed
- Cache success rate
- Most or least requested devices
- Observed restraint

The `sp_sysmon` can even give advice like "it is recommended to increase the cache procedure" or "it is desirable to increase the user log cache size".

The opportune moments to launch a `sp_sysmon` are:

- Before and after a major change in the dataserver configuration.
- During periods of high activity.
- When customers complain about slowness.

Monitoring tables

There are 89 non-essential tables (they are not system tables because of their letter in the `status` column of the `sysobjects` table: "U") but very useful nevertheless. They are all located in the `master` database. To read them, you must have the "my_role" role:

```
grant role mon_role to lbolnet
```

They provide analytical information on the instance. The data from these tables are not really present inside the tables: they are proxy tables that point to the ASE kernel.

They are officially called "MDA tables". The most useful one is myProcessSQLText. It is a table that plays the same role as `dbcc sqltext`:

it contains the texts of the queries that have been executed on the instance. Other notable tables are myLicense, myErrorLog, myDeviceSpaceUsage.

The MDA tables are powered by the ASE core with real-time information. Before ASE 15.7 these tables were not installed by default. Now they appear after executing the `installmaster` script.

But whether or not they are powered, you must first configure several parameters with `sp_configure` in the [Monitoring] category, otherwise you will receive an error message:

```
1> select * from myProcessSQLText
2> go
Msg 12052, Level 17, State 1:
Server 'TACTILOU', Line 1:
Collection of monitoring data for table 'monProcessSQLText' requires that
the 'enable monitoring', 'max SQL text monitored', 'SQL batch capture'
configuration option(s) be enabled.
 To set the necessary configuration, contact a user who has the System
Administrator (SA) role.
(0 rows affected)
```

Statistics

Statistics are one of the three elements on which an optimizer relies to design the execution plan of a query. They are stored in the system tables `sysstatistics` and `systabstats`. These tables are not readable "with the naked eye". They represent the global face of a table: number of rows, distribution of distinct values in a column, etc...

They contain numerical information about this:

- The tables.
- The rows.
- The partitions.
- The indexes.
- The columns.

To keep the optimizer informed, they must be up to date. To know if a table has changed a lot since its last update statistics, ASE offers the datachange() function. This function is not very clear or reliable, but it is the only tool available to indicate "obsolete" statistics. It is supposed to return a number between 0 and 100 to indicate the "percentage change" of a table, partition or column.

Let's create an empty table and check its datachange:

```
1> create table saturday (id int, name char(30))
2> go
1> select datachange( saturday,null)
2> go
 --------------------------
                  0.000000
```

Now let's add 5000 rows and remove 917 rows.

```
1> insert into samedi values (42, newid())
2> go 5000
(1 row affected)
5000 xacts:
1> delete from Saturday where name > "d"
2> go
(917 rows affected)
```

And let's check the datachange again:

```
1> select datachange( saturday,null)
2> go


 ---------------------------
                144.917952
```

This means that Sybase considers the table to have changed by 144% from its last update stats. Let's restart an update statistics:

```
1> update statistics Saturday
2> go
1> select datachange( saturday,null)
2> go
```

177

```
    ---------------------------
                144.917952
```

It seems that the update statistics command does not bring much interest. Let's try another one.

```
1> update all statistics samedi
2> go
1> select datachange( saturday,null)
3> go
    -------------------------
                0.000000
```

The command `update all statistics` is therefore very effective. In fact, it can last a very long time on large tables. This is why we usually only need an `update index statistics`.

Note: it is completely useless to launch an `update index statistics` after the creation of an index because any index creation necessarily updates the statistics of a table.

There is a fourth syntax:

```
update table statistics Saturday
```

> **Opinion of the author.** In the future, the ASE editor should simplify the jungle of update stats syntax and stick to a single syntax.

It is preferable to run the `update statistics` outside of business hours, but fortunately, this kind of processing does not lock the table.

To go faster, one can also perform only a sample of statistics:

```
update index statistics authors with sampling = 10
percent
```

178

There are two ways to view the statistics of an object. The `optdiag` tool and the stored procedure `sp_showoptstats`.

```
1> sp_showoptstats city
2> go
```

```
<?xml version="1.0" encoding="UTF-8"?>
 <optStats>
     <version>sp_showoptstats/1.1/AnyPlatform/AnyOS/Thur
     <ServerVersion>Adaptive Server Enterprise/15.7/EBF 21339
     <serverName>TACTILOU</serverName>
     <specifiedDatabase>example</specifiedDatabase>
     <specifiedTableOwner></specifiedTableOwner>
     <specifiedTable>city</specifiedTable>
     <specifiedCol></specifiedCol>
     <tables
         <tableOwner>dbo</tableOwner>
         <nametable>city>/nametable>
         <tableStats>
             <nametable>city>/nametable>
             <Stats.
                 <pgCnt>1</pgCnt>.
                 0</emptyPgCnt>0</emptyPgCnt>
                 <rowCnt>9.0000000000000000</rowCnt>
                 <fwdRowCnt>0.0000000000000000</fwdRowCnt>
                 <delRowCnt>0.0000000000000000</delRowCnt>
                 <CRCnt>0.0000000000000000</CRCnt>
                 <oamAllocPgCnt>2</oamAllocPgCnt>
                 0</firstExtDataPgs>0</firstExtDataPgs>
                 <dataRowSz>64.0000000000000000</dataRowSz>
                 <joinDegree>0.0000000000</joinDegree>
                 6</unusedPgCnt>6</unusedPgCnt>
                 <oamPgCnt>1</oamPgCnt>
                 <derivedStats>
...
```

Another method of evaluating statistics is to check the date of the statistics in a table or column. These dates are available in the system tables.

```
select statmoddate from systabstats
```

```
select moddate from sysstatistics
```

To delete the statistics contained in the `sysstatistics` table, the command is

```
delete statistics nameoftable
```

Execution plan

SQL is a declarative language, which means that the users communicate in SQL to say what they wants and not how they want it.

The optimizer's job is to set up an action plan to respond to the request.

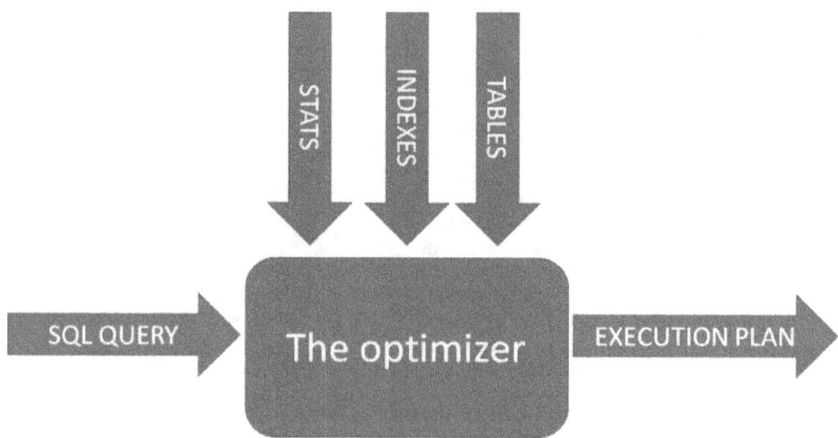

Figure 36 : The optimizer use 3 types of information to make its decision

The optimizer is both a strategist and a servant: it uses the information it has in its hands to respond to the request that is submitted to it.

Figure 37 : ASE optimizer must have strategies

To see the execution plan of a query you are about to enter, you need to make a `set showplan on` or a `set statistics plancost on` before launching the query. It can be useful to see an execution plan without actually executing a query: set `noexec on`.

There are two even more verbose instructions to understand what's going on in the head of the optimizer:

```
dbcc traceon(3604)
go
set plan for show_exec_xml to client on
go
```

And

```
set option show on
go
```

To see the execution plan of a query not belonging to me, you have to make a `sp_showplan <spid>`.

In both cases, we get an indented diagram that explains what the optimizer will do: it consists of several "operators".

An operator is an algorithm that fits into a hierarchical tree structure: it performs its work in order to report to a superior (operator). In order to perform its work it needs to receive data from its subordinate.

The most common operators

The highest operator in the plan is usually "**EMIT**": it is the operator who sends the data to the customer. While one of the lowest operators in the hierarchy is "**SCAN**: the operator** who reads the data from the disk.

Analogy. An analogy can be seen with the different hierarchical strata of a food company: at the bottom of the ladder, the farmers who work the raw material and at the very top of the pyramid, the people in contact with the customers.

An operator can be qualified by the number of subordinates it has:

Number of subordinates	Qualifier	Example of operator
0	" NULLARY "	Scan
1	"UNARY "	Restrict, Spell
2	"BINARY "	Merge joined
3 or more	"N-ARY "	Nested loop join

There are two types of SCAN: the table path and the index path. Table scan is an undesirable operation especially if the table contains many records: it looks at each row of the table, from the first to the last. It is the haunting of execution plans. On the other hand, index browsing is often a very fast operation since in a few readings of pages, the desired data is found.

Analogy. *The difference between the table scan and the index scan is similar to the comparison between VHS and DVD. The first one forces us to go through the whole tape to choose a scene. While the second allows us to jump directly to a chapter of the film.*

Now let's take the example of a very simple implementation plan:

```
1> select * from country
2> go

QUERY PLAN FOR STATEMENT 1 (at line 3).
Optimized using Serial Mode

     STEP 1
          The type of query is SELECT.

          1 operator(s) under root

          |ROOT:EMIT Operator (VA = 1)
          |
          | |SCAN    Operator (VA = 0)
          | |    FROM TABLE
          | |    country
          | |    Table Scan.
          | |    Forward Scan.
          | |    Positioning at start of table.
          | |    Using I/O Size 2 Kbytes for data pages.
          |    | With LRU Buffer Replacement Strategy for data
pages.

Total estimated I/O cost for statement 1 (at line 3): 83.
```

id	name	government
1	FRANCE	75
2	SPAIN	79
3	ITALY	75
4	UNITED KINGDOM	79
5	CHINA	11
6	SOMALIA	41
7	CANADA	76

This execution plan is composed of only 2 operators: there is SCAN which is in charge of going to the disk to retrieve the rows of the country table. And there is EMIT which simply sends the result to the client who typed the request.

Now let's sort the table by country name:

```
1> select * from pays order by nom
2> go

QUERY PLAN FOR STATEMENT 1 (at line 1).
Optimized using Serial Mode

    STEP 1
        The type of query is SELECT.

        2 operator(s) under root

        |ROOT:EMIT Operator (VA = 2)
        |
        |  |SORT     Operator (VA = 1)
        |  |    Using Worktable1 for internal storage.
        |  |
        |  |SCAN        Operator (VA = 0)
        |  |    |    FROM TABLE
        |  |    |    country
        |  |    |    Table Scan.
        |  |    |    Forward Scan.
        |  |    |    Positioning at start of table.
        |  |    |    Using I/O Size 2 Kbytes for data pages.
        |     |    | With LRU Buffer Replacement Strategy for
data pages.


Total estimated I/O cost for statement 1 (at line 1): 97.
```

id	name	government
7	CANADA	76
5	CHINA	11
2	SPAIN	79
1	FRANCE	75
3	ITALY	75
4	UNITED KINGDOM	79
6	SOMALIA	41

A third operator came to help: it is located between SCAN and EMIT. It is called SORT and will sort the data that SCAN entrusts to it and give the result to EMIT. A real team's work. When a query contains an order by clause, the optimizer has 3 ways to provide a sorted result:

1. If the table is in **allpages** and has a **clustered** index, it knows that the table is physically sorted on the disk so a simple TABLE SCAN is enough.
2. If the table is in **DOL** and/or has a **non-clustered** index, the INDEX SCAN operator is used.
3. If the table does not have **an index**, two operators follow one another: TABLE SCAN + SORT.

This can be summarized in a table:

	Index clustered	Index nonclustered	No index
APL	SCAN TABLE	INDEX SCAN	TABLE SCAN + SORT
DOL	INDEX SCAN	INDEX SCAN	TABLE SCAN + SORT

Let's continue our study by asking only the first 3 rows of the previous query:

```
1> select top 3 * from pays order by nom
2> go

QUERY PLAN FOR STATEMENT 1 (at line 1).
Optimized using Serial Mode

    STEP 1
        The type of query is SELECT.

        3 operator(s) under root

        |ROOT:EMIT Operator (VA = 3)
```

```
|
| Top     Operator (VA = 2)
| |       Top Limit: 3
| |
| |       SORT    Operator (VA = 1)
| |       |       Using Worktable1 for internal storage.
| |       |
| |       |       |SCAN    Operator (VA = 0)
| |       |       |    FROM TABLE
| |       |       |    country
| |       | |          Table Scan.
| |       |       |    Forward Scan.
| |       |       |    Positioning at start of table.
| |       |       |    Using I/O Size 2 Kbytes for data pages.
| |               |    With LRU Buffer Replacement Strategy for
data pages.
```

Total estimated I/O cost for statement 1 (at line 1): 97.

id	name	government
7	CANADA	76
5	CHINA	11
2	SPAIN	79

We see that a fourth operator comes into play: TOP has the role of limiting the data before providing it to EMIT. It is thanks to TOP that we receive only 3 rows.

Let's get to the heart of the matter with the joints. A join is a query involving several tables.

Let's make a joint on the country table and the government table:

```
1> select * from pays p, gouvernement g where p.gouvernement =
g.id order by p.nom
2> go

QUERY PLAN FOR STATEMENT 1 (at line 1).
Optimized using Serial Mode


    STEP 1
        The type of query is SELECT.
```

```
        4 operator(s) under root

       |ROT:EMIT Operator (VA = 4)
       |
       | |SORT     Operator (VA = 3)
       | |    Using Worktable1 for internal storage.
       | |
       | NESTED    LOOP JOIN Operator (VA = 2) (    Join Type:
Inner Join)
         | |    |
         | |    |   |SCAN    Operator (VA = 0)
         | |    |   |   FROM TABLE
         | |    |   | |   government
         | |    |   |   g
         | |    | |   Table Scan.
         | |    |   |   Forward Scan.
         | |    |   |   Positioning at start of table.
         | |    |   |   Using I/O Size 2 Kbytes for data pages.
         | |         |   With LRU Buffer Replacement Strategy for
data pages.
         | |    |
         | |    |   |SCAN    Operator (VA = 1)
         | |    |   |   FROM TABLE
         | |    |   |   country
         | |    |   |   p
         | |    | |   Table Scan.
         | |    |   |   Forward Scan.
         | |    |   |   Positioning at start of table.
         | |    |   |   Using I/O Size 2 Kbytes for data pages.
         | |         |   With LRU Buffer Replacement Strategy for
data pages.


Total estimated I/O cost for statement 1 (at line 1): 206.
```

id	name	government id
name		
7	CANADA	76
76 Governor		
5	CHINA	11
11 Single Party		
2	SPAIN	79
79 Monarchy		
1	FRANCE	75
75 Republic		

187

```
        3  ITALY                                    75
75  Republic
        4  UNITED KINGDOM                              79
79  Monarchy
        6  SOMALIA                         41
41  Unstable
```

This join gives us the opportunity to see a binary operator, i.e. one that has two subordinates: NESTED LOOP JOIN. This operator needs the results of the two scans (one per table) to be able to try all combinations of rows between the two.

If the first SCAN gives N rows and the second SCAN gives J rows, the NESTED LOOP JOIN operator will compare N x J pairs of results to see if they match the join criterion located in the WHERE clause. It is said that this operator performs a "Cartesian product".

NESTED LOOP JOIN is therefore very repetitive since it compares each row in table 1 as many times as there are rows in table 2. Its performance is sometimes very poor. If the tables had 20,000 rows each, there would be 400 million comparisons to make!

Over the course of the releases, Sybase has developed additional joint algorithms for greater efficiency and speed. MERGE JOIN, for example, is known to be much faster than NESTED LOOP JOIN. "Merge" means merge or match.

Merging is an algorithm that works only if the 2 tables are sorted in the order of the columns concerned by the join criterion. The principle of MERGE is to advance row by row each table in order to compare once for all each row of each table without ever starting again. The other requirement of MERGE is that at least one of the tables has a single column.

Since the 2 tables are sorted according to the same criteria, it is enough to scroll one table then the other one alternatively to match pairs of data without having to start all over again at each row:

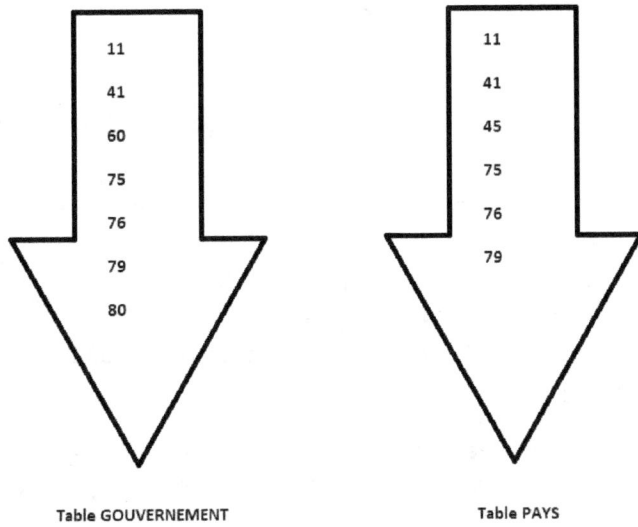

Table GOUVERNEMENT	Table PAYS

Figure 38 : Merging to tables

The SCAN operator always indicates a very important information: the use of the table or one of its indexes. When a table has an index, the execution plan avoids using the SORT operator.

```
1> select * from pays order by gouvernement
2> go

QUERY PLAN FOR STATEMENT 1 (at line 1).
Optimized using Serial Mode

    STEP 1
        The type of query is SELECT.

        1 operator(s) under root

        |ROOT:EMIT Operator (VA = 1)
        |
        | |SCAN    Operator (VA = 0)
        | |    FROM TABLE
        | |    country
```

189

```
    |  |         Using Clustered Index.
    |  |         Index: IDX
    |  |         Forward Scan.
    |  |         Positioning at index start.
    |  | Using I/O Size 2 Kbytes for index leaf pages.
    |  | With LRU Buffer Replacement Strategy for index
leaf pages.
    |  |         Using I/O Size 2 Kbytes for data pages.
    |  | With LRU Buffer Replacement Strategy for data
pages.
```

The optimizer knew that there was already an index on the government column of the country table, so it refrained from using the operator in charge of sorting (SORT). Indexes are particularly important on columns affected by a foreign key.

It is usually the optimizer that chooses whether it will use an index or not. But it is possible to force it to use or ignore an index:

select * from nameoftable (index nameoftable) →to ignore all indexes.

select * from nameoftable (index nameofindex) →to force the use of an index.

Some developers often do it but it is necessary to avoid making useless WHERE clauses. For example, this one below called RESTRICT whereas the WHERE 1=1 clause is strictly useless:

```
1> select * from pays p where 1 = 1
2> go

QUERY PLAN FOR STATEMENT 1 (at line 1).
Optimized using Serial Mode

    STEP 1
        The type of query is SELECT.

        2 operator(s) under root

    |ROOT:EMIT Operator (VA = 2)
```

190

```
      |
      | |RESTRICT      Operator (VA = 1)(4)(0)(0)(0)(0)(0)(0)
      | |
      | |SCAN          Operator (VA = 0)
      | |       |      FROM TABLE
      | |       |      country
      | |       |      Table Scan.
      | |       |      Forward Scan.
      | |       |      Positioning at start of table.
      | |       |      Using I/O Size 2 Kbytes for data pages.
      |     |   | With LRU Buffer Replacement Strategy for
data pages.


Total estimated I/O cost for statement 1 (at line 1): 35.

 id            name                              government
 ----------- ----------------------------- ------------
           5 CHINA                                   11
           6 SOMALIA                                 41
           1 FRANCE                                  75
           3 ITALY                                   75
           7 CANADA                                  76
           2 SPAIN                            79
           4 UNITED KINGDOM                                79
```

RESTRICT is the operator in charge of **filtering**. It is therefore necessarily part of the game when a query contains WHERE, LIKE, etc... It is also responsible for simple calculations as in the example below:

```
3> select *, 2015 - year from age
4> go
QUERY PLAN FOR STATEMENT 1 (at line 3).
Optimized using Serial Mode


      STEP 1
          The type of query is SELECT.

          2 operator(s) under root

          |ROOT:EMIT Operator (VA = 2)
          |
          | |RESTRICT      Operator (VA = 1)(0)(0)(0)(0)(0)(0)(3)
          | |
          | |SCAN          Operator (VA = 0)
```

191

```
      | |      |    FROM TABLE
      | |      |    age
      | |      |    Table Scan.
      | |      |    Forward Scan.
      | |      |    Positioning at start of table.
      | |      |    Using I/O Size 2 Kbytes for data pages.
      |     |     | With LRU Buffer Replacement Strategy for
data pages.
```

```
Total estimated I/O cost for statement 1 (at line 3): 81.
```

```
   first name      year
   ----------   -----------  -----------
   LIONEL          1984           31
   ERIC            1990           25
   SEVERINE        2001           14
```

There is a small sentence that appears at the end of all ASE implementation plans: "Total estimated I/O cost for statement...". This sentence means "Total estimated I/O cost for this query...". The number that is mentioned next is an integer that indicates the "cost" of the query. The cost is not expressed in Euros or US Dollars. It is a virtual value but it makes a lot of sense for the optimizer. It calculates it in the following way:

```
Cost = (Physical IO) X 25 + (Logical IO) X 2 + CPU X 0.1
```

An IO is an operation consisting in reading a page of data contained on the hard disk (physical IO) or in the RAM memory (logical IO). Empirically, Sybase estimates that reading information from a hard disk takes 12.5 times longer than reading from RAM.

Analogy. *The hard disk is like a basement of a building and the RAM memory is like an apartment. It's boring to store things in a basement but you have to do it because that's where there's room. You can't keep everything in your apartment! Each time that we want to use something which is in the cellar, we have to take the keys, go down the stairs, rummage in the cellar then go back up in the apartment with this thing: that takes a lot of time. By analogy, French-speaking DBAs often use the terms "getting the data down to disk" and "getting the data back up to memory".*

It is obvious that the optimizer always tries to choose the least "expensive" execution plan, i.e. the one that requires the least I/O.

To find out why an index is not used, it may be useful to make the command "set showplan on" even more verbose.

```
dbcc traceon(3604, 302)
go
set showplan on
goset
noexec ongo

select * from resources where nom='6e5fbc3e5e'
go

set noexec offgoset
showplan offgo

dbcc traceoff(3604,302)
go
```

User requests are stored in a cache called the "statement cache" and the associated execution plans are stored in the "procedure cache".

To view them, use sp_sysmon or dbcc prsqlcache or dbcc prsqlcache(ssql_id,1).

If the cache procedure is not large enough, the optimizer will be forced to delete execution plans that could have been used often.

Recommended values in production:

- 120 MB for the statement cache
- 1 GB for the cache procedure.

Syntax:

```
sp_configure "statement cache size" , 60
go
```

```
sp_configure "procedure cache size" , 500
go
```

Parallelism

When a request is made in parallel, another operator appears: EXCHANGE. This is the operator that brings together all the operators who have worked in parallel. It is called "exchange" because it transforms a multitude of producers into consumers. The producers are the operators who have worked for EXCHANGE and the consumers are the operators for whom EXCHANGE works.

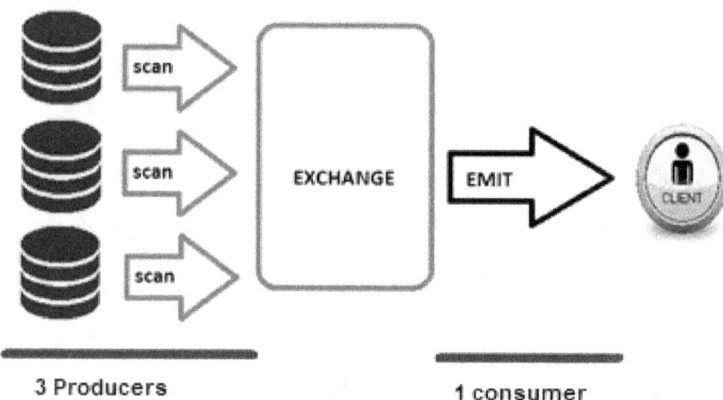

For example, if a table is partitioned and parallelism is enabled, it is certain that if the customer makes a SELECT, the optimizer will try to ask several "producers" to scan each partition. These producers may return their result in a mess each time. The word "ORDER BY" becomes even more important in this case.

STORE Operator

Sometimes, for some shots, the optimizer itself creates temporary clustered indexes! This kind of situation highlights the lack of indexes on a table. The operator that creates temporary tables and then clustered indexes on them is STORE. Forbidding the STORE operator can considerably slow down a request because the optimizer will be forced to do NESTED LOOP instead.

```
QUERY PLAN FOR STATEMENT 1 (at line 1).
Optimized using the Abstract Plan in the PLAN clause.

STEP 1
 The type of query is SELECT.

 7 operator(s) under root

 |ROOT:EMIT Operator (VA = 7)
 |
 | |SEQUENCER Operator (VA = 6) has 2 children.
 | |
 | | STORE Operator (VA = 5)
 | | | Worktable1 created, in allpages locking mode, for
REFORMATTING.
 | | | Creating clustered index.
 | | |
 | | | INSERT Operator(VA = 4)
 | | | | The update mode is direct.
 | | | |
 | | | | |SCAN Operator(VA = 0)
 | | | | | FROM TABLE
 | | | | | | | | bigun
 | | |   | | b
 | | | | | Table Scan.
 | | | | | Forward Scan.
 | | | | | Positioning at start of table.
 | | | | | Using I/O Size 2 Kbytes for data pages.
 | | | | | With LRU Buffer Replacement Strategy for data pages.
 | | | |
 | | | | TO TABLE (VA = 3)
 | | | | Worktable1.

...
```

Operator SEQUENCER

SEQUENCER is the operator who coordinates two other operators one after the other. It does not "do" anything special. It just states that one action must be performed after another.

Inserts execution plan

The notion of execution plan is especially useful for `SELECT`, `UPDATE` and `DELETE`. But there are many execution plans for some `INSERTs`: when there is a foreign key on the table, the optimizer has to do a `SELECT` on the index of another table to know if the foreign key constraint is well respected.

Abstract plans

Abstract plans are a complementary language to SQL but are intended exclusively for Sybase ASE instances. Its role is to give orders to the optimizer. In the absence of an abstract plan, an optimizer usually does what it thinks is best. To contradict it is to expose oneself to performance degradations (especially if one does not know what one is doing).

Figure 39 : Getting the upper hand on the optimizer is like driving "manual gearbox".

However, there may be times when it is necessary to contradict the optimizer. In this case, it is necessary to communicate with the optimizer. In the previous section, the command to force or forbid the use of indexes showed a simplified aspect of abstract plans.

Here is how to reproduce the same behavior with the language of abstract plan. The necessary syntax is `plan "(...)"`.

To launch a query without using any index:

```
select * from nameoftable plan "(t_scan nameoftable)"
```

To launch a query using a particular index:

```
select * from nameoftable plan "(i_scan nameofindex nameoftable)"
```

Les autres mots de ce langage sont: `append_union_all`, `distinct`, `distinct_hashing`, `distinct_sorted`, `distinct_sorting`, `group`, `group_hashing`, `group_inserting`, `group_sorted`, `h_join`, `hash_union_distinct`, `hints`, `i_scan`, `in`, `join`, `m_join`, `m_scan`, `merge_union_all`, `merge_union_distinct`, `nested`, `nl_join`, `prop`, `scalar_agg`, `scan`, `sequence`, `sort`, `store`, `store_index`, `subq`, `t_scan`, `table`, `these`, `union`, `work_t`, `xchg`.

For joints, it may also be interesting to know which method will be the least expensive among all the joint algorithms.

`nl_join` is the instruction forcing the optimizer to make a NESTED LOOP JOIN. While `m_join is the instruction` of the MERGE. Attention, for there to be "merge" in an ASE instance, this parameter `sp_configure` "enable merge" must be `enabled , 1`.

For example:

```
select * from ville v, pays p where v.codepays = p.id
map "(nl_join(i_scan idx city)(i_scan idx country))")
go
```

or

```
select * from ville v, pays p where v.codepays = p.id
map "(m_join(i_scan idx city)(i_scan idx country))")
```

```
go
```

The reader is invited to learn more about this subject in the official ASE documentation.

Switches

They are another lever to influence the execution plans manually. To see the list of switches:

```
sp_options show
go
```

To modify a switch

```
set switch on <nameofswitch>
go
```

Slow-responding query

A slow query is a query (usually SELECT) whose execution time exceeds what the user is entitled to expect. Here are the 7 most common reasons for a slow query:

Fragmented table

It is a table with a small number of rows compared to the number of pages. The table contains a lot of pages and therefore is more demanding in terms of io. To avoid this, regular reorg (defragmentation) must be run on the table.

Unbalanced index

It is an index that is no longer symmetrical enough to perform efficient searches. To avoid this, it is sometimes necessary to drop and recreate table indexes. Or reorg rebuild.

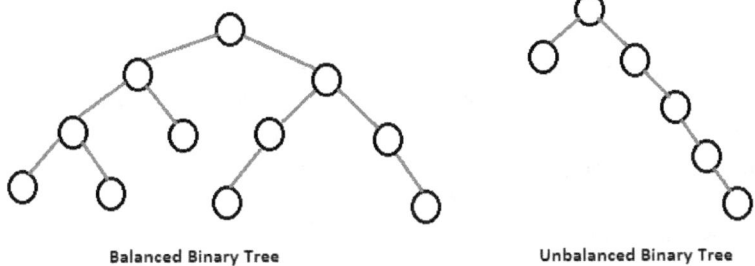

Balanced Binary Tree   Unbalanced Binary Tree

Figure 40 : Trees

Obsolete statistics

When the optimizer has a misrepresentation of the table, it is more likely to choose inefficient execution plans. The statistics are then said to be "obsolete". For example, a table with statistics indicating that it has 5 rows when in reality it contains 15 million rows is more likely to have an inadequate execution plan. To avoid this, you need to play regular table statistics updates.

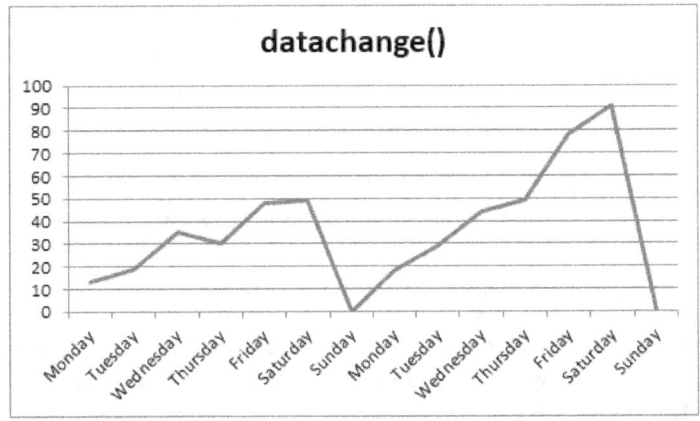

Figure 41 : The more the data changes, the more a new stats update is necessary.

Cache too small

A cache is used to avoid having to fetch pages of data from the hard disk too often. If the cache is too small, the optimizer will have to go back and forth between it and the hard disk a lot, which will inevitably lengthen the duration of the request.

Wrong locking pattern

When a table is locked by another process, it is partially or totally unavailable to others. The 3 locking schemes proposed by ASE offer different levels of flexibility. The solution is to always have tables locked in datapages or datarows.

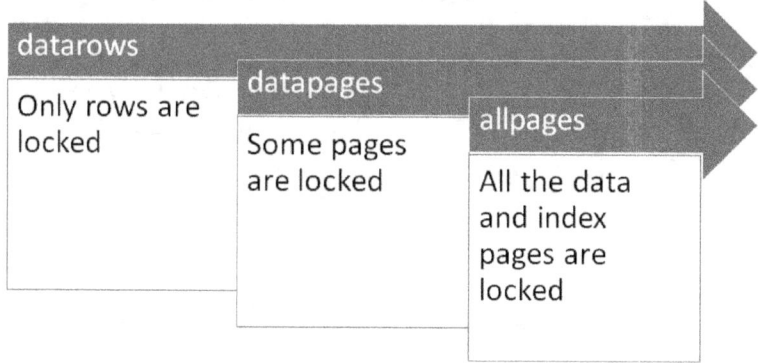

Figure 42 : Distinction of the lock schemes

Number of rows is too high

It is obvious that if a table contains a lot of rows, a select query on it will be long. There are two solutions to have fewer rows in a table. The first is simply to purge old data: this is a choice that can only be made by the application manager (a DBA should not purge data itself!). The second solution is to apply semantic partitioning to move away without purging.

Thanks to the *pruning partition,* the optimizer will only work with the partition containing the data useful to the `select`.

Badly written request

Finally, one of the most common reasons for slowness is that the request is poorly written. Even with correct syntax, a query can be a performance disaster. The use of `group by` with the wrong number of columns or forgetting the aggregation functions, badly strung joins, forgetting the `where` clause, misuse of `distinct` or `order by` can cause gigantic Cartesian products.

$$Cartesian\ Product$$
$$= number\ of\ rows\ in\ tableA$$
$$* number\ of\ rows\ in\ table\ B$$

The sum of it all

By cumulating these 7 problems, it is not impossible that a request will never "give up", i.e. after 48 hours, it still hasn't finished its work.

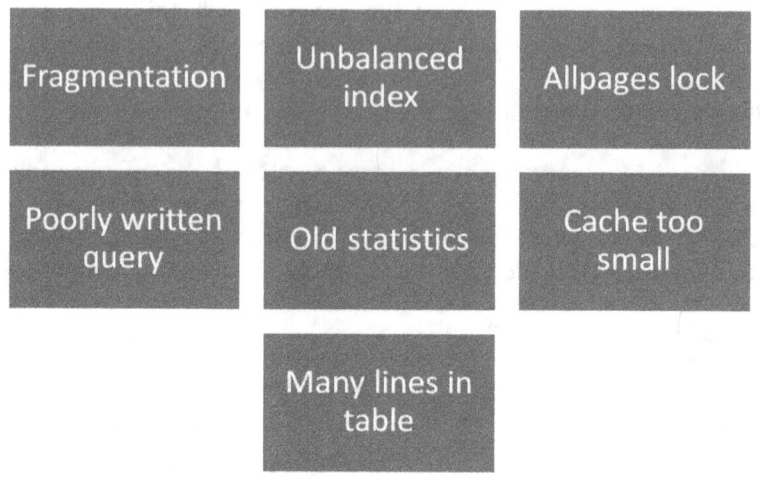

Fragmentation

Unbalanced index

Allpages lock

Poorly written query

Old statistics

Cache too small

Many lines in table

Figure 43 : The 7 main causes of a slow request.

Query processing metrics

Metrics are values that are measured during the execution of a query. The discipline of measurement science is called "metrology".

Figure 44 : A metric is a system or standard of measurement.

The ASE metrics are:

- Processor load duration
- Duration of the request
- Number of logical IOs
- Number of physical OIs
- Number of times the query is executed
- Number of times the query failed

To activate the metrics census, do:

```
sp_configure "enable metrics capture", 1
```

These metrics are used to identify...

- Poor performance,
- Expensive requests,
- Frequent requests,
- Slow requests.

The metrics can be found in the `sysquerymetrics` system view. The most important columns of this view are:

- exec_avg: average CPU time.
- elap_avg: average request duration.
- pio_avg: average number of IO.
- cnt: number of times a query has been executed.

Parallelism

Parallelism is the principle of performing several sub-tasks at the same time in order to deliver a faster result to the user.

For example, sorting a large table will be faster if it is sorted in parallel.

Parallelism imposes many requirements. Materially, to begin with, it is necessary to have several processors on the machine that hosts ASE.

Then, in ASE, you have to start several engines. Because the degree of parallelism will never be higher than the number of engines started on the instance. To see the started engines:

```
select * from master..sysengines
```

Then, you have to configure all the parameters that frame this concept:

```
-- Maximum number of worker process of a query can
mobilize

sp_configure "max parallel degree".

go

-- Number of tasks that can be executed at the same time
in the whole instance

sp_configure "worker process

go
```

Then, it is necessary to know in which cases parallelism can intervene. Generally, it is associated with the existence of **partitions** on a table but it is not mandatory. Each partition of a table can be sorted at the same time as the others and then, a last operation will consist in sorting the whole.

To ask the optimizer to process a request in parallel, the syntax looks like this example:

```
select * from entreprises (parallel) order by id
```

We can add this syntax to the syntax of index forcing:

```
select * from toto (index IDX1 parallel 2)
```

Huge pages

Sybase ASE supports Linux Huge Pages. This support improves the performance of the instance. But for this, the parameter must already be enabled at the operating system level.

How to see if it is active (on unix):

```
grep Huge /proc/meminfo
```

```
grep Huge errorlog.log
```

Raw device vs filesystem

Sybase ASE supports both storage systems.

A **filesystem** is an overlay that the operating system provides. For the user, a filesystem is seen as a tree structure: files are grouped in directories (a concept used by most operating systems). These directories contain either files or recursively other directories. So, there is a root directory and subdirectories. Such an organization generates a hierarchy of directories and files organized in a tree.

Conversely, the **raw** device does not offer any user support. The user must use byte positioning functions to read and write. There are no files or folders, just a linear succession of bytes.

On ASE, the raw device is known to offer much better performance than the filesystem.

To know which devices are created on filesystem and which are created on raw devices, Sybase offers a stored procedure `sp_helpdevice` and a `getdevicetype()` function.

The `getdevicetype()` function is not officially documented but it does exist. It must be called by putting the path of a file in brackets. It then returns 0, 1, 2 or 3:

- 0 = File not found
- 1 = raw device
- 2 = block device
- 3 = file system device

Indexes

An **index** is a complementary device to a table. The simple definition of an index is "list ordered according to one or more columns". Its roles are

- Enable **quick search for** a value in a table
- **Sort** the table
- **Prohibit** duplicates
- Helping the **joints**
- Facilitate the concept of **foreign key**.

Its disadvantages are:

- Disk space usage.
- Long time and locks set during their creation.
- Index maintenance i.e. they can slow down UPDATE, INSERT and DELETE.

At Sybase ASE, there are 3 categories of indexes:

	Allows NULL values	Allows DOUBLES
Classic index	YES	YES
Constraint of uniqueness	YES	NO
Primary Key	NO	NO

Trees

At Sybase ASE, indexes are computer trees. They are structures that allow you to follow the shortest path to the data you are looking for. Here is an illustrated example of an index and its 13-row table:

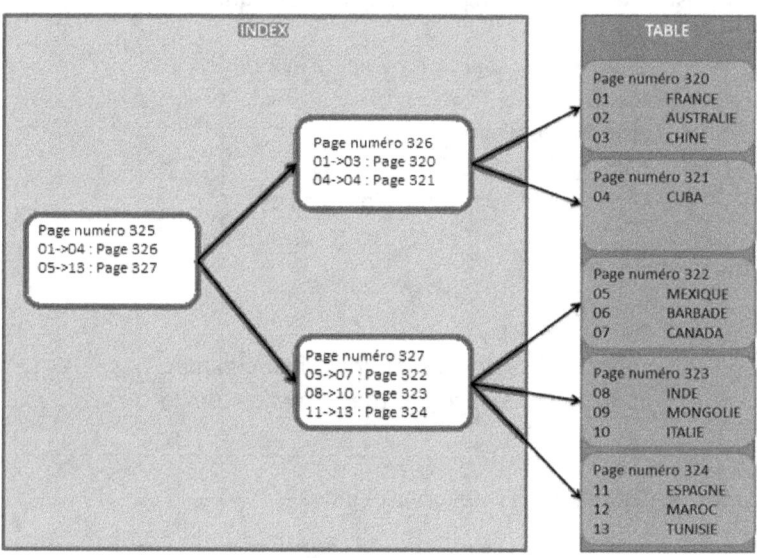

Figure 45 : Example of index use

In this illustration, the table occupies 5 pages and the index occupies 3 pages. The index has 2 levels: the level of page 325 and the level of pages 326 and 327. Each level acts as an orientation table to find the data you are looking for.

Classic index

Here is the simplest syntax for creating an index:

```
create index index1 on table1(id)
```

But there are 4 other more detailed syntaxes:

```
create unique clustered index index1 on table1(id)

create unique nonclustered index index1 on table1(id)

create clustered index index1 on table1(id)

create nonclustered index index1 on table1(id)
```

The words "clustered" and "nonclustered" have no translation in French. Their characteristics will be explained in the following pages.

Their deletion syntax is:

```
drop index table1.index1
```

Uniqueness constraint index

The indexes that are created to apply a uniqueness constraint have the following syntax:

1. Either "in row", next to the column name when creating the table

```
create table toto (unique id int)
```

2. Either at the end of the block for creating a table. Practical when several columns are involved.

```
create table toto (id int, type int, unique (id, type))
```

3. Or during an alter table.

```
alter table toto add unique (id)
```

4. Or during an alter table by specifying the name given to this uniqueness constraint.

```
alter table toto add constraint c1 unique (id, type)
```

The deletion requires to know the name of the constraint:

```
alter table toto drop constraint c1
```

Primary Key Index

The indexes that are created to apply a primary key have the following syntax:

1. Either "in row", next to the column name when creating the table

```
create table toto (id int primary key)
```

2. Either at the end of the block for creating a table. Practical when several columns are involved.

```
create table toto (id int, type int, primary key (id, type))
```

3. Or during an alter table.

```
alter table toto add primary key (id)
```

4. Either during an Alter table by specifying the name given to this primary key.

```
alter table toto add constraint c1 primary key (id, type)
```

The deletion requires to know the name of the constraint:

```
alter table toto drop constraint c1
```

Clustered index

For APL tables, the **CLUSTERED INDEX** is a balanced tree whose leaves are the pages of sorted data. The CLUSTERED INDEX **physically moves** the data from the table like a librarian who would arrange his/her books alphabetically by moving them on the shelves.

Therefore, there can only be one clustered index on a table.

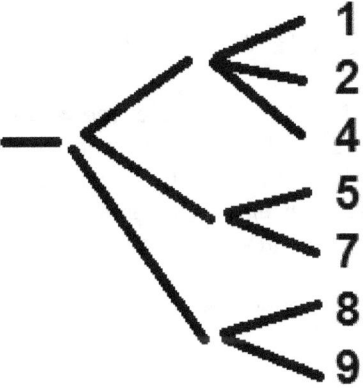

Figure 46 : A clustered index

On the other hand, for DOL tables, the clustered index works like a non-clustered index.

 Opinion of the author. The author advises against the use of clustered indexes for 5 reasons:

    a.   They cause the data in their table to be moved and

thus **fragmented at** each `insert` or `update`.

b. When they are modified, they also **impact,** in their wake, the other indexes.

c. They take **longer** to create than non-clustered ones.

d. Most **competing DBMS** do not offer this mechanism.

e. In **DOL**, they function as non-clustered.

Nonclustered index

The **NONCLUSTERED INDEX** is a balanced tree whose leaves are pointers to the data pages in the table. There can be several non-clustered indexes on a table (which remains disordered). That's why it is always necessary to create the non-clustered indexes **after** the clustered index because the data moves when a clustered index is created.

The non-clustered index is therefore a simple **statement of the positions of the data pages.**

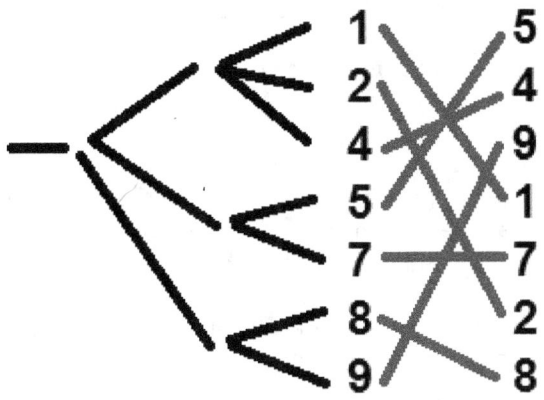

Figure 47 : A nonclustered index

Clustered vs Nonclustered

Comparative experiment n°3

"Clustered and non-clustered index".

Let's create two APL tables, of identical structure, but one with a clustered index and the other with a non-clustered index.

```
create table rouge (id int, nom char(40) primary key
clustered)
```

```
create table jaune (id int, nom char(40) primary key
nonclustered)
```

Then, let's insert 5000 rows (whose values are totally disordered) in each of the tables.

Observations:

213

- The Red (rouge) Table occupies **177** pages of data.

- The Yellow (jaune) table occupies **120** pages of data.

Explanation:

The red table has a clustered index and is therefore reworked at each insert to always remain in the sort order. This permanent reshuffling causes a great fragmentation of the data (because of *row forwarding*).

Conversely, the yellow table has a non-clustered index and therefore is never reworked. It is not fragmented.

However, here are the sizes of the indexes:

- The clustered index of the Red Table occupies **9** pages.

- The non-clustered index of the Yellow table occupies **179** pages.

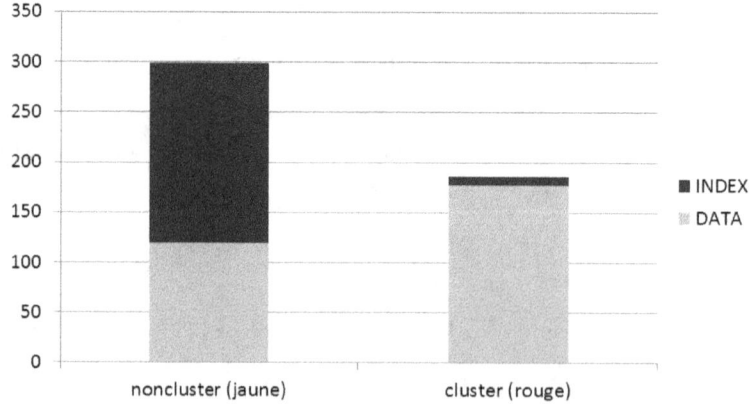

Figure 48 : Admittedly, this experience confirms that a table with clustered index (right) occupies less space than a table with non-clustered index (left), but the fragmentation rate of the table with clustered index is really disappointing!

The more rows there are in a table, the heavier the non-clustered index weighs. This is one of the few drawbacks of the non-clustered index.

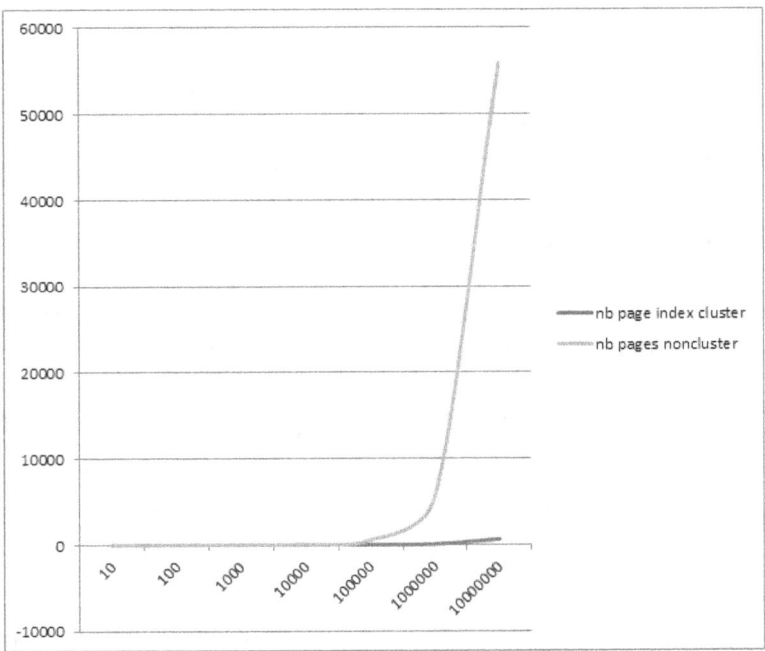

Figure 49 : Logarithmic scale showing that beyond 1 million rows, a non-clustered index becomes very heavy.

Generally speaking, we can conclude that clustered indexing is **long to create** and vulnerable to table **fragmentation** but is very disk space **efficient** (less than 1% of a table volume). Conversely, the non-clustered index is **fast to** create and **maintain** but very disk space **consuming.** Beyond 10,000 rows, a non-clustered index accounts for 30% of the volume of a table!

Obviously, the more columns there are in an index, the more disk space it takes up. It is possible to put all the columns of a table in an index. In these cases, the index weighs more than the data.

	Index clustered	Index nonclustered
Occupied disk space	Low	Important
Creation	Slow	Fast
Fragmented	Yes	No

Index covering

Usually, the index is used to indicate the pages of data needed to complete a query. But in some cases, the index is self-explanatory and the optimizer doesn't even need to look at the data pages. This happens when the query asks if a value exists but does not ask for the rest of the row associated with that value.

For example, if a COMPANY table has an index on the ID column:

```
select count(1) from ENTREPRISE where ID = 5
```

Just by consulting the index of this table, it is possible to know if the value 5 exists in the ID column. No need to go to the table. In this case, the index is said to be "covering".

An index can concern one or more columns of the table. In previous versions of ASE, the order in which they were listed was important because the first column mentioned in a `create index` was the "leading column", i.e. it could be searched for alone but not the others. Today, this is no longer the case: regardless of the position of a column in the index, the index can be searched on that column only.

For example, when creating the index below:

```
create index IDX on buyer(first name, last name, city)
```

There is no need to create the following indexes:

```
create index IDX_1 on buyer(first name)

create index IDX_2 on buyer(name)

create index IDX_3 on buyer(city)
```

Function index

The creation of an index on a column can be useless if during the selections, this column is systematically encapsulated in a function.

For example, if a table has an index on a val column, queries such as `select * from matable order by cos(val)` will be unable to do so because there is no obvious relationship between a value and its cosine. To be useful, the index should have been built on cos(val). This is possible with this syntax:

```
create index IDX_COS on matable(cos(val))
```

ASE will "secretly" create a computed column that will contain the calculation of cos(val) and hide this column. We will see it anyway in `sp_help`:

```
Name              Owner
------------------
dbo math

(1 row affected)
Column_name Type
----------- -----
id          int
val         float
sybfi3_1    float
```

The secret columns of ASE are all those that answer this query:

```
select name from syscolumns where status3 = 1
```

217

ASE does not tolerate that people try to make queries on it:

```
1> select sybfi3_1 from mathematiques
2> go
Msg 11738, Level 15, State 1:
Server 'TACTILOU', Line 1:
Name 'sybfi3_1' is reserved for internal use by Adaptive
Server.
```

Tables that have a function-based index have one more disadvantage than others: if a new column is added, the whole table has to be rebuilt using the "select into" method, which is very expensive in terms of disk space, locks and processing time. Whereas a normal table usually does not need to be recopied to add a null column.

For no apparent reason, you get the following message:

```
1> alter table example3 add new char(1) null
2> go
Msg 11052, Level 16, State 1:
Server 'TACTILOU', Line 1:
The 'select into' database option is not enabled for
database 'exemple'. ALTER TABLE with data copy cannot be
done. Set the 'select into' database option and re-run.
```

Heap

A **heap** is the name given to a table that has no index. They are justified in 3 situations:

- Table in which one INSERT massively but one does not SELECT often.
- Table in which you never need to sort or search for a particular row.
- Table containing less than 500 rows.

Index options

There are 3 possible options for indexes: ignore_dup_row, allow_dup_row and ignore_dup_key. They are applicable in the following cases:

Index	Unique	Not unique
Clustered	ignore_dup_key	allow_dup_row
		ignore_dup_row
Nonclustered	ignore_dup_key	-

Nonclustered indexes have no problem with two rows of a table being identical. While clustered indexes only tolerate this if the "allow_dup_row" option is specified.

```
1> select * from country
2> go
 id          name
 ----------- ------------------------------
           1 FRANCE
           9 SPAIN
           7 ITALY
           3 CHINA
           0 INDIA
           3 CHINA

(6 rows affected)
1> create clustered index IDX on country(id)
2> go
Msg 1508, Level 16, State 2:
Server 'TACTILOU', Line 1:
Create index aborted on duplicate rows. Primary key is
'3'
1> create clustered index IDX on pays(id) with
allow_dup_row
2> go
```

The `ignore_dup_row` option means that if a whole duplicate row is encountered, ASE deletes it and continues without error. →So, it is a perfect anti-double row mechanism.

```
1> select * from table3
2> go
 id          name
 ----------- ------------------------------
           4 LIONEL
           5 LUCILE
           7 KEVIN
           2 JULY
           2 JULY
(5 rows affected)
1> create clustered index IDX on table3(id) with
ignore_dup_row
2> go
Warning: deleted duplicate row. Primary key is '2'
Warning: Clustered index 'IDX' has been created with
ignore_dup_row

1> select * from table3
2> go
 id          name
 ----------- ------------------------------
           2 JULY
           4 LIONEL
           5 LUCILE
           7 KEVIN
```

The `ignore_dup_key` option is yet another concept. It means that when inserting a duplicate key, ASE must reject the whole row and not fall into error (when inserting or updating). This is not valid at the time of index creation.

```
4> select * from table4
5> go
 id          name
 ----------- --------------------
           1 RED
           3 BLUE
```

```
         8 GREEN
         0 BROWN

(4 rows affected)


1> create unique index idx on table4(id) with
ignore_dup_key
2> go
1> insert into table4 values (8 , "VIOLET")
2> go
Duplicate key was ignored.
(0 rows affected)
```

Estimates

Creating an index is a time-consuming operation that takes up disk space.
There is a system stored procedure capable of estimating the future size of
an index.

```
sp_estspace <table name> , <number of rows>
```

Users

Logins

A **login** is an authentication account allowing access to an ASE **instance.** It is a couple login/password. So, when a person wants to log in, they must, at least and at most, know the login name and password.

Main features

A login is composed of 18 fields of which the best known are:

- Name = its name
- Password = its password
- Suid = its primary key
- Status = its login lock status

The primary key that identifies the logins is "suid", which means Server User ID. Simply put, Sybase could have called it LID (Login ID).

To find out more

> **Opinion of the author**. Against all expectations, there is no stored system procedure to list all the logins of a dataserver. It is advisable to create it yourself and call it sp_helplogin. It is proposed in the Appendix.

To list all the logins of a database, the simplest query is:

```
select name, suid from master..syslogins order by name
```

To inquire about a particular login, the procedure to use is `sp_displaylogin` followed by the name of a login.

```
1> sp_displaylogin sa
2> go
Suid: 1
Loginame: sa
Fullname:
Default Database: master
Default Language:
Auto Login Script:
Configured Authorization:
        sa_role (default ON)
        sso_role (default ON)
        oper_role (default ON)
        sybase_ts_role (default ON)
        my_role (default ON)
        sa_serverprivs_role (default ON)
        new_role (default OFF)
Locked: NO
Date of Last Password Change: Nov 1 2013 12:50PM
Password expiration interval: 0
Password expired: NO
Minimum password length: 6
Maximum failed logins: 4
Current failed login attempts: 0
Authenticate with: AUTH_DEFAULT
Login Password Encryption: SHA-256
Last login date: Jul 29 2015 4:00AM
Exempt inactive lock: 0
(return status = 0)
```

Syntax for creating, modifying and deleting

Example of creation syntax:

```
create login RAYMOND
with password TOTO123
default database etudes
```

Example of password change syntax:

223

```
alter login RAYMOND
with password MyPassword
modify password NewPassword
```

Example of deletion of a login:

```
drop login toto
```

There is also, since ASE version 15.7, a way to create a login with an encrypted password. This is particularly useful when a DBA needs to recreate an account that already exists on another dataserver. Simply read the password of the existing account:

```
1> select password from master..syslogins where name =
'lbolnet'
2> go
 password
0xc007485ad71f7d3a594c41556fae4cb7941e34f99
```

Then repeat this password when creating the account on the other instance:

```
create login lbolnet with encrypted password
0xc007485ad71f7d3a594c41556fae4cb7941e34f99
```

Default base

The default base of a login is the base in which the users are located in when they log in. It is best to set the master database as the default database for all logins because there are several occasions when choosing a default database can generate error messages:

For example, if the login has no user in its default database:

```
C:\>isql -U simon -P ZSR784
Msg 10351, Level 14, State 1:
Server 'TACTILOU':
Server user id 8 is not a valid user in database
'newyork'
Msg 4001, Level 11, State 1:
```

```
Server 'TACTILOU':
Cannot open default database 'newyork'.
```

For example, if the default database is not available:

```
C:\>isql -U simon -P ZSR784
Msg 930, Level 14, State 1:
Server 'TACTILOU':
Database 'newyork' cannot be opened because either an
earlier system termination
left LOAD DATABASE incomplete or the database is created
with 'for load' option.
Load the database or contact a user with System
Administrator (SA) role.
Msg 4001, Level 11, State 1:
Server 'TACTILOU':
Cannot open default database 'newyork'.
```

Even the "-D" option does not prevent problems:

```
C:\Users\Lionel>isql -U simon -P ZSR784 -D master
Msg 930, Level 14, State 1:
Server 'TACTILOU':
Database 'newyork' cannot be opened because either an
earlier system termination
left LOAD DATABASE incomplete or the database is created
with 'for load' option.
Load the database or contact a user with System
Administrator (SA) role.
Msg 4001, Level 11, State 1:
Server 'TACTILOU':
Cannot open default database 'newyork'.
```

Language

The language of a login is the language in which error and warning messages should be displayed. To change it, the syntax is like this:

```
alter login JDurand modify default language french
```

Login script

A "login script" (also called a login trigger) is a stored procedure that runs right at the time a login is connected. However, it is useless to create a login script containing a `select` request because when connecting to the instance, nothing will be displayed on its screen. Login scripts are usually used to trigger certain session parameters for a particular login or to forbid a login to connect during certain time slots, or even to intervene on the optimizer. Anything is possible: just code what you want as behavior in a stored procedure and then define it as a login script:

```
alter login lbolnet modify login script RestrictProc
```

To know the login script of a login, you must either make a `sp_displaylogin` or consult the procid column of `syslogins`. Some conditions must be respected for the logins scripts to work:

1. The stored procedure of a login script must necessarily be in the **default login** database.
2. The login must be assigned the rights to execute it with `grant execute`.
3. The login must have **a user** to enter its default database.

The sa login

The DBA login is "**sa**" and means "system administrator". It is the login that has the most power. Its password must therefore be a well-kept secret. If the password "sa" is locked, lost or forgotten by everyone, you must

1. Stop the instance abruptly, i.e. with a kill command from the operating system.
2. Add the options " -p sa -u sa" in the runfile and restart the instance.

A new password appears in the standard output (but not in the errorlog!).

```
00:0002:00000:00001:2015/07/15 10:15:28.87 server Checking
external objects
00:0002:00000:00001:2015/07/15 10:15:28.94 server The
transaction log in th
00:0002:00000:00001:2015/07/15 10:15:28.94 server Database
'sybsystemprocs'.
New SSO password for sa:ergcbdwvcyefs1
00:0002:00000:00011:2015/07/15 10:15:29.00 kernel server will
listen on all
00:0002:00000:00011:2015/07/15 10:15:29.00 kernel network name
Tactilou, in
00:0002:00000:00011:2015/07/15 10:15:29.00 kernel network name
Tactilou, in
00:0002:00000:00011:2015/07/15 10:15:29.00 kernel network name
Tactilou, in
00:0002:00000:00011:2015/07/15 10:15:29.00 kernel network name
Tactilou, in
```

Recording Attempts

To log in the errorlog all successful or unsuccessful connection attempts, use these settings:

```
sp_configure 'log audit logon failure' , 1
go
sp_configure 'log audit logon success' , 1
go
```

Users

A **user** is an account allowing to enter a **database**. It does not have a password. Each user is, in principle, linked to a login. It is useless to know the name of the user to enter a database. A user can be in a group (and only one).

Main features

A user is composed of 4 main characteristics:

- Uid = this is the user's primary key

227

- Suid = this is the foreign key pointing to a login
- Name = this is the name of the user
- Gid = this is the foreign key pointing to the user's group

To find out more

To see the list of users of a database or to get information about a particular user, you have to call the stored procedure `sp_helpuser` followed or not by a user name.

```
2> sp_helpuser
3> go
 Users_name ID_in_db Group_name Login_name
 ---------- -------- ---------- ----------
 JDurand         4 public      Jdurand
 dbo             1 public      sa
 lbolnet         5 public      lbolnet
```

Syntax for creating, modifying and deleting

Example of syntax for creating a user:

```
sp_adduser RAYMOND, RAYMOND, READERS
```

The procedure `sp_adduser` allows to create a user in a database. It is mandatory to provide it with a login name. It is optional to provide a user name. It is also optional to provide a group name.

Example of group change of a user:

```
sp_changegroup WRITERS, RAYMOND
```

Example of syntax for deleting a user:

```
sp_dropuser RAYMOND
```

Groups

Groups are containers of users. They allow you to assign privileges to several users at the same time.

Example of creation of a group:

```
sp_addgroup WRITERS
```

Example of deleting a group:

```
sp_dropgroup WRITERS
```

Example of consultation of the users of a group:

```
sp_helpgroup WRITERS
```

How it works

A user is not really the equivalent of a key (because it does not contain a password). It is rather a kind of "facial recognition".

Indeed, to enter a database, you just have to request access with "use" and the database itself authorizes or denies access.

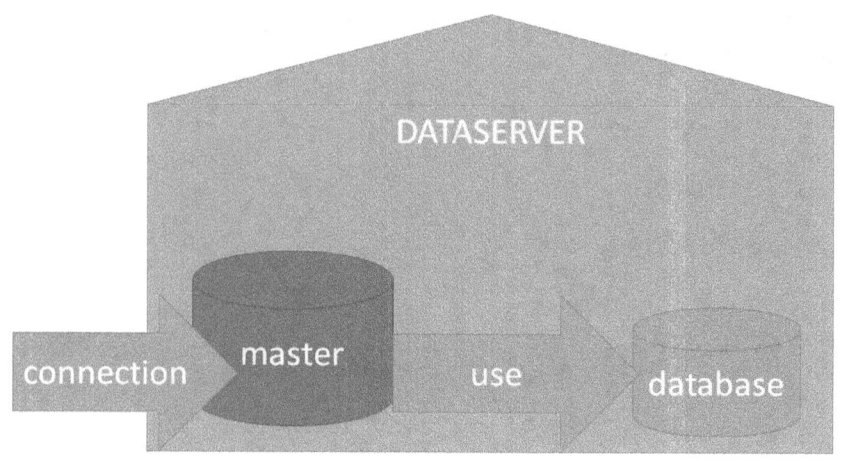

Figure 50 : Metaphor of users and logins with a building security

Analogy. The notion of login and user is very similar to security in a residential building: to enter the building, you need to have the key and to know the digicode.

Once inside, the visitors are in the entrance hall.

To go further, they have to ring the doorbell of one of the apartments and the people living in the apartment will decide whether or not they can come in.

Alias

An alias is a kind of "legal identity theft" that the database grants to a login provided that it does not already have a user in the database.

One login can then be mistaken for another.

Main features

The aliases are located in the `sysalternates` table:

- SUID: login who wants to enter the database but has no user.
- ALTSUID: login that already has a user in the database.

The most frequent use of aliases is to give several logins the right to behave like the **dbo** (owner) of the database. This is a simple way to give "all rights" on a base without getting tired.

Creation and deletion syntax

Example of creation of an alias:

```
sp_addalias RAYMOND , dbo
```

Example of deleting an alias:

```
sp_dropalias RAYMOND
```

To find out more

By calling `sp_helpuser` followed by a user name, it is possible to see all its aliases.

Opinion of the author. Against all expectations, there is no stored system procedure to list all the aliases of a database. It is advisable to create it yourself and call it sp_helpalias. It is proposed in the Appendix.

Not to be confused

There is another form of identity theft sometimes used by DBAs: pretending to be a user without knowing their password is possible with the `setuser` command. This allows on the one hand to diagnose privilege problems on database objects. But it also allows dropping indexes of tables belonging to another user.

Example:

```
1> select user_name()
2> go
 ------------------------------
 dbo

(1 row affected)
1> setuser "JDurand
2> go
1> select user_name()
2> go

 ------------------------------
 JDurand
```

Relationship between login, alias and user

Interbase relationship

Users and aliases are entities that point to logins. It is an interbase relationship.

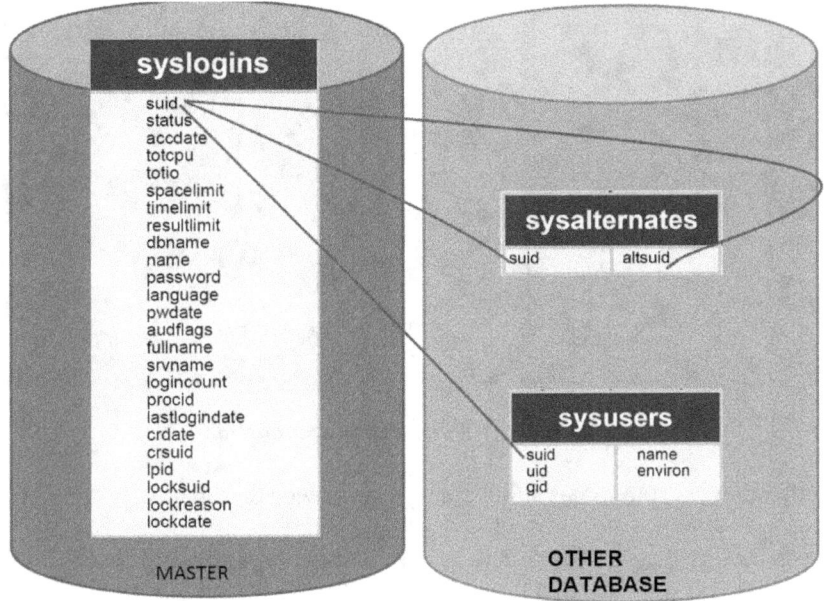

Figure 51 : The syslogins, sysalternates and sysusers tables maintain close links.

Desynchronization

Suid and uid are real puzzles when it comes to

- Dump/Load
- Replication.

These two practices have the disadvantage of leading to a displacement of the databases (and thus of the users) but not of the master (and thus of the logins).

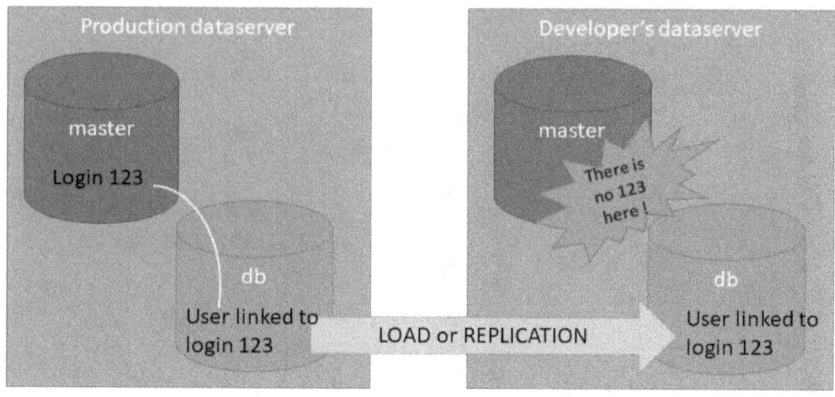

Figure 52 : Login/user desynchronization

Refreshments sometimes suffer from the following 3 problems:

User that points to a login that does not have a SUID. → This user is then totally useless!

Login that is not linked to any user. → Impossibility to enter the refreshed database.

User who points to a bad login →it is possible to connect and enter the database but you risk being mistaken for someone else and therefore having bad rights.

Decision trees of ASE towards users

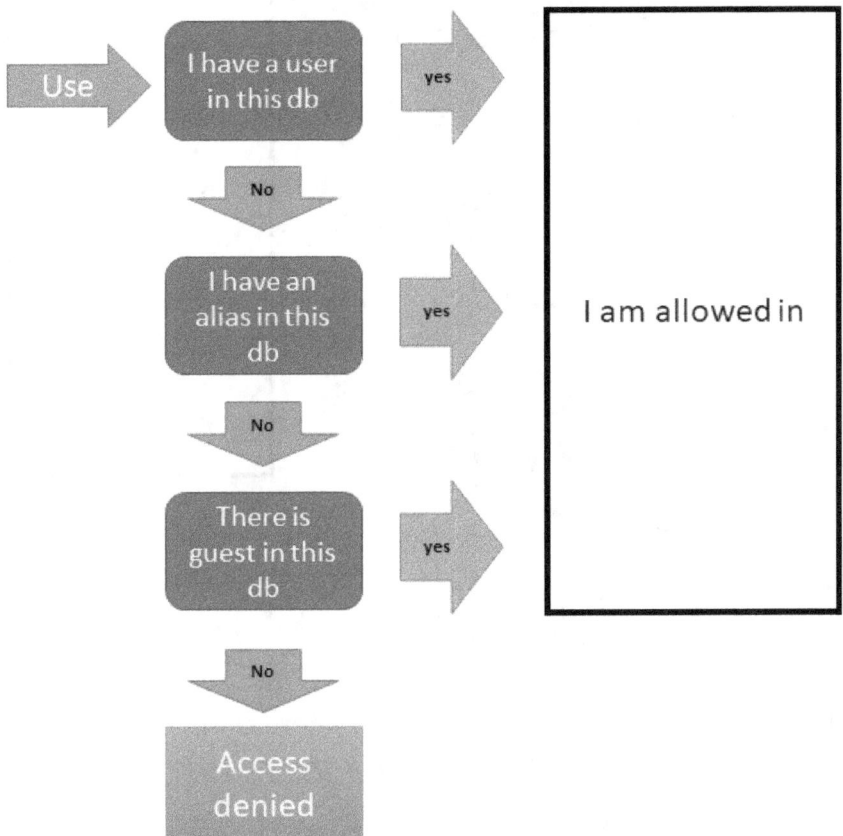

Figure 53 : decision to allow or deny an access

235

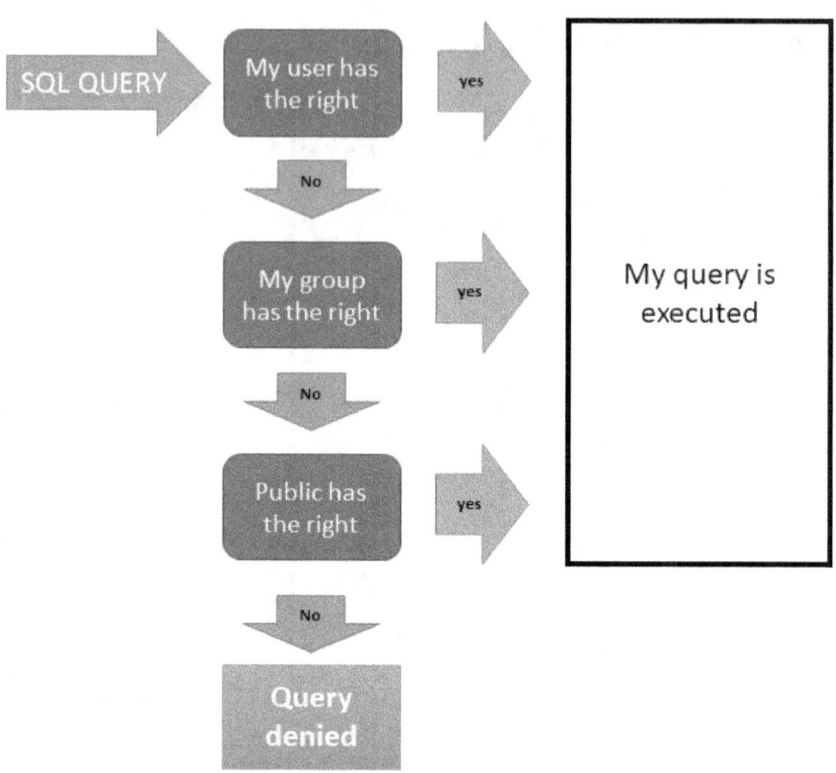

Figure 54 : ASE decision tree to allow a query

236

Guest and Public

Guest

Guest is a special kind of **user** that you can find in some bases only.

It's a user that allows anyone to enter, even without a dedicated user or alias.

The master database always has a guest, that's why all logins can always enter a dataserver.

Public

Public is the **group** in which all users are in.

All the people who were able to enter the database are in the public group. A user can only be in one group + public.

Roles

A role is an entity that confers powers to certain logins. A login can have several roles and a role can be assigned to several logins. The purpose of the role is to be granted privileges that the logins linked to it will automatically benefit from. Roles allow a real segregation among the people who can log in to ASE.

The system procedure `sp_displayroles` allows you to see the roles of your own login. And since not all the roles that a login has are active, you can use `sp_activeroles` to view active roles only.

As soon as a dataserver is created, there are many system roles:

sa_role, sso_role, oper_role, sybase_ts_role, navigator_role, replication_role, dtm_tm_role, ha_role, mon_role, js_admin_role, messaging_role, js_client_role, js_user_role, webservices_role, keycustodian_role, sa_serverprivs_role.

This is the stored procedure sp_helprotect which details the privileges of each role. Here are the privileges of sa_role, the most powerful role of ASE:

```
grantee action type
------- ----- ----------------------------------
sa_role Grant Allow Exceptional Login
sa_role Grant Checkpoint Any Database
sa_role Grant Connect
sa_role Grant Create Database
sa_role Grant DBCC Checkalloc Any Database
sa_role Grant DBCC Checkcatalog Any Database
sa_role Grant DBCC Checkdb Any Database
sa_role Grant DBCC Checkindex Any Database
sa_role Grant DBCC Checkstorage Any Database
sa_role Grant DBCC Checktable Any Database
sa_role Grant DBCC Checkverify Any Database
sa_role Grant DBCC Fix_text Any Database
sa_role Grant DBCC Indexalloc Any Database
sa_role Grant DBCC Reindex Any Database
sa_role Grant DBCC Tablealloc Any Database
sa_role Grant DBCC Textalloc Any Database
sa_role Grant DBCC Tune
sa_role Grant Dump Any Database
sa_role Grant Kill Any Process
sa_role Grant Load Any Database
sa_role Grant Manage Any Database
sa_role Grant Manage Any ESP
sa_role Grant Manage Any Execution Class
sa_role Grant Manage Any Thread Pool
sa_role Grant Manage Cluster
sa_role Grant Manage Data Cache
sa_role Grant Manage Disk
sa_role Grant Manage Dump Configuration
sa_role Grant Manage Hadr
sa_role Grant Manage Lock Promotion Threshold
sa_role Grant Manage Opt Goal
sa_role Grant Manage Resource Limit
```

```
sa_role Grant Manage Server
sa_role Grant Manage Server Configuration
sa_role Grant Manage Server Permissions
sa_role Grant Map External File
sa_role Grant Mount Any Database
sa_role Grant Online Any Database
sa_role Grant Own Any Database
sa_role Grant Quiesce Any Database
sa_role Grant Select
sa_role Grant Select
sa_role Grant Select
sa_role Grant Select
sa_role Grant Set Switch
sa_role Grant Set Tracing Any Process
sa_role Grant Show Switch
sa_role Grant Shutdown
sa_role Grant Unmount Any Database
```

It is possible to create roles with the following syntax:

```
create role new_role
```

To be even more careful, you can create a role that is only activated if you enter a specific password:

```
create role veryverysecure with passwd EPD585Y
```

After assigning these two roles to a user, they will have to activate them (with password if necessary) to be able to enjoy them:

```
1> set role nouveau_role on
2> go
1>
2> sp_activeroles
3> go
 Role Name
 -----------------------------
 sa_role
 sso_role
 oper_role
 sybase_ts_role
```

```
 my_role
 sa_serverprivs_role
 new_role

(7 rows affected)
(return status = 0)
1> set role veryverysecure on
2> go
Msg 11141, Level 16, State 1:
Server 'TACTILOU', Line 1:
Password required to set role 'veryverysecure' on.
```

For a role to be active as soon as the login is connected, it must be specified with the following syntax:

```
sp_modifylogin sa , "add default role" , veryverysecure
```

For a role to be inactive as soon as the login is connected, it must be specified with the following syntax:

```
sp_modifylogin sa , "drop default role" , veryverysecure
```

Roles are stored in an set of several tables:

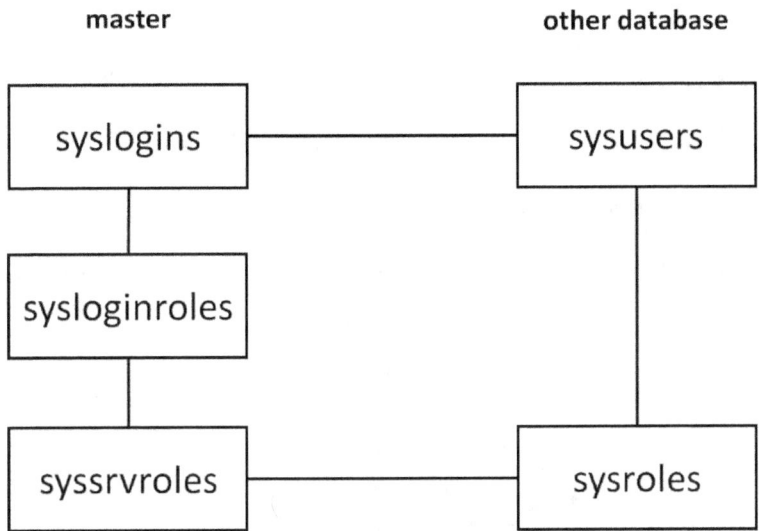

Figure 55 : Relation between system tables

sysroles: correspondence table between local role (lrid) and role defined at the dataserver level (srid or id).

sysusers: table in which the roles are stored. The primary key is uid and suid is always -2.

syslogins: table containing the list of logins. Primary key: suid.

sysloginroles: correspondence table between roles defined at the dataserver level and logins.

syssrvroles: list of roles defined at the dataserver level.

The two most powerful roles of ASE are sso_role and sa_role. By using `sp_helprotect,` we can discover the privileges of these roles.

sso_role: use any database, select in syslogins...

sa_role: create database, dbcc, dump, kill, load, online, shutdown...

The list of privileges can be found in the sysprotects table:

- uid = role, user or group
- id = object identifier
- action = type of privilege among the 368 possible ones (select, update ...)

Figure 56 : the two default roles in ASE

The "sa" account always has the sso_role and the sa_role. Some privileges are common to these two very powerful roles.

The act of giving a role or privilege is called "GRANT". You can grant a role to a role or a role to a login, or a privilege to a login or a privilege to a role.

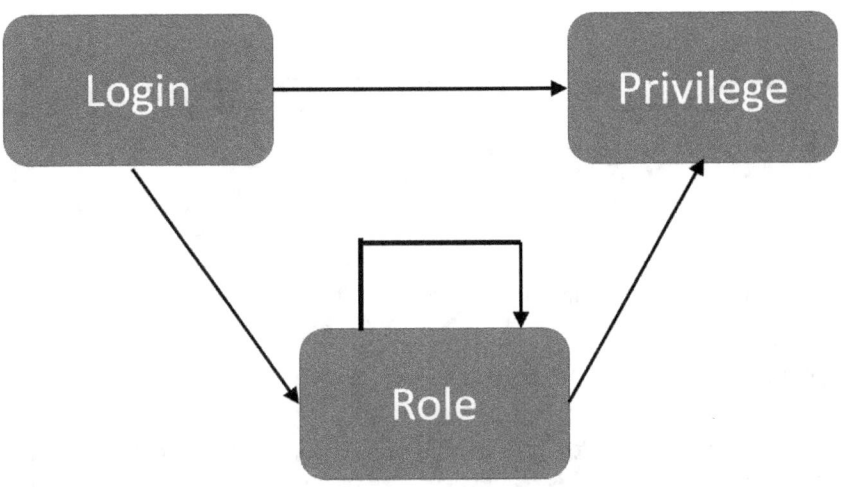

Figure 57 : A prilivege can be granted to a login or a role. A role can be granted to another role. A role can be granted to a login.

Sessions, Processes and Transactions

Three concepts are similar but nevertheless different.

Sessions

Sessions are a concept that only applies to the High Availability functionality of Sybase ASE (Sybase Failover). The `syssessions` table ensures connection failover from one node to another. Many DBAs, including the author of this book, misuse the word "session" to mean the same as the word "process".

Processes

Processes (processes), also called **connections,** or by abuse of language, **sessions** or **spid** are all the connections open on an instance. Some processes are issued by the ASE kernel itself. These are very important indicators to monitor because they are a sign of the activity of the instance. There are processes that are "doing nothing", there are processes that are waiting for something and there are processes that are performing a task.

`sp_who`

The famous stored procedure that informs a DBA about all running processes is `sp_who`. It gets its content from the `sysprocesses` table.

Here are the columns of the sp_who from left to right:

```
 fid spid status     loginame origname hostname blk_spid dbname      tempdbname cmd
block_xloid threadpool
 --- ---- -------- -------- -------- -------- -------- ----------- ---------- -------
---------- ----------- ----------------
   0    2 sleeping NULL     NULL     NULL NULL            0 master     tempdb
DEADLOCK TUNE            0 syb_default_pool
   0    3 sleeping NULL     NULL     NULL NULL            0 master     tempdb
SHUTDOWN HANDLER         0 syb_default_pool
   0    4 sleeping NULL     NULL     NULL NULL            0 master     tempdb
KPP HANDLER              0 syb_default_pool
   0    5 sleeping NULL     NULL     NULL NULL            0 master     tempdb
ASTC HANDLER             0 syb_default_pool
   0    6 sleeping NULL     NULL NULL         NULL        0 master     tempdb
CHECKPOINT SLEEP         0 syb_default_pool
   0    7 sleeping NULL     NULL NULL         NULL        0 master     tempdb
HK WASH                  0 syb_default_pool
   0    8 sleeping NULL     NULL     NULL NULL            0 master     tempdb
HK GC                    0 syb_default_pool
   0    9 sleeping NULL     NULL NULL         NULL        0 master     tempdb
HK CHORES                0 syb_default_pool
   0   10 sleeping NULL     NULL     NULL NULL            0 master     tempdb
DTC COMMIT SVC           0 syb_default_pool
   0   11 sleeping NULL     NULL     NULL            0 sybsecurity tempdb
AUDIT PROCESS            0 syb_default_pool
   0   12 sleeping NULL     NULL NULL         NULL        0 master     tempdb
PORT MANAGER             0 syb_default_pool
   0   13 sleeping NULL     NULL     NULL         0 master     tempdb
NETWORK HANDLER          0 syb_default_pool
   0   14 sleeping NULL     NULL     NULL NULL            0 master     tempdb
NETWORK HANDLER          0 syb_default_pool
   0   15 sleeping NULL     NULL     NULL NULL            0 master     tempdb
NETWORK HANDLER          0 syb_default_pool
   0   16 sleeping NULL     NULL     NULL NULL            0 master     tempdb
NETWORK HANDLER          0 syb_default_pool
   0   17 running sa       sa       TACTILOU         0 master     tempdb
INSERT                   0 syb_default_pool
   0   19 sleeping NULL     NULL     NULL NULL            0 master     tempdb
LICENSE HEARTBEAT        0 syb_default_pool
```

fid: family of SPID. When a treatment is carried out in parallel, several processes work for it. They are all grouped under the same fid. If fid is equal to zero, it means that the process is not included in a parallel treatment.

spid: unique identifier of a process.

status: indicates what the process is currently doing.

- Sleeping = "writing to disk in progress" or "system process at rest". Sleeping is a misleading term. Most of the time, a sleeping process is working to write large amounts of data to disk.
- Running = "Optimizer working".

245

- Runnable = "Processing pending processor availability".
- Sync sleep = "Expectation of other processes in the fid family".
- Recv sleep = "Waiting for a next order from the customer". This is the only expectation that depends on user intervention.
- Send sleep = "Waiting for the end of the sending of the result by the network".
- Lock sleep = "Waiting for a lock to be released".

`loginame`: login of the person who started this process. If it's null, it's the ASE system.

`origname`: Usually the same as loginame.

`hostname`: machine that hosts the client.

`blk_spid`: Very important. It's the process spid that blocks the process. If it's zero, no one is blocking it.

`dbname`: this is either the current database in which the login is connected or the database that is being dropped, created, altered, put online, *dumped* or loaded by this process (all these actions can only be performed in the master database).

`tempdbname`: This is the temporary database linked to this session.

`cmd`: Very useful! This is the command currently executed by the process. If it's "AWAITING COMMAND", it means that nothing is running. It doesn't mean that a transaction is not in progress. It may very well be waiting for a commit or rollback.

sysprocesses

This table is even more complete than `sp_who`. It is still in the master database. It has 36 columns that give a maximum of information about each process. Note that some of the information is identifiers and not names, such as dbid, suid, which can be transformed into a literal name using the `suser_name()` and `db_name()` functions respectively.

pssinfo()

The `pssinfo()` function is a good complement to `sp_who` and `sysprocesses`. It needs to be given two parameters between brackets: the spid of a process and a request for information. Among what we can ask it:

- `"ipaddr"` - Customer's IP address.

- `"ipport"` - Customer's port number.

- `"isolation_level"` - Isolation level of the session.

- `"tempdb_pages"` - Number of pages of the tempdb used.

For example:

```
select spid,
pssinfo(spid,"ipaddr"),pssinfo(spid,"ipport"),pssinfo(spi
d,"isolation_level"), pssinfo(spid,"tempdb_pages") from
sysprocesses
```

Transactions

Transactions are yet another concept. A transaction is a set of SQL statements to be committed in a single block or rolled back in a single block.

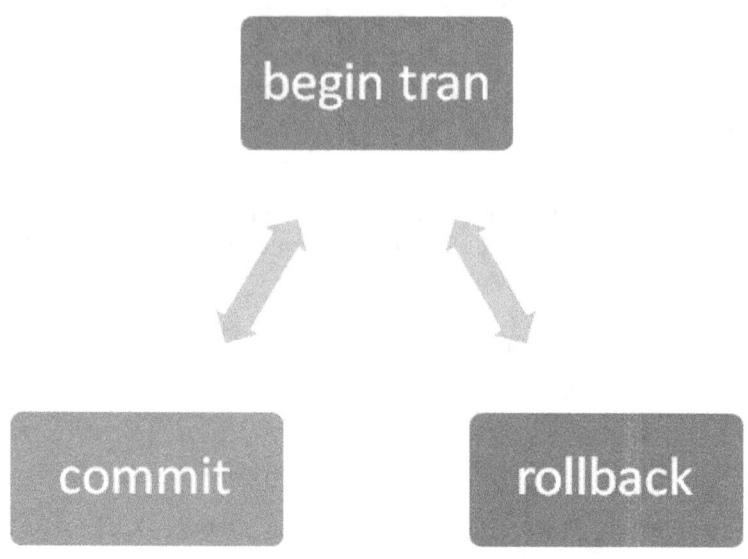

Figure 58 : The two only ending for a transaction

As soon as a transaction is completed (*committed* or *rolledback*) it no longer appears in the `systransactions` table. A transaction is always linked to a process by its spid. Conversely, a process is not always linked to a transaction.

A transaction must prevent any uncertainty in a DBMS because a transactional database must never show uncommitted information. It must refrain from considering as final what has not yet been completed or rolled back.

Anything that cannot be rolledback is prohibited in a transaction:

- `disk init...`
- `truncate table...`
- `alter database...`
- `create database...`

If the `commit` instruction never arrives, for various reasons (network outage, dataserver shutdown, login disconnection, etc...), then an implicit `rollback` will be automatically executed. The rollback is an unraveling job that can take a very long time: ASE must return all data as it was before the `begin tran` instruction.

Analogy. *It is like a man who paints his white house all in pink: he paints his walls square meter by square meter, face by face, and suddenly he discovers that he does not like this color. He is then forced to roll back with a bucket of white paint until the house is white as before. The transaction will have cost 2 times of work time and 2 times of resources (paint). Whereas "committing" would have been simpler. During all the painting work, this person puts up opaque tarpaulins so that no one could see the house during the work. So, no one knew that the house was pink for a few hours.*

For the list of the current transactions on the instance, you have to call the procedure `sp_transactions`.

To track the status of a transaction, the system variable `@@transtate is used`.

- 0 = My transaction is in progress.
- 1 = My last transaction was committed.
- 2 = My last instruction gave an error. However, the transaction is still in progress.
- 3 = My last transaction was rolled back.

This means that a person who connects to an instance and runs `select @@transtate` should normally see this:

```
1> select @@transtate
2> go

 -----------
           1
```

Then, if the person writes `begin tran,` they will see this:

```
1> begin tran
2> go
1> select @@transtate
2> go
 -----------
            0
```

SQL objects

Objects

An object is a computer element contained in a database. The list of objects is available in the `sysobjects` table. It contains...

- ° User tables (U)

- ° System tables (S)

- ° Defaults (D)

- ° Views (V)

- ° Stored procedure (P)

- ° Trigger (TR)

- ° Rule or check constraint (R)

- ° Extended procedure (XP)

- ° User Functions (SF)

- ° Computed column (C)

- ° SQLJ function (F)

- ° Log (L)

- ° Referential constraint (RI)

- ° Partition condition (N)

Conversely, some entities are not objects:

- ○ Logins
- ○ Users
- ○ Indexes
- ○ Types
- ○ Unique constraints
- ○ Devices
- ○ Roles
- ○ Caches
- ○ Segments
- ○ Fragments
- ○ Bases
- ○ Primary keys
- ○ Partitions

Owner

The owner of a table is usually the user who created it. Within the same database, it is allowed to create several tables with the same name as long as their owners are different.

```
1> sp_help
2> go
 Name                Owner Object_type
```

```
----------------     ------  -----------
CASTOR              fifi    user table
CASTOR              riri    user table
CASTOR              loulou user table
```

By typing `select * from CASTOR`, the 3 users below will see different tables.

To specify the table you want to consult, you must write the complete syntax:

```
select * from mabase.riri.CASTOR
```

When the owner of an object is dbo, you can leave a blank between the 2 points:

```
select * from mabase..CASTOR
```

Functions

A function is an operator that performs a transformation from an incoming value to return an outgoing value. The incoming value can be null.

A function can belong to the system or be created by a user or DBA.

Here is an example of creating a function whose role is to translate a day in French from the English word:

```
create function traduit_jour (@day char(20))
returns char(20)
as
    begin
    declare @jour char(20)
    if(@day = "Monday") set @jour = "Lundi"
    if(@day = "Tuesday") set @jour = "Mardi"
    if(@day = "Wednesday") set @jour = "Mercredi"
    if(@day = "Thursday") set @jour = "Jeudi"
    if(@day = "Friday") set @jour = "Vendredi"
    if(@day = "Saturday") set @jour = "Samedi"
    if(@day = "Sunday") set @jour = "Dimanche"
    return @jour
```

```
      end
go
```

Example of use (non-system functions must always be prefixed with the owner name)

```
1> select dbo.traduit_jour("Tuesday")
2> go

 --------------------
 Mardi
```

Triggers

A trigger is a piece of computer program coded in SQL that is automatically triggered after a given event.

For example, the next trigger will insert a row in the CITIES table each time a row is inserted in CITIES.

```
create trigger villes_cities on VILLES
for insert
as
insert into CITIES values (1, 'test')
```

To activate or deactivate a trigger, you can write this:

```
alter table Cities enable trigger villes_cities
alter table Cities disable trigger villes_cities
```

To use the values that have just been deleted or inserted, two temporary tables dedicated to triggers can be used:

```
select * from inserted
select * from deleted
```

Finally, it is interesting to know that a trigger can be modified without dropping the previous trigger with the same name: it is a kind of "*create or replace*".

It is forbidden to create a trigger on a system table.

There can only be one trigger per table and per action.

Computed columns

These are columns that are not filled in by the database users but rather automatically *computed*. Let's take the example of a table with a unit_price column and a quantity column, then we can create a computed column which will be the multiplication of the two previous ones.

ID	UNIT_PRICE	QUANTITY	AMOUNT
1	17.50	4	70.00
2	02.50	10	25.00
3	03.00	1	03.00

The syntax for creating a calculated column is:

```
alter table purchases add amount
compute (unit_price * quantity)
```

It is obviously not allowed to modify this kind of column since it is updated automatically.

```
Msg 11067, Level 16, State 1:
Server 'TACTILOU', Line 1:
```

```
Cannot directly insert into or update computed column
'montant'.
```

Surprisingly, a calculated column is considered as an object in its own right because it can be seen in the list of objects displayed by sp_help.

```
Name                          Owner  Object_type
------------------------       -----  ----------------
sysquerymetrics               dbo    view
purchases                     dbo    user table
...
achats_montan_1984007068      dbo    computed column
```

There are two ways for ASE to manage these columns:

- Materialize them.
- Virtualize them.

Virtual column

These are columns that do not really exist on the hard disk. Only when you make a select on the table, the optimizer calculates the content of the virtual columns.

For example, let's take a table containing many rows:

```
1> sp_spaceused toto
2> go
 name rowtotal reserved data     index_size unused
 ---- -------- -------- ------ ---------- ------
 toto 5000       302 KB   296 KB 0 KB        4 KB
```

And now, let's add a rather simple virtual calculated column:

```
alter table toto add tenmilleid compute (10000 * id)
```

Let's measure the volume of the table again:

```
1> sp_spaceused toto
2> go
 name rowtotal reserved data      index_size unused
```

| ---- | -------- | -------- | ------ | ---------- | ------ |
| toto 5000 | | 302 KB | 296 KB | 0 KB | 4 KB |

If the table hasn't gained weight despite the addition of a column it's because this column doesn't really exist.

Under these conditions, the column does not really exist, so ASE refuses to create indexes based on it:

```
1>  create index IDX_virtual on toto(tenmilleid)
2>  go
```

Msg 1777,... Cannot create index on a virtual computed column (dixmilleid).

Materialized column

This is the opposite of the virtual column concept. The new column is actually created and saved to disk. During SELECT queries, the optimizer has nothing to calculate because the column really exists. The role this time is quite different: this mechanism can be used as a timestamp in tables.

```
create table employe

(id int identity, nom char(30), date_arrivee as getdate()
materialized)
```

Then, by making 4 data insertions by filling in only the name column:

```
1> insert into employe (name) values ("Jack Matthews")
2> insert into employe (name) values ("Raymond Picolo")
3> insert into employe (name) values ("Mike Flech")
4> insert into employe (name) values ("Hyke Luppo")
5> go
(1 row affected)
(1 row affected)
(1 row affected)
(1 row affected)
```

The result is a column that fills itself with the date of insertion.

257

```
2> select * from employe
3> go
 id              name              date_arrival
 -----------     ----------------   -------------------
           1 Jack Matthews      Jun 27 2015 2:12PM
           2 Raymond Picolo     Jun 27 2015 2:12PM
           3 Mike Flech         Jun 27 2015 2:12PM
           4 Hyke Luppo         Jun 27 2015 2:12PM
```

ASE even allows an index on this kind of column. But updates are still forbidden.

Integrity constraints

An integrity constraint is a device that restricts what can be inserted as information in a table. There are 7 forms:

1. Null or not null: allows or not empty values.
2. Default: this is what will be saved if no value is mentioned.
3. Rule: this is a formula that the value must respect.
4. Unique: duplicates are not allowed in a column.
5. Type: the value must belong to a specific data type.
6. Check constraint: the values of the same row must comply with a certain rule.
7. Foreign key: the values must belong to those of another table

The primary keys are the addition of 2 contrains: Unique and NOT NULL.

Rule and Check constraint are two related concepts. The rule is a format constraint for a column. While the check constraint is a constraint that imposes the respect of a certain equation between two or more columns.

Let's take an example to distinguish them. This insertion in a table:

```
insert into enfant (id, age, arrivee, depart) values (42,
3, '20120202', '20150202')
```

It respects the rule that says age < 4 and the check constraint that says arrival < departure.

Here are the syntaxes:

```
create table enfant (id int, age int, arrivee datetime, depart
datetime)
go
alter table enfant add constraint coherence check (arrivee <
depart)
go
create rule roul1 as @x < 4
go
sp_bindrule roul1 , "enfant.age".
go
```

Types

A type is a computer representation of a set of values: numbers, character strings, dates, etc...

On Sybase ASE 15.7, there are more than 30 data types.

But users and DBAs can also invent them by combining existing types and dimensional values.

Examples

```
sp_addtype first name, "varchar(30)".
sp_addtype trigram , "char(3)".
sp_addtype "row_id", "numeric(10,0)", "identity
```

A type can contain even more information. In total, a user-type can be the combination of:

- Type
- Dimensional value (for char and varchar or numeric)
- Null or not null

- Default
- Rule
- Access rule
- Identity

Example

```
1> create default DefCel as "Single".
2> go
1> sp_addtype maritalstatus , "char(50)". not null
2> go
Type added.
(return status = 0)
1> sp_bindefault DefCel , marital status
2> go
Default bound to datatype.
The new default has been bound to columns(s) of the specified
user datatype.
(return status = 0)
```

numeric

The numeric(X , Y) type is often used by developers. It means number of X digits in total of which Y is after the decimal point.

For example:

numeric(4,2) can be 97.52 or 5.20

numeric(5,0) is an integer between 0 and 99999

numeric(5,5) is a real number between 0 and 1.

Difference between char and varchar

The char type and varchar type are different but few people understand why.

`char(n)` allocates n bytes of data regardless of the true length of the string you want to write.

While `varchar(n)` only allocates the number of useful bytes to store our string.

For this reason, the varchar type is known to be more economical than the char type. It is a mistake to think that. In fact, the varchar type forces the table to contain a small additional field to note the true length of the data. So, it is an "overhead": i.e. a part of extra space.

Comparative Experience #4

"Char vs Varchar"

The following experiment tries to convince the reader: let's create two identical tables except the name field which will be in varchar or char.

```
create red table (id int, name varchar(32))
go
create yellow table (id int, name char(32))
go
```

Then fill the 2 tables with 10000 rows filled to the brim (an integer + a string of characters of length 32). We expect to observe the same size for these two tables and yet this is not the case.

- Red, the table using the `varchar` type, weighs **228** pages.
- Yellow, the table using the `char` type, weighs **200** pages.

Observation: at equal string length, the varchar type weighed more than the char type (+14%).

Conclusion: when all the fields of a string are used, the CHAR type occupies less space than the VARCHAR type.

Views

A view is a `select` query that behaves like a table. You can make `select` queries on it as if it was a real table when in fact it has no hardware existence.

The syntax for creating a view is

```
create view mavue as select * from matable
```

When using select *, the star is immediately replaced by the real column list when the view is created. This means that in case of future changes to the table, the view may be invalid.

```
1> create table Example (id int, name char(20))
2> go

1> create view viou as select * from Exemple
2> go

1> alter table Example drop name
2> go
(0 rows affected)

1> select * from viou
2> go
Msg 207, Level 16, State 4:
Server 'TACTILOU', Line 1:
Invalid column name 'name'.
```

To inquire about a view, you can use `sp_help` and `sp_helptext`.

Note: it is forbidden to put an `order by` clause in the text of a view:

```
1> create view viou as select * from test order by id
2> go
Msg 154, Level 15, State 4:
Server 'TACTILOU', Line 1:
An ORDER BY clause is not allowed in a view.
```

Defaults

A default value is a value that is automatically placed in a record when no other has been specified.

There are two types of default values at ASE. There is the object and the local value.

You can create a default that can be used by several tables. It then takes the form of an object that can be consulted in `sp_help`.

```
create default_year_by_default as 2000
```

This object can then be linked to one or more columns:

```
1> sp_bindefault year_by_default , "birth.year".
2> go
Default bound to column.
```

There is another syntax, simpler and more local:

```
create table naissance (id int, annee int default 2000
null)
```

When a column can be null but has a default, the following subtlety must be understood:

```
insert into naissance (id, year) values (30, null)
```

Gives this:

```
id          year
----------- -----------
         30         NULL
```

While:

```
insert into naissance (id) values (40)
```

Gives this:

```
id              year
----------- -----------
          40         2000
```

Remove a default

Either remove the link that links a column to a default:

```
sp_unbindefault "naissance.annee" (birth.year)
```

Either make an alter on the table:

```
alter table naissance replace annee default null
```

Large objects

LOB, BLOB, Large objects, TEXT and IMAGE are different terms but describe the same thing: they are types of columns that are designed to absorb a large number of bytes (files, very long text, images...). By a set of pointers, these large data are moved out of the table and can therefore be freed from the limits of "normal" rows. Normal values are strings of characters, dates and numbers.

Illustration:

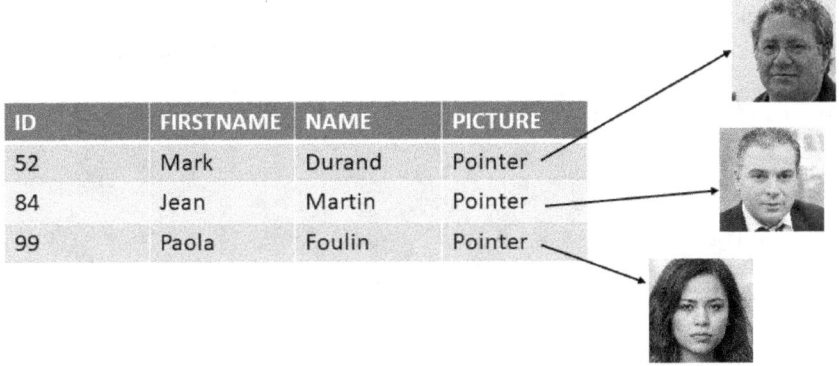

ID	FIRSTNAME	NAME	PICTURE
52	Mark	Durand	Pointer
84	Jean	Martin	Pointer
99	Paola	Foulin	Pointer

Figure 59 : Example of a table containing pictures

The two most commonly used types of large objects are TEXT and IMAGE.

TEXT allows you to store text of almost unlimited length. Ten thousand, a hundred thousand, a million characters, or even more. Whereas no char or varchar field would ever have tolerated more than 1200 characters.

These types of data impose many constraints:

- convert() function not applicable
- MAX(), MIN(), AVG() functions not applicable
- Creation of indexes impossible on this kind of columns,
- Group by inapplicable
- Order by inapplicable
- Union inapplicable (but UNION ALL yes)
- Distinct inapplicable
- Impossible joints on these columns
- Unenforceable rules
- Inapplicable concatenations
- Degraded performance.

To manipulate these particular columns, there are adapted commands: `readtext` and `writetext` allow to read or write in these fields.

You can also use hexadecimal!

For example:

```
1> create table ecole (id int, name image)
2> go
1> insert into ecole values (1, 0x01000F)
2> go
(1 row affected)
```

Among all types of the Large Object genre, the difference between `text` and `unitext` is the capacity and character set.

`text` →2 billion bytes maximum

`unitext` →1 billion bytes maximum

There is a subtlety between large objects and update null. By default, ASE does not empty the pages written by a large object after an `update <table> set <champtext> = null`. However, it does it with `DELETE` and `TRUNCATE TABLE`.

For example, let's take a table with a "text" field:

Event	Size in pages
Insertion of 5000 rows	5086
After a DELETE without where	2
After a TRUNCATE TABLE	2

After an update ... set ... = null	5086

The worst is that even after a `reorg rebuild`, the lost space is not recovered. The reorg has no control over the TEXT fields.

To encourage ASE to clean up unnecessary pages after an update set null, an option on the:

```
sp_chgattribute matable , dealloc_first_txtpg , 1
go
```

You can also activate this option in the entire database:

```
sp_dboption mabase , 'deallocate first text page ' , true
go
```

Foreign keys

A foreign key is a constraint that forces the values in one column to belong to those in another column in another table. For example, in a list of people, the postal code of their address must necessarily exist in the postal code table:

ABONNES				VILLES	
ID	NOM	CODEPOSTAL		ID	COMMUNE
1	DURAND	75001		75001	PARIS
2	RAYMOND	78180		06000	NICE
3	MARTIN	94200		78180	MONTIGNY-LE-BRETONNEUX
4	BOLNET	92400		94200	IVRY-SUR-SEINE
5	OLIVO	78180		92400	COURBEVOIE

Example of syntax:

```
create table abonnes (ID int, NOM char(40), CODEPOSTAL
int references villes(ID))
```

or

```
alter table abonnes add constraint contrainte1 foreign
key (CODEPOSTAL) references villes (ID)
```

It is mandatory to have a unique index on a column so that it is referenced by a foreign key:

```
Msg 1711, Level 16, State 1:
Server 'TACTILOU', Line 1:
There is no unique constraint on the referenced columns
in the referenced table 'villes' specified in referential
constraint declaration on the table 'abonnes'.
Msg 2761, Level 16, State 4:
Server 'TACTILOU', Line 1:
Failed to create declarative constraints on table
'abonnes' in database 'exemple'.
```

And afterwards, the single index cannot be deleted as long as the foreign key of the other table exists.

```
1> drop index cities.idv
2> go
Msg 3712, Level 16, State 2:
Server 'TACTILOU', Line 3:
Cannot drop index 'villes.idv' because it still has
referential integrity constraints.
```

To find out if there are foreign or primary keys on a table:

```
sp_helpconstraint <delatablename>
```

Stored procedures

A stored procedure is an object that executes a succession of SQL queries. The syntax is:

```
create procedure <procedurename> as <sql query>
```

For example:

```
create procedure nbindex
as select count(1) from sysindexes
go
```

Thanks to the option set deferred name resolution, it is possible to create stored procedures using objects that do not exist.

For example:

```
set deferred_name_resolution on
go
drop table toto
go
create procedure example
as
select * from toto
go
```

Identity columns

An identity column is an integer column that increments itself at each insertion.

Next_identity function

The next_identity() function announces the next number that will be entered when a row is inserted. If this function returns NULL, it can mean either that the table does not have an identity column or that the object mentioned in brackets cannot be found or is not a table.

Obviously when a new and empty table has an identity column, the next_identity() function returns 1.

Negative numbers are prohibited.

Identity gaps

The identity gap is a problem that usually occurs after a sudden shutdown of the ASE instance (`shutdown with nowait`, kill -9, power outage, stacktrace...).

When the instance restarts, the RAM has been emptied! Not knowing anymore where it had stopped counting, the identity of the table is confused. At the next insert, it then takes the number 5,000,002.

Explanation: the counter is in memory, so in case of a sudden stop of the instance, the counter does not have the opportunity to go down to the disk.

When the instance is restarted, Sybase takes the last counter that was saved to disk and adds 5 million because it wants to avoid creating duplicates by taking over numbers that it might have already assigned before the shutdown.

To put everything back in order, there is a small procedure to follow.

Beforehand: check the dependencies of this table because the DBA is about to modify numbers in a table. This could generate inconsistencies with other tables!

1. Enable permission to edit identity columns:

```
set identity_update nameoftable on
```

2. Modify all rows that have a high ID:

```
update toto set id = id - 4000000 where id > 5000000
```

3. Check the current status of the counter:

```
select next_identity("labelname")
```

4. Decrease the table counter:

```
sp_chgattribute "nameoftable", "identity_burn_max", 0, "desired_number"
```

5. Mitigate future identity gaps should it happen again:

```
sp_chgattribute "nameoftable", "identity_gap", 500
```

And all this rather in a quiet period because these actions are very much hindering access competition.

The theory is simple but the practice is much less so because you have to perform all these steps at once and it is very long and it is impossible to run `sp_chgattribute` in a transaction.

Cursors

A cursor is an entity located in memory. As its name indicates it is a small device that allows you to position yourself in the results of a `select` query.

Normally, when a `select` query is executed without a cursor, the result appears immediately (subject to performance and lock issues) and it is up to the client to deal with any returned rows.

The cursor, on the other hand, allows the database server to support navigation within the `select` results.

The cursor is composed of two variables in memory:

- The result set
- The position

On the other hand, a cursor can have several modes of operation:

- `Insensitive`: the data in the result set will never change again from the execution of the query.
- `Semi-sensitive` (by default): the data in the result set will be affected by certain modifications to the table.
- `Scroll`: you can scroll through the result set from top to bottom and from bottom to top.
- `No scroll` (default): you can only scroll through the result set in one direction without ever going back.

Here are some examples of syntax. Let's start by declaring a cursor to browse a table:

```
declare chihuahua cursor for

select id, prenom, nom from clients order by id
```

At this stage, nothing is really done by the instance. But it is possible to see this cursor in sp_cursorinfo.

```
Cursor name 'chihuahua' is declared at nesting level '0'.
The cursor is declared as NON-SCROLLABLE cursor.
The cursor id is 1572873.
The cursor has been successfully opened 0 times.
The cursor will remain open when a transaction is
committed or rolled back.
The number of rows returned for each FETCH is 1.
The cursor is read only.
The cursor is read only because it contains an ORDER BY
clause.
This cursor is using 8099 bytes of memory.
```

The cursors are very personal, no one can see the cursors from other sessions. They are not objects. They do not exist on the hard disk.

Then, to really trigger the query itself, you have to open the cursor:

```
open chihuahua
```

Now the request has an execution plan. All that remains is to retrieve the data row by row. Since this cursor is, by default, in `no scroll`, it is only possible to browse all the results in one direction. Just write:

```
fetch chihuahua
```

And this for each row to the last. To go faster, it is possible to set a session parameter indicating a wish to `fetch` from 6 to 6:

```
1> Set cursor rows 6 for chihuahua
2> go
1> fetch chihuahua
2> go
 id          first                                   name last name
 ----------- --------------------------------------- ----------------------------
           4 3ec6381ca3a74326b57defd4e238c8 fde03869522549c9aad2efd4e238c
           5 574b1c9c1ea14ad88e0aefd4e238c8 e2f58a3ce4414af383a7efd4e238c
           6 3742bbb098f34e1cb48defd4e238c8 36ae0cf8640d4319b8bfefd4e238c
           7 414fb8bc407d4e23b107efd4e238c8 15eed05d57cc48b6a796efd4e238c
           8 3ef61958b9f840dba61eefd4e238c8 8f4da740fed8499db779efd4e238c
           9 5ceb240840ea49238eadefd4e238c8 13416f1dd9784d1283f9efd4e238c
```

For cursors in `scroll` mode, there is a range of navigation syntax:

- `fetch absolute 10 cursor_name`

- `relative fetch 10 cursor_name`

- `fetch first cursor_name`

- `fetch last name_of_cursor`

- `fetch prior cursor_name`

- `fetch next cursor_name`

It is also possible to save the `fetch` results in variables. For example:

```
fetch cursor into @mavariable1, @mavariable2
```

It is also possible to update a row at the current cursor position:

```
update clients set nom = "Bertrand" where current of
chihuahua
```

Finally, you have to close the cursor plus un-allocate it:

```
close chihuahua
deallocate cursor chihuahua
```

Concurrency control

Cursors have one thing in common with transactions: they cause restraint problems due to the amount of locks they pose. This restraint will depend on:

- of the table locking scheme

- `scroll` or `no scroll` **mode**

- `sensitive` or `semi-sensitive` **mode**

- `for read only` **ou** `for update` **mode.**

With `sp_who`, it is not possible to detect a session that sets a lock because of an open cursor. And neither `sp_transactions` nor the `systransactions` table contain any trace of the blocking session. You have to fall back to the `syslocks table` or the stored procedure `sp_lock`.

In the syslocks table, the columns are as follows:

- id = id of the locked object
- dbid = base
- page = id of the locked page or 0 otherwise

- type = type of lock. If the value contains 256 then it is a lock that is blocking another session at the moment.
- Class = indicates whether the lock is set by a cursor or not.

The stored procedure sp_cursorinfo will not be able to help the diagnosis because it only gives indications on cursors opened by the user's session only. Unfortunately, sp_showplan does not help the DBA with cursors either:

"the query plan for spid 85 is unavailable.

To unblock a situation, just close the cursor or *kill* the session.

Proxy tables

A proxy table is a virtual table that draws its contents from another table existing in another remote dataserver. It is like a symbolic link.

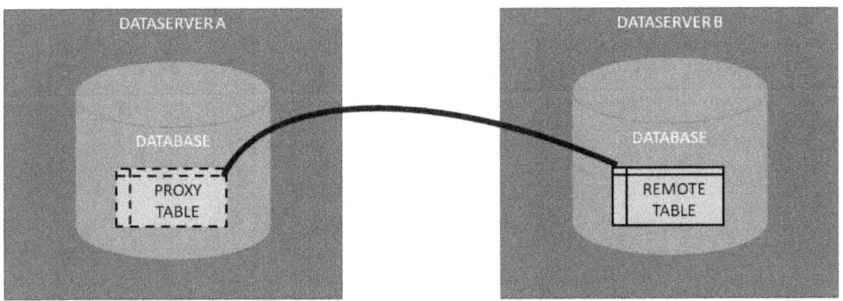

Figure 60 : A proxy table is a "ghost" table showing the content of another table located remotely

Syntax to create them:

```
create existing table <nameoftable> (<structure>)
at "INSTANCE>.<BASE>.<OWNER>.<TABLE>"
```

Example:

```
create existing table Ventes_NY (id int, product
char(40))
at "NEWYORK.marketing.dbo.Sales"
```

By using `sp_help` without arguments, proxy tables are not different from normal tables. But if you specify their name when calling `sp_help`, you know more:

```
1> sp_help Sales_NY
2> go
 Name            Owner Object_type Object_status       Create_date
 ------------    ----- ----------- -------------------- --------------------
 Ventes_NY       dbo    user table keep first text page Jun 30 2015 11:21PM

(1 row affected)
 Column_name Type Length Prec Scale Nulls Not_compressed Default_name
Rule_name
 --------------- ---------- ----- ----- -------------- ------------ ---
 ------
 id             int     4 NULL NULL      0                0 NULL
NULL NULL NULL
 name           char   40 NULL NULL      0                0 NULL
NULL NULL NULL

Object is Remote/External
--------------------------
NEWYORK.marketing.dbo.Sales

Object created with 'existing' option

Object does not have any indexes.
No defined keys for this object.
 name            type        partition_type partitions partition_keys
 ------------ ---------- -------------- ---------- --------------
 Sales_NY     base table roundrobin              1 NULL

 partition_name                partition_id compression_level pages row_count
segment
 --------------------------- ------------ ------------------ ----- --------- --
 -----
 Sales_NY_1497053338          1497053338 none                     0         0
default
```

It is well mentioned that they do not contain any rows or pages. All the rows they return come from the remote table. In case of a network failure, the data is no longer accessible:

```
1> select * from Ventes_NY
2> go
Msg 11206, Level 16, State 9:
Server 'PARIS', Line 1:
Unable to connect to server 'NEWYORK'.
Command has been aborted.
(0 rows affected)
```

Distant does not mean public! It is important to have a login in the remote dataserver otherwise access to the proxy table is compromised:

```
3> select * from Ventes_NY
4> go
Msg 4002, Level 14, State 1:
Server 'NEWYORK', Line 3:
Login failed.
Msg 11206, Level 16, State 1:
Server 'PARIS', Line 3:
Unable to connect to server 'DUBAI'.
```

These problems in accessing a remote ASE require attention to the system procedures sp_helpexternlogin and sp_helpremotelogin.

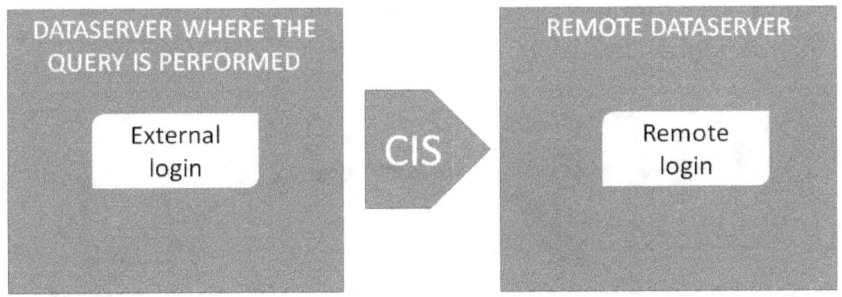

Figure 61 : One must understand the difference between an external login and a remot login

Once you have the right logins, passwords and privileges, you can consult the proxy table like any other table and even insert or delete. Be careful, the data will transit through the network: slowness is to be expected.

277

To know the list of proxy tables of a database, you have to use the `sysobjects` system table as follows:

```
select name from sysobjects where sysstat2 & 1024 = 1024
```

It is even possible to point the proxy table to a stored procedure:

```
create existing table personne_NY (prenom char(10), nom
char(20)) external procedure at
"NEWYORK.marketing.dbo.Personnel"
```

It is not mandatory to use a remote body. A proxy table can also point to a local object. To do this, you simply need to create a loopback server in the dataserver that points to itself.

```
sp_addserver loopback, null, BUCAREST

go

create existing table exemple2 (nom char(40)) external
procedure at "loopback.disneyland.dbo.exemple1"
```

Finally, a proxy table can even get its data from a simple file.

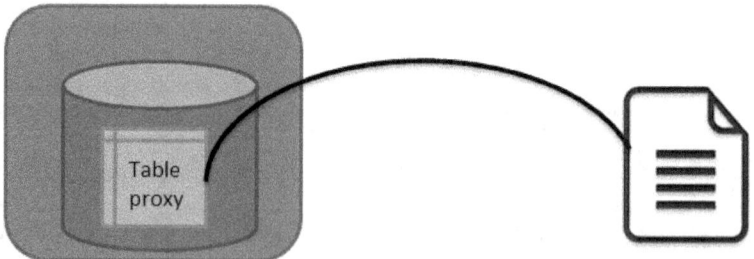

Figure 62 : A simple file can be read as if it was a table

This feature makes possible a very practical trick: the transposition of the ASE errorlog to the table in the master database.

Here is the necessary syntax:

```
use master
go
sp_configure 'enable file access' , 1
go
create table errorlog (line varchar(500))
external file at @@errorlog
go
```

From now on, the errorlog can be consulted like any table, without even having to connect to the machine hosting the instance!

```
select top 5 * from errorlog
go
 00:0006:00000:00009:2015/01/01 15:13:57.76 kernel Begin processing to
generate RSA keypair.
 00:0006:00000:00009:2015/01/01 15:14:00.45 kernel Completed processing to
generate RSA keypair.
 00:0006:00000:00009:2015/01/01 15:14:00.45 kernel Begin processing to
generate RSA keypair.
 00:0006:00000:00009:2015/01/01 15:14:00.48 kernel Completed processing to
generate RSA keypair.
 00:0006:00000:00009:2015/01/02 21:19:49.86 kernel Begin processing to
generate RSA keypair.
```

Proxy bases

To go beyond the proxy table concept, Sybase offers proxy bases. The principle is the same: to give the user of an instance the impression of using a local database when in fact the data is remote.

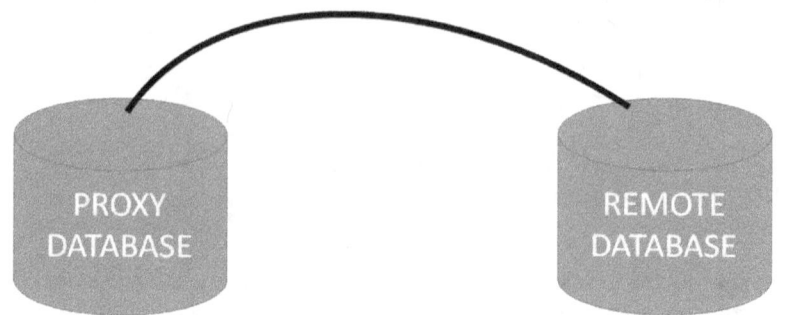

Figure 63 : A proxy database is a ghost representing the data contained in a remote database

For example, it may be useful to allow branch offices to access data from the head office of a large company. Or to ensure that certain data shared by several teams is always identical.

Here is an example of how to create a proxy database:

```
create database BaseDeConnaissance_Paris
with default_location = "PARIS.BaseDeConnaissance.dbo.".
for proxy_update
go
```

Do not forget the end point in the string of characters of the "default location".

There are many limitations:

- Only the tables are accessible through proxy databases. Views or procedures stored in the remote database will not be visible in the proxy database.
- Tables that are created in the remote database after setting up the proxy database will not appear in the proxy database. To see them, you have to drop the proxy database and recreate it.

- It may seem stupid but the opposite is possible: if a table is created in the proxy database, it immediately appears in the remote database, even though it is the source!

To find out if a database is a proxy, use `sp_helpdb` followed by its name.

```
1> sp_helpdb KnowledgeBase_Paris
2> go
 name                             db_size          ow
 ------------------------         ---------------
 BaseDeConnaissance_Paris          8.0 MB sa

(1 row affected)
 device_fragments                      size
 ------------------------------   ----------
 disneyland_dat05                         8.0
 device             segment
 ---------------    ----------
 disneyland_dat05 default
 disneyland_dat05 logsegment
 disneyland_dat05 system
 remote location
 ----------------------------------------
 TACTILOU.disneyland.dbo.
(return status = 0)
```

Links

Sybase makes extensive use of the concept of binds.

A **cache** can be linked to a base, a table or an index.

A **tempdb** can be linked to a login or an application.

A **rule** can be linked to a column or a type.

A **default** can be linked to a column or a type.

A **type** can be linked to a column.

This kind of links must be carefully monitored because if an object is deleted, it may either generate an error message or cause a future problem.

Example:

```
1> sp_addtype first name, "char(30)"
2> go
Type added.

1> create table client (id int, first name first name)
2> go

1> sp_droptype first name
2> go
Msg 17541, Level 16, State 1:
Server 'TACTILOU', Procedure 'sp_droptype', Line 145:
Type is being used. You cannot drop it.
```

T-SQL language

This book does not pretend to describe the whole SQL language or even Transact-SQL. It only lingers on some rather peculiar syntaxes. For the rest, the reader is invited to turn to the official documents of Sybase ASE 15.7.

go

In T-SQL, there is a concept that baffles novices and/or those who are used to working with competing DBMS: the "**go**".

To send a query that has been typed on the keyboard, you have to do a carriage return and type go (without any space before the go). No semicolons are allowed.

```
select @@version
go
```

DBA's job is also to remind everyone who calls the hotline of this practice by asking why "it doesn't work! ».

The "GO" in capital letters is allowed but not very common.

Typing the go command next to the query without carriage return will not work.

Few people know this but it is totally allowed to write several requests on the same line!

```
1> select @@servername select db_name() select getdate() select
pi()
2> go
```

```
------------------------------
TACTILOU

(1 row affected)

------------------------------
master

(1 row affected)

------------------------------
          Jul 15 2015 2:30PM

(1 row affected)

--------------------------
                  3.141593
```

Messages of success

Unlike most other DBMS, at Sybase ASE, the `create table`, `create index`, `create login`, `create view`, `drop login`, `drop view`, `drop table`, `disk init` **and** `truncate table` **statements do not issue any messages if successful. This can be confusing because you don't know if the request was successful.**

```
3> create login toto with password ZFSD78484
4> go
1>
2> create table example (id int)
3> go
1>
2> create index indD on example(id)
3> go
```

On the other hand, the commands `select`, `update`, `insert`, `delete`, `create database` **and** `alter table` **return a confirmation message at the end of execution.**

```
3> insert into example values (13)
4> go
```

```
(1 row affected)
1> select * from example
2> go
 id
 -----------
           13
(1 row affected)
1> create database toto on master = 10
2> go
CREATE DATABASE: allocating 5120 logical pages (10.0
megabytes) on disk 'master' (5120 logical pages
requested).
Database 'toto' is now online.
```

Top

top is a word that allows you to delete, update or select the first n rows of a result. It is very useful.

Examples:

```
select top 500 * from persons
delete top 500 from schools
update top 500 companies set name = "XXXX
```

Having

Having is a clause of the SQL. It can be used in 2 cases: in association with Group By or alone. But in all cases, it requires the use of an aggregation function (like max, min, avg or count).

If we want to display the row of a table "having" the largest number in a column, we need this syntax. For example, to display the dean of a list of people:

```
1> select name from person
2> having birth = min(birth)
3> go
```

```
name
--------------------
Lionel
```

Many users tend to use WHERE and are disappointed with the result:

```
1> select name from person
2> where birth = min(birth)
3> go
Msg 147, Level 15, State 1:
Server 'TACTILOU', Line 1:
An aggregate function may not appear in a WHERE clause unless it
is in a subquery that is in a HAVING clause, and the column
being aggregated is in a table named in a FROM clause outside of
the subquery.
```

Truncate table

The `truncate table` control is an alternative to DELETE without WHERE. It is an instruction that empties all the rows of a table but without logging the lost rows in the transaction log.

However, it should not be thought that this operation is a "weakly logged operation". Truncate table does not prevent from doing dump transactions on the base.

Example:

```
1> use example
2> go
1>
2> select tran_dumpable_status("example")
3> go

   -----------
             0

(1 row affected)
1>
2> truncate table A1
3> go
1>
```

```
2> select tran_dumpable_status("example")
3> go


-----------
           0

(1 row affected)
```

On the other hand, it is impossible to rollback a truncate table (because the lost rows are not in the transaction log). That's why transactions prohibit it:

```
1> begin transaction
2> go
1> truncate table A1
2> go
Msg 226, Level 16, State 1:
Server 'TACTILOU', Line 1:
TRUNCATE TABLE command not allowed within multi-statement
transaction.
```

All and any

ALL and ANY are keywords dedicated to nested queries. These words are translated as "All" and "None".

For example, to see the list of companies whose city is not the address of any employee:

```
select * from company
where ville <> all (select ville from employe)
```

This syntax is particularly unreadable. It is therefore preferred this one:

```
select * from company
where ville not in (select ville from employe)
```

Case when

case when is a **word that allows you to modify the rows of a result according to several criteria. It is like a "if" but applied to the SQL code.**

Example of use:

```
select "Minister" =
      case
              when minister = 1 then "YES"
              when minister = 0 then "NO"
      end
from hommespolitiques
```

or

```
select "Minister" =
      case
              when minister = 1 then "YES"
              else                      "
      end
from hommespolitiques
```

= ,*= and =*

The entries =, *= and =* can be equivalent to the words join, left join and right join.

Examples of syntax:

```
select * from tableA, tableB where ida = idb
-- Gives the same result as
select * from tableA join tableB on ida = idb

select * from tableA, tableB where ida *= idb
-- Gives the same result as
select * from tableA left join tableB on ida = idb

select * from tableA, tableB where ida =* idb
```

```
-- Gives the same result as
select * from tableA right join tableB on ida = idb
```

Like

`like` is a powerful tool because it can be an efficient search engine. The word like reveals its interest when coupled with wildcards such as:

- **%:** means "any character and any number of characters".
- **_:** means "any character. Only one character ".
- **A-D]:** means any letter between A and D.
- **AD]:** means either A or D.

If you really want to use "%" as a real character and not as a wildcard, you have to frame it with square brackets: [%].

It is even possible to make joints with the LIKE operator:

```
1> select * from rate
2> go
 category rates
 -------- ---------------- --------
 BOBD%                   .    200000
 BOBJ%                   .    800000

(2 rows affected)
1> select * from articles
2> go
      price id
 ----- --------------------------
 BOBD1                    170.0000
 BOBD2                    177.0000
 BOBDW                     22.300000
 BOBJ2                    188.300000
 BOBJ9                    250.020000

(5 rows affected)
```

```
1> select id , rate * price from items a, rate t
2> where a.id LIKE t.category
3> go
 id
 ----- --------------------------
 BOBD1                 204.0000
 BOBD2                 212.400000
 BOBDW                  26.760000
 BOBJ2                 338.940000
 BOBJ9                 450.036000
```

ASE specific commands

kill

The only thing you can kill in ASE is a process. The victim session is then immediately rolled back and the person is disconnected. But he or she can reconnect.

The syntax is very simple:

```
kill <spid>
```

Some recommendations

It is impossible to *kill* your own process. To disconnect its process, the command is `select syb_quit()`.

It is strongly not recommended to kill a process in the system, i.e. all those whose loginame in `sp_who` is NULL. There are always about twenty of them.

```
1> sp_who
2> go
 fid spid status    loginame origname hostname blk_spid dbname
tempdbname cmd
 --- ---- -------- --- -------- -------- -------- -----------
---------- ---------------
    0     2 sleeping NULL     NULL     NULL NULL                  0
master      tempdb      DEADLOCK TUNE
    0     3 sleeping NULL NULL NULL 0
master tempdb SHUTDOWN HANDLER
    0     4 sleeping NULL NULL NULL NULL 0
master tempdb KPP HANDLER
    0     5 sleeping NULL NULL NULL NULL 0
master tempdb ASTC HANDLER
```

```
    0     6 sleeping NULL NULL NULL NULL 0
master tempdb CHECKPOINT SLEEP
    0     7 sleeping NULL NULL NULL NULL 0
master tempdb HK WASH
    0     8 sleeping NULL       NULL       NULL                    0
master       tempdb      HK GC
    0     9 sleeping NULL NULL NULL NULL 0
master tempdb HK CHORES
    0    10 sleeping NULL     NULL      NULL NULL                0
master         tempdb      DTC COMMIT SVC
    0    11 sleeping NULL     NULL      NULL NULL                0
sybsecurity tempdb        AUDIT PROCESS
    0    12 sleeping NULL NULL NULL NULL 0
master tempdb PORT MANAGER
    0    13 sleeping NULL NULL NULL 0
master tempdb NETWORK HANDLER
    0    14 sleeping NULL NULL NULL NULL 0
master tempdb NETWORK HANDLER
    0    15 sleeping NULL NULL NULL NULL 0
master tempdb NETWORK HANDLER
    0    16 sleeping NULL NULL NULL NULL 0
master tempdb NETWORK HANDLER
    0    19 sleeping NULL NULL NULL 0
master tempdb LICENSE HEARTBE.
```

It is recommended to always know exactly what a process was doing before *killing* it, because ASE will never be able to give information about a process that has disappeared. Getting information about a process requires at least the following commands:

```
dbcc traceon(3604)
go
dbcc sqltext(<spid>)
go
dbcc traceoff(3604)
go
sp_who "<spid>"
go
select * from master..sysprocesses where spid = <spid>
go
sp_showplan <spid>
go
```

In appendix, a procedure named `sp_kill` proposes to collect all the information about a process then kills this process and announces the estimated duration of its rollback.

If a *killed* process takes a long time to completely disappear it is because it must necessarily undo everything it started. It is a "kill rollback". To follow the evolution of this rollback, ASE provides this syntax. It even indicates the remaining duration of the rollback.

```
kill <spid> with statusonly
```

For example:

```
1> kill 17
2> go
1>
2> kill 17 with statusonly
3> go
Transaction rollback in progress for spid 17 for 0 seconds.
Estimated remaining rollback time is 10 seconds.
Completed scanning: 22562 / 98001 log records (23%); 45 MB / 15
MB log space (300%).
```

connect

The word connect allows a user from one dataserver to connect to another via the "CIS" (Component Integration Services) platform, i.e. the same device that makes proxy databases and proxy tables possible. It is important that the other dataserver is present in the server table.

Example:

```
C:\Users\Lionel>isql -w1000 -Usa -S TACTILOU -P lionel
1> sp_addserver DUBAI, ASEnterprise , DUBAI
2> go
Adding server 'DUBAI', physical name 'DUBAI'
Server added.
(return status = 0)
1> connect to DUBAI
```

```
2> go
Entered passthru mode to server 'DUBAI'.
1>
2>
3> select @@servername
4> go
 ------------------------------
 DUBAI
(1 row affected)
```

To disconnect, the instruction is simply `disconnect`.

```
3> select @@servername
4> go

 ------------------------------
 DUBAI

(1 row affected)
1> disconnect
2> go
Exited passthru mode from server 'DUBAI'.
1> select @@servername
2> go

 ------------------------------
 TACTILOU
```

In sp_who, there is no indication that the user has logged in to another instance.

```
1> sp_who
2> go
 fid spid status       loginame origname hostname blk_spid dbname
tempdbname cmd
 --- ---- ---------- -------- -------- -------- -------- ----------- ----
------ ----------------
   0    2 sleeping   NULL     NULL     NULL NULL              0 master
tempdb    DEADLOCK TUNE
   0    3 sleeping   NULL     NULL     NULL              0 master
tempdb    SHUTDOWN HANDLER
   0    4 sleeping   NULL     NULL     NULL NULL              0 master
tempdb    KPP HANDLER
   0    5 sleeping   NULL     NULL NULL     NULL              0 master
tempdb    ASTC HANDLER
   0    6 sleeping   NULL     NULL NULL     NULL              0 master
tempdb    CHECKPOINT SLEEP
   0    7 sleeping   NULL     NULL NULL     NULL              0 master
tempdb    HK WASH
```

```
        0     8 sleeping    NULL       NULL       NULL NULL          0 master
tempdb        HK GC
        0     9 sleeping    NULL       NULL       NULL NULL          0 master
tempdb        HK CHORES
        0    10 sleeping    NULL       NULL       NULL NULL          0 master
tempdb        DTC COMMIT SVC
        0    11 sleeping    NULL       NULL       NULL NULL          0
sybsecurity tempdb         AUDIT PROCESS
        0    12 sleeping    NULL       NULL NULL      NULL           0 master
tempdb        PORT MANAGER
        0    13 sleeping    NULL       NULL       NULL           0 master
tempdb        NETWORK HANDLER
        0    14 sleeping    NULL       NULL       NULL NULL          0 master
tempdb        NETWORK HANDLER
        0    15 sleeping    NULL       NULL       NULL NULL          0 master
tempdb        NETWORK HANDLER
        0    16 sleeping    NULL       NULL       NULL NULL          0 master
tempdb        NETWORK HANDLER
        0    19 sleeping    NULL       NULL       NULL NULL          0 master
tempdb        LICENSE HEARTBEAT
        0    26 running     sa         sa         TACTILOU          0 master
tempdb        INSERT
        0    27 recv sleep sa          sa         TACTILOU          0 master
tempdb        AWAITING COMMAND
```

execute

It is an instruction that triggers the call of a stored procedure. It is therefore the counterpart of the SELECT instruction used to read tables and views.

You can write exec or execute.

Execute is optional to invoke a stored procedure unless you want to invoke several procedures in the same transaction:

For example:

```
exec sp_helpdb
exec sp_who
go
```

While without exec, you get an error:

```
sp_helpdb
sp_who
go
Msg 17590, Level 16, State 1:
Server 'TACTILOU', Procedure 'sp_helpdb', Line 103:
The specified database does not exist.
```

reorg

Reorganizing a table means, in common parlance, defragmenting it. Indeed, during its life, a table undergoes DELETE, INSERT and UPDATE which are the only 3 commands that make changes to data in a table.

__Analogy.__ Like a student's notebook that would spend its time crossing out, scratching, putting TippEx on, the table will start to become very disorganized and contain a lot of "holes".

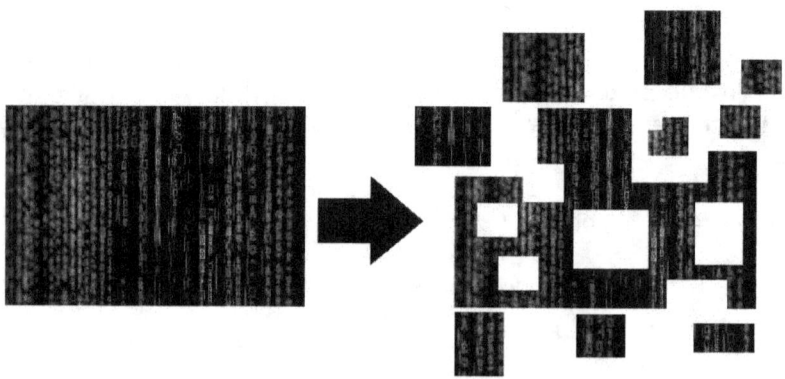

Figure 64 : After many delete, update the data are fragmented

The harmful consequences of fragmentation are mainly:

- The table takes up more space than necessary →loss of space.

- The data is so spread out that it takes longer to retrieve it when it is needed - a →waste of time.

Reorganization is an operation that must be attempted away from business hours for two reasons:

1. The table is (usually) **not usable** during a reorg.
2. The operation has an **impact on the performance of the instance.**

There are 4 syntaxes to trigger a reorg.

- `reorg compact nameoftable`
- `reorg forwarded_rows nameoftable`
- `reorg reclaim_space nameoftable`
- `reorg rebuild nameoftable`

Without going into too many technical details, it is necessary to know in which cases each reorg syntax is used:

	Locked table in APL	Locked table in DOL
Base with select into TRUE option	`reorg rebuild only`	`The 4 syntaxes work`
Base with select into FALSE option	`No reorg syntax works`	`Reorg compact` `Reorg forward...` `Reorg reclaim...`

Here is an example of error messages obtained when trying to perform the 4 types of reorg on a table locked in allpages in a database without select into option:

```
1> reorg rebuild company
2> go
Msg 11919, Level 16, State 1:
Server 'TACTILOU', Line 22:
You cannot run REORG REBUILD in this database because the
'select into/bulkcopy' o
1>
2> reorg compact enterprise
3> go
Msg 11903, Level 16, State 4:
Server 'TACTILOU', Line 2:
You cannot run REORG on a table which uses allpages locking.
REORG COMPACT of 'entreprise' terminated due to error or user
interrupt.
1>
2> reorg forwarded_rows company
3> go
Msg 11903, Level 16, State 4:
Server 'TACTILOU', Line 2:
You cannot run REORG on a table which uses allpages locking.
REORG FORWARDED_ROWS of 'entreprise' terminated due to error or
user interrupt.
1>
2> reorg reclaim_company space
3> go
Msg 11903, Level 16, State 1:
Server 'TACTILOU', Line 2:
You cannot run REORG on a table which uses allpages locking.
REORG RECLAIM_SPACE of 'entreprise' terminated due to error or
user interrupt.
```

To get around this limit, there are two solutions:

1. **Create then drop a clustered index** on this table. Be careful, this does not mean that clustered indexes are ramparts against fragmentation. It's just when you create them that you can be sure that the data will be reorganized during the sorting. Conversely, if the table already has a clustered index, just drop it and recreate it.
2. Or, simpler, **temporarily enable the** select into **option** on the base and remove it at the end of the reorg rebuild.

ASE versions 15.7 brought many innovations to reorg treatments.

A fifth reorg syntax was released with ASE 15.7 SP100: `reorg defrag`. It acts step by step, row by row, and not at all in a bundled way, so that nobody is locked out. It is reserved for DOL tables and requires that the table has an index.

A DBA will use the `resume` and `time` options if he/she knows that reorganizing a table may take too much time and therefore interfere with the availability of the table. `time` allows to launch a reorg by specifying a maximum duration. While the word `resume` indicates that a previous reorg should be restarted from where it stopped. Before that, many companies were reluctant to use reorg because it was unstoppable.

The unit for limiting the duration of a reorg is the minute:

```
reorg compact nameoftable with time = 30
```

The other major innovation of 15.7 is the option to perform a reorg rebuild while allowing users to use the table simultaneously:

```
reorg rebuild nameoftable with online
```

Example of a problem that occurs when a user launches a `select` on a reorganized table without the "online" option.

```
3> select * from table2
4> go
Msg 8233, Level 16, State 1:
Server 'TACTILOU', Line 3:
REORG operation is in progress on the object 'table2'
```

 Opinion of the author. The ASE editor has obviously decided to drown DBAs under the syntax of "reorg"!

The Sybase DBA will have to choose from among the 5 syntaxes, which one best suits their needs. One thing is for sure, the oldest syntax, `reorg`

`rebuild` induces a lot of inconveniences and is to be banned except for a tiny table.

It can be interesting to quantify the effects of a reorg: the simplest method is to perform a `sp_help` on the table before and after the reorg. This will show the number of pages in the table. If the number has decreased after the reorg, it means that the table was fragmented.

Before:

```
1> sp_help fragmentee
2> go
 Name         Owner Object_type Object_status         Create_date
 ----------   ----- ----------- --------------------- -----------------
 fragmentee   dbo   user table  keep first text page  Jul 12 2015  2:55

(1 row affected)
 Column_name Type Length Prec Scale Nulls Not_compressed Default_nam
 ----------- ---- ------ ---- ----- ----- -------------- -----------
 id          int       4 NULL NULL      0                0 NULL
 nom         char     50 NULL NULL      0                0 NULL
Object does not have any indexes.
No defined keys for this object.
 name        type         partition_type partitions partition_keys
 ----------  ----------   -------------- ---------- --------------
 fragmentee  base table   roundrobin              1 NULL

 partition_name         partition_id compression_level pages row_count
 --------------------   ------------ ----------------- ----- ---------
 fragmentee_217048778     217048778 none                461      3068
```

After:

```
1> sp_help fragmentee
2> go
  Name          Owner Object_type Object_status         Create_date
  ----------    ----- ----------- --------------------  --------------------
  fragmentee dbo    user table   keep first text page Jul 12 2015   2:55P

(1 row affected)
  Column_name Type Length Prec Scale Nulls Not_compressed Default_name
  ----------- ---- ------ ---- ----- ----- -------------- ------------
  id           int      4 NULL NULL     0                0 NULL
  nom          char    50 NULL NULL     0                0 NULL
Object does not have any indexes.
No defined keys for this object.
  name          type         partition_type partitions partition_keys
  ----------    ----------   -------------- ---------- --------------
  fragmentee base table roundrobin                  1 NULL

(1 row affected)

  partition_name        partition_id compression_level pages row_count
  -------------------   ------------ ----------------- ----- ---------
  fragmentee_217048778    217048778 none                 96      3068
```

And even before launching a reorg, it is already necessary to know if a table is fragmented or not. There are 3 ways to know it:

1. The command **dbcc checktable** <delatablename>.
2. Since ASE 15.7 SP100, there is the **sp_helpdefrag** procedure.
3. In the appendix of this book, there is a stored procedure capable of measuring the fragmentation of a table: **sp_help_frag**.
4. The following **theoretical calculation:**

$$\frac{\text{Number of rows X Width of a row}}{\text{Number of pages X size of page}}$$

Example 1: a very fragmented table

A table of 2889 rows on 459 pages in a 2048 bytes page dataserver with a structure composed of an INT(4) column and a CHAR(50) column:

301

Occupancy rate = (2889*54)/(459*2048) = **17%.**

Example 2: a table with little fragmentation

A table of 5000 rows on 122 pages in a 2048 bytes page dataserver with a structure composed of two CHAR(20) columns:

Occupancy rate = (5000*40)/(122*2048) = **80%.**

Backups and loads

General

At Sybase ASE 15.7, backups and reloads have remained a simple process. There are two main commands to be aware of:

```
dump database to 'path to a file'.
```

and

```
load database <base> from 'path to file>'.
```

The rest is up to the DBA. The **backup strategy** is specific to each company and each DBA. However, the most common practice is to perform `dump databases` at least once a day and `dump transactions` every 30 minutes.

To reload the master database, first stop and then start the instance with the "-m" option. It is rare to have to *load* the master but it can be useful if you have a corruption of the master database.

Best practices

Some DBAs always perform a `dbcc checkdb` just before a dump database to make sure they are not going to create a backup containing corrupted data. It would be a shame to find this out 10 years later.

As a precaution, it is strongly discouraged to try to interrupt or *kill* a dump database or a load database. Risk of basic corruption, risk of phantom process, risk of losing the port of the Backup Server...

Follow the progress of dumps and loads

There are three ways to view the progress of a backup or reload.

1. The first is to look at the **errorlog of** the Backup Server.
2. The second is to look at the io generated by the dump or load process in `sysprocesses: select spid, cmd, physical_io from master..sysprocesses where cmd like "LOAD%" or cmd like "DUMP%"`.
3. The third is to query the stored procedure `sp_who of` the Backup Server: `SYB_BACKUP...sp_who` (yes, there are 3 points).

Backup server

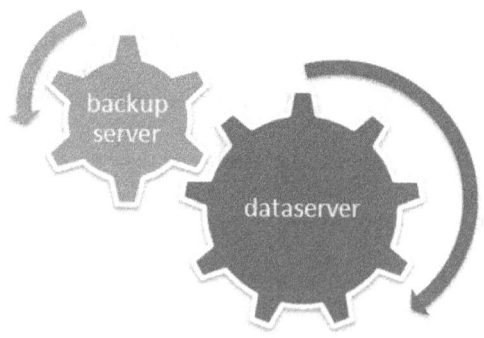

Figure 65 : Correlation between dataserver and backup server

ASE needs only one binary to work... Except when it comes to `dump` and `load`. These operations necessarily require the start of an additional binary called "Backup Server". Its architecture is similar but simpler than that of the dataserver.

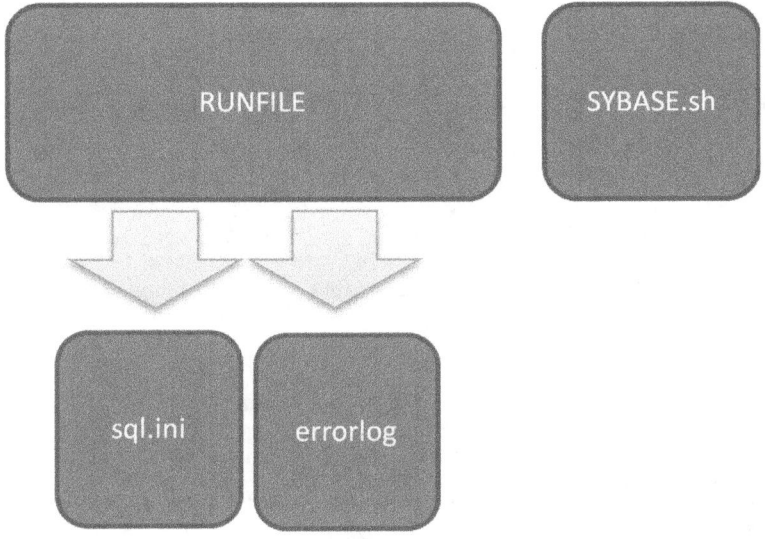

Figure 66 : Required files for the backup server

Runfile

This is the startup file of the Backup Server. But it also acts as a configuration file because it is the only file in which you can influence the performance of the Backup Server. There are 2 parameters to be monitored:

- **-P** tracking the number of dumps strips
- **-m** followed by the memory allocated to the Backup Server (in megabytes)

If these parameters are not chosen, the Backup Server sets them to 48 each. This will mean that each stripe will be entitled to 1 Megabyte of RAM during dumps and loads. It is advisable not to leave these default values, to choose a "-P" that corresponds to slightly more than the number of stripes in the dumps, and to set "-m" to 5 times the value of "-P". The typical error that can occur when -P is incorrectly configured is *"cannot create an open server thread as the maximum number of service threads configured has already been reached. Increase the value via -P command line. »*

Here is an example of the Runfile of Backup Server, under Windows:

```
rem
rem Backup Server Information:
rem name:                      DUBAI_BS
rem errorlog:                  C:\Sybase\ASE-
15_0\install\DUBAI_BS.log
rem interfaces:                C:\Sybase\ini\sql.ini
rem location of multibuf:      C:\Sybase\ASE-
15_0\bin\sybmbuf.exe
rem language:                  us_english
rem character set:            cp850
rem
rem
"C:\Sybase\ASE-15_0\bin\bcksrvr.exe" -SDUBAI_BS -
e"C:\Sybase\ASE-15_0\install\DUBAI_BS.log" -
I"C:\Sybase\ini\sql.ini" -M"C:\Sybase\ASE-15_0\bin\sybmbuf.exe"
-Lus_english -Jcp850
```

Here is an example of the Runfile of Backup Server, under Unix:

```
#!/bin/sh
#
# Error log path:
/abricot/sgbd/TACTILOU/errorlog/TACTILOU_BK.log
# Maximum number of network connections:        25
# Maximum number of server connections: 20
# Multibuf executable path:
/abricot/sgbd/TACTILOU/ASE157/ASE-15_0/bin/sybmultbuf
# Backup Server name:    TACTILOU_BK

/abricot/sgbd/TACTILOU/ASE157/ASE-15_0/bin/backupserver \
-e/abricot/sgbd/TACTILOU/errorlog/TACTILOU_BK.log \
-N25 \
-C20 \
-M/abricot/sgbd/TACTILOU/ASE157/ASE-15_0/bin/sybmultbuf \
-STACTILOU_BK \
-m1500 \
-P128 \
```

SYBASE.sh (or sybase.bat on Windows)

This is the file that contains all environment variable declarations.

sql.ini or interface

The interface files (for Unix) and sql.ini (for Windows) contain the list of ASE instances and also the Backup Servers that can be reached via the network. Each instance is identified by a name and indicates the machine and port through which a client can reach them.

For example, under Windows:

```
[DUBAI_BKP]
      master=NLWNSCK,Tactilou,5005
      query=NLWNSCK,Tactilou,5005
```

For example, under Unix:

```
DUBAI_BKP
      query tcp ether Tactilou 5005
      master tcp ether Tactilou 5005
```

Starting a Backup Server

Under Unix: `startserver -f runfile_du_backup_server`

Under Windows: you have to start the service or run the runfile.bat.

Stopping a Backup Server

Connect to the corresponding ASE instance and launch a `SYB_BACKUP shutdown`. However, stopping a backup server requires the right to use the `shutdown` instruction. The error to avoid is to connect to a Backup server to stop it. It is possible but it doesn't work because a Backup Server doesn't "understand" SQL.

```
C:\Users\Lionel>isql -w1000 -STACTILOU_BS
Password:
1> shutdown
```

```
2> go
No language handler installed.
Language cmd:
shutdown
```

Connecting to a Backup Server

It is possible to connect to a Backup Server with the isql tool. No matter the login and no matter the password: you can put anything. Regardless of the login and password, the Backup Server will respond positively if it can be reached. So, it's a good way to make sure it's up and running and reachable.

Example of a reachable Backup Server:

```
C:\Users\Lionel>isql -U Barack -P Obama -S TACTILOU_BS
1>
2>
3> exit
```

Example of unreachable Backup Server:

```
C:\Users\Lionel>isql -U Barack -P Obama -S DUBAI_BS
CT-LIBRARY error:
        ct_connect(): network packet layer: internal net
library error: Net-Lib protocol driver call to connect two
endpoints failed
```

Three types of backup

Since Sybase ASE 15.7, there are 3 types of database backups:

Full backups:

```
dump database disneyland to "c:/disneyland.full"
```

Cumulative backups, i.e. containing only the pages that have changed since the last dump database:

```
dump cumulative disneyland to "c:/disneyland.inc"
```

Transaction log backups:

```
dump transaction disneyland to "c:/disneyland.tran"
```

In all three cases, a storage location for the dump (the backup file) must be specified. Usually a file is specified as in the 3 examples above.

But it is possible to save a filename permanently in the `sysdevices` table and then use an alias to make the dumps:

```
sp_addumpdevice
"disk","SauvDisneyland","C:/sauvegarde_disneyland.dmp"
```

then

```
dump database disneyland to SauvDisneyland
```

Dump transaction

There are several reasons why a `dump transaction` may not be executed:

- If the transaction log is not on a separate device,
- If the base is in "trunc log on checkpoint",
- If weakly logged operations have taken place,
- If someone made a dump tran with truncate only,
- If the database has never been dumped.

To find out the reason, there is a stored procedure `sp_tran_dumpable_status` as well as a `tran_dumpable_status()` function.

It is because their log segment is not on a device except that it is never possible to perform a `dump transaction` on system databases like master or tempdb:

```
1> use master
2> go
1>
2> sp_tran_dumpable_status
3> go
 bit              description

 ----------- -----------------------------
-------------------------------------------
              2 Log is not on its own device

             32 Log has been truncated
```

Three types of loading

Load database

The main command to reload (*or* refresh) a database is `load database`. It has a syntax very similar to its sister command `dump database`:

```
load database <base> from 'path to file>'.
```

But, in addition has two features to simply read the descriptive information of a dump file:

```
1> load database model from
"c:/TACTILOU_petitebase_15.07.08_004129.dmp" with listonly
2> go
Backup Server session id is: 8. Use this value when executing
the 'sp_volchanged' system stored pr
Backup Server: 4.34.1.1: Device
'c:/TACTILOU_petitebase_15.07.08_004129.dmp':
Volume name:'          '
Backup Server: 4.36.1.1: Device
'c:/TACTILOU_petitebase_15.07.08_004129.dmp':
File name:          'itebase15189009C7'.
Create date & time:       Wednesday, Jul 8, 2015, 00:41:43
Expiration date & time: Wednesday, Jul 8, 2015, 00:00:00:00
```

```
Database name: 'petitebase                          '.
Backup Server: 6.30.1.3: Device
c:/TACTILOU_petitebase_15.07.08_004129.dmp: Volume cataloguing
com

1> load database model from
"c:/TACTILOU_petitebase_15.07.08_004129.dmp" with headeronly
2> go
Backup Server session id is: 10. Use this value when executing
the 'sp_volchanged' system stored p
Backup Server: 6.28.1.1: Dumpfile name 'itebase15189009C7'
section number 1 mounted on disk file '
This is a database dump of database ID 5, name 'petitebase',
from Jul 8 2015 12:41AM. ASE version
sp101/3439/64-bit/OP. Backup Server version: Backup Server/15.7
SP101/EBF 21339/P/X64/Windows Serv
Database contains 7168 pages; checkpoint RID=(Rid pageid =
0x193f; row num = 0x1a); next object ID
Database log version=7; database upgrade version=35; database
durability=UNDEFINED.
segmap: 0x00000003 lstart=0 vstart=[vpgdevno=11 vpvpn=0]
lsize=5120 unrsvd=4208
segmap: 0x00000004 lstart=5120 vstart=[vpgdevno=12 vpvpn=0]
lsize=2048 unrsvd=2031
The database contains 7168 logical pages (14 MB) and 7168
physical pages (14 MB).
dbdevinfo: devtype=0 vdevno=11 devname=disneyland_dat05
physname=C:\Sybase\data\disneyland_dat05.d
dbdevinfo: devtype=0 vdevno=12 devname=disneyland_dat06
physname=C:\Sybase\data\disneyland_dat06.d
This is the SYSDATABASES row of database ID 5, name 'petitebase'
from the dump header. Status:0x00
dflags:0x0000. Deftabaud:0. Defvwaud:0. Defpraud:0.
Def_remote_type:0. Status3:0x20000. Status4:0x
This is the SYSATTRIBUTES row for the database 'petitebase' from
the dump header. Flmode:0x0000.
```

When the dump consists of several files (or stripes), the syntax is:

```
load database TOTO
        from "c:/Sybase/dump_TOTO.1.dmp"
stripe on "c:/Sybase/dump_TOTO.2.dmp"
stripe on "c:/Sybase/dump_TOTO.3.dmp"
stripe on "c:/Sybase/dump_TOTO.4.dmp
go
```

311

One of the most rigid constraints of the `load database` is the fact that the destination database must be at least the same size as the database used to generate the dump.

On the other hand, ASE strictly forbids the use of a dump of the master database to reload a database that is not master:

```
1> load database example2 from
"c:/TACTILOU_master_15.07.25_184843.dmp"
2> go
Msg 3109, Level 16, State 1:
Server 'TACTILOU', Line 1:
This dump was created from the Master database. A dump
from Master can only be loaded as part of the Restore
Master procedure.
```

Cumulative load

The second way to reload a base is the `cumulative load` command. This command must follow a load database because it is an increment. A cumulative reload only modifies the pages of data that have **changed** since the last load database. This results in a saving of disk space. But not a saving of time, because to use it, you have to reload the 2 dumps one after the other.

Dump Database
500 Mo

Dump Cumulative
320 Mo

Load transaction

Unlike `cumulative load`, `load transaction` existed long before version 15.7. It is a command that saves a piece of the transaction log to a file. Its main role is to replay transactions that have been committed since the last `dump database`. `Dump transaction` can for example be triggered every 30 minutes. This will result in 48 transaction files in a directory. With these 48 files, it will be possible to reload the database and put it back to the time you want, to the nearest 30 minutes, like a time machine.

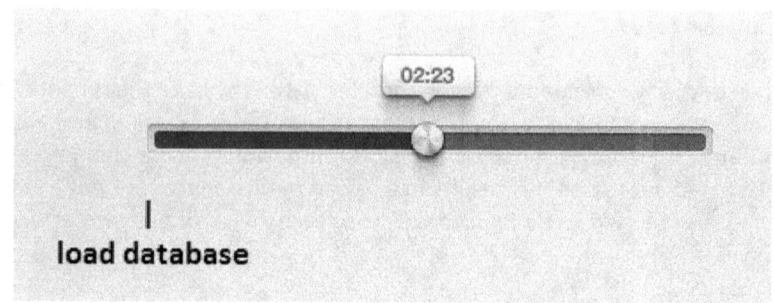

Figure 67 : You can set a database to a previous state if you have dumps

It is possible to reload a `dump database`, then a `cumulative dump` and then as many `dump transactions as` you wish. The final act that will make the database available is the `online database` command.

For example:

```
load database example from "C:\Backup\example_Sunday.dmp"
go

load cumulative example from "C:\Backup\example_incl.dmp"
go

load transaction example from "C:\Backup\example_100.trn"
go

load transaction example from "C:\Backup\example_101.trn"
go

load transaction example from "C:\Backup\example_102.trn"
go

online database example
go
```

Once the `online database is` completed, it is not possible to reload other transaction files.

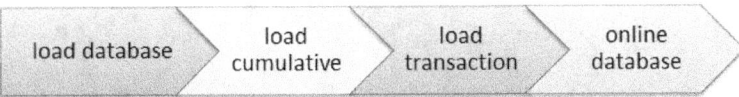

Figure 68 : Order of the load commands

The files produced by dump database, cumulative dump and dump transaction lead DBAs to be able to go back in time to put the database in a more or less accurate state in the past.

Online database

It is a command that finalizes the loads and opens the database to users.

This operation does not require the assistance of the Backup Server and therefore cannot be logged in the errorlog of the Backup Server.

This operation usually takes a very long time without "progress bar", especially the part "*Recovery of database xxxxx will undo incomplete nested top actions*". So, be careful not to claim victory too early at the end of a load. Moreover, if the version of the dump is different from the version of the instance, there is +20% of time spent converting the dump to make it compatible.

Problem that can happen

The error message "*Database XXXX cannot be brought online because it has replicated tables that may not be completely transfered...*" is due to another Sybase product: Replication Server. This book is not about Sybase Replication.

The solution is as follows:

```
1.  dbcc dbrepair(example,ltmignore)
2.  online database example
3.  use example
4.  sp_reptostandby example , 'NONE'.
```

Redo and Undo

"Redo" and "Undo" are common terms in the database field.

The redo is usually done at the end of the `load database while the` undo is done at the end of the `online database.`

Redo

The entire transaction log is browsed and everything it describes is **re-populated** on the data pages to make sure there is consistency between data and log. Indeed, the transaction log may contain transactions that the data does not yet contain.

Undo

The entire transaction log is scanned for the word "commit". All actions not ending in `commit` must then be undone in the data pages.

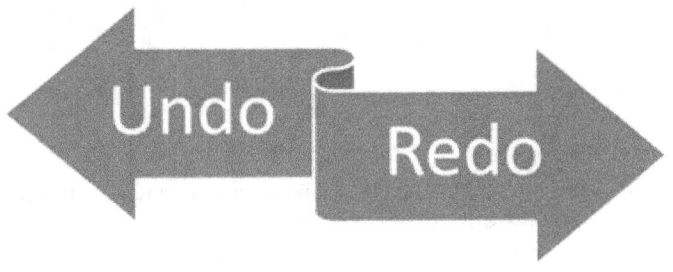

Figure 69 : Undo and redo are ways to move across time

Log and data arrangement

We know that a `load database` can only work if the destination database is the same size or larger than the source database. In the past, it was also necessary to provide a database with strictly the same alternation of log and data fragments as the database used to generate the dump file (the same DDL to put it simply).

Figure 70 : Since the first version of ASE, the load database command simply copied and pasted the data and log pages, "hoping" that the DBA had provided identical source and destination configurations.

Since version 15.7 SP100, ASE supports dispatching but requires adequate log and data sizes:

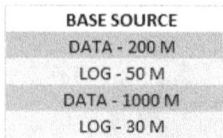

BASE SOURCE
DATA - 200 M
LOG - 50 M
DATA - 1000 M
LOG - 30 M

BASE DESTINATION
DATA - 1000 M
LOG - 50 M
LOG - 30 M
DATA - 200 M

Figure 71 : Since version 15.7 SP100, ASE manages to match logs with logs and data with data. The only requirement is that the sizes must match.

This feature is called Automatic Physical Database Rearrangement in Sybase 15.7 SP100.

For example:

Dump coming from a base constituted like this:

```
disneyland_dat1 100.0 MB data only
disneyland_dat2 100.0 MB data only
disneyland_log1 10.0 MB log only
disneyland_log2 50.0 MB log only
```

Load in a base made up like this:

```
parcasterix_dat1 60.0 MB data only
parcasterix_log1 200.0 MB log only
```

There is an error message:

The data segment in the target database 'parcasterix' is too small (60 MB) to accommodate the data segment from the dumped database (200 MB).

It is therefore mandatory to provide a data segment of at least the same size as the source.

For the log segment it would have been the same:

The log segment in the target database 'parcasterix' is too small (50 MB) to accommodate the log segment from the dumped database (60 MB).

Last backup

There are three methods of determining the last date a database was dumped.

Method 1: The DBCC command

```
dbcc traceon(3604)
go
dbcc dbtable("mabase")
go
```

The result of this command is very verbose. You have to look for the following line:

```
dbt_backup_start: ... Dec 9 2014 11:49:02:570PM
```

Method 2: the load database command

The following command is used to time stamp a dump:

```
load database ... with headeronly
```

Example of use:

```
1> load database exemple from
"c:/TACTILOU_petitebase_15.07.08_004129.dmp" with
headeronly
2> go
Backup Server session id is: 30. Use this value when
executing the 'sp_volchanged' system
Backup Server: 6.28.1.1: Dumpfile name
'itebase15189009C7' section number 1 mounted on dis
This is a database dump of database ID 5, name
'petitebase', from Jul 8 2015 12:41AM. ASE...
```

Method 3: the errorlog

The errorlog file always indicates the date of the dump at the end of a reload. You have to look for a line like this one:

```
Log contains all committed transactions until 2015/06/14
04:05:16.95 for database parc2.
```

Refresh cross-platform

A *cross-platform refresh* is a data refresh performed with a backup from another operating system.

Specifically, cross-platform is considered to exist when two operating systems have a different "*endianness*".

Operating Systems "Little-endian"	Operating Systems "Big-endian"
Linux x86	Linux SPARC
Solaris x86	Solaris SPARC
Windows	AIX

Here is the procedure to follow to carry them out:

1. Interrupt all activity on the source base.
2. Perform a `sp_flushstats` on the source database.
3. *Dump* the source database.
4. *Loader* the target base. (Duration longer than a classical load)
5. Put the target database online.

6. Make a `sp_post_xpload` in the target database. (Very long duration)
7. Make a `sp_indsuspect` in the target database.

Cessation of activity

It is preferable that the bases you want to migrate are not in use.

Several methods: kill all users and prevent their reconnection by changing the port number of the dataserver or by locking all logins, suspend incoming replication, perform the operation during the night, put the database in single-user mode.

This first step is an annoying constraint in a production environment: getting the certainty that no transaction will take place in the base during the entire duration of the dump requires a trick.

This trick involves an intermediary base that is sure to have no activity. There are several ways to prevent the intermediate base from being active: dbo use only, single, non-broadcast network port, machine isolated from users ...

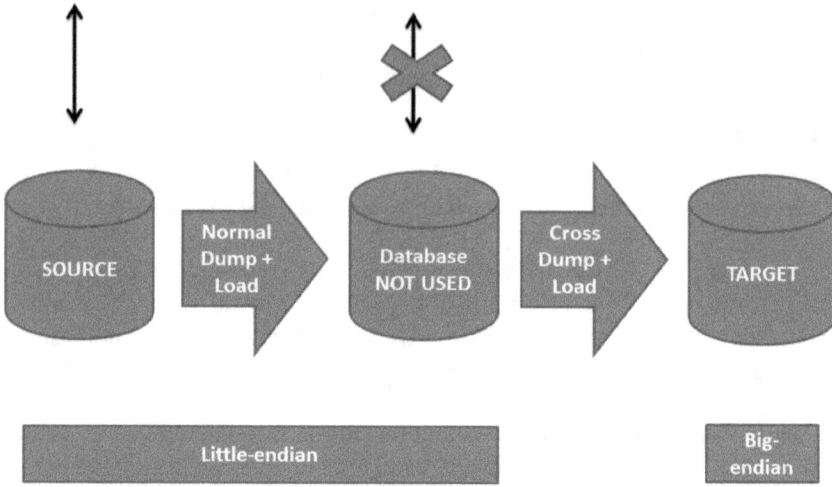

Figure 72 : To perform a cross platform load , you might need an intermediary database not used at all

`sp_flushstats`

Before *dumpering* a database, it is prudent to perform a "`sp_flushstats`". This is an operation that does not erase the statistics as its name suggests but just brings them back to the disk. Performing a checkpoint right afterwards is also a best practice.

`sp_post_xload`

This stored procedure is important after a cross-platform load: it drops and recreates all non-clustered indexes. It is a step that can be extremely long. It is prudent to perform a `tran dump with truncate_only` right afterwards because the `sp_post_xload` fills the transaction log.

Check the indexes

In spite of the `sp_post_xpload` procedure, there may still be suspicious indexes. This is what happens when the database is too small to allow the reconstruction of certain indexes.

You have to list them with the system procedure `sp_indsuspect`.

Remote Backup

It is possible to avoid the dump copy by "scp" by performing a remote dump. The instruction to perform remote dumps is "AT".

Subject to adequate information in the **hosts.allow** files and **interfaces**, it is possible to make a backup that does not use the local Backup Server.

For example:

```
dump database model to "c:/test.dmp" at BCK_DISTANT
```

You can also use multiple Backup Servers for the same dump. To do this, simply create new runfiles and add entries with different ports in the interfaces file. There is no need to make additions with `sp_addserver`.

For example:

```
dump database model
to         "c:/test.1.dmp" at BCK_DISTANT_1
stripe on "c:/test.2.dmp" at BCK_DISTANT_2
stripe on "c:/test.3.dmp" at BCK_DISTANT_3
stripe on "c:/test.4.dmp" at BCK_DISTANT_4
```

Dump compression

When backing up a database, it is possible to specify a compression level to reduce the size of the dump file. The syntax is as follows:

```
dump database mabase to
"C:/sauvegardes/mabase_20150714.dmp" with compression = 1
```

The number after "with compression =" is the compression level. It can be chosen between 0 and 9 or 100 or 101. Here are a few examples of dumps of the same base at different compression levels:

Compression level	Dump duration	File Size
0	66 seconds	112 Mb
1	78 seconds	20 Mb
2	80 seconds	19 Mb
3	80 seconds	18 Mb

Compression level 1 offers a good compromise between time and disk space saving.

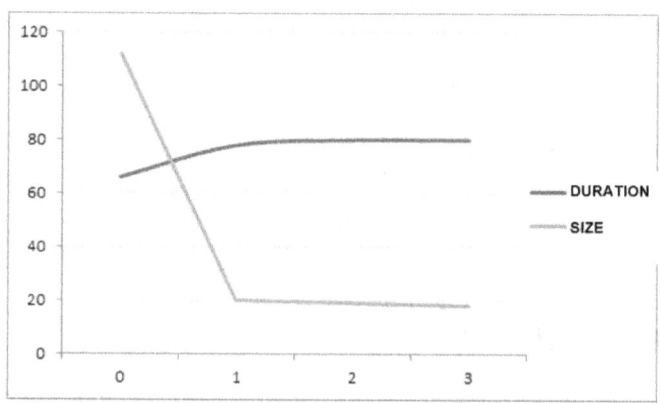

Figure 73 : Duration vs size of backup for each level of compression

Table compression

General

ASE 15.7 provides a feature to compress data contained in a dataserver. Like any compression mechanism, its interest lies in saving storage space, saving cache memory and improving performance.

Figure 74 : Compression icon

Compression requires the purchase of the ASE_COMPRESSION license.

Be careful, this compression is to be distinguished from the compression of dump database which, it existed well before version 15.7 and does not require a particular license.

How it works

Only the **tables** are concerned by compression.

Surprisingly, Sybase allows a table to contain a mixture of compressed and uncompressed data.

It is possible to compress some columns and not others.

It is possible to compress some partitions and not others.

For non-LOB columns, there are two compression scales: the "page" level and the "row" level.

For LOB columns (text, image, ...): the compression strategy is a number between 1 and 9 or 100 or 101. These numbers indicate the algorithm and the compression power. 9 = maximum compression but heavy CPU usage. 100 and 101 use little CPU and compress quickly.

There is no mechanism for compressing an entire base. However, it is possible to tell a base that all its future tables must be compressed.

Syntax

DML commands remain unchanged: whether a table is compressed or not, SELECT, DELETE, UPDATE and INSERT queries keep their classic syntax.

The syntax for compression is as follows.

Creation of a compressed table at row level:

```
create table example (id int, first name char(50))
with compression = row
```

Creation of a compressed table at page level:

```
create table example (id int, first name char(50))

with compression = page
```

Creation of a database by indicating that future tables should be compressed at the row level.

```
create database example on dev_exmple_dat01 = 1000

with compression = page
```

NB: This is only a default parameter that can be contradicted by the two previous syntaxes.

Changing the compression mode of a database

```
alter database example set compression = row
```

Stop table compression

```
alter table example set compression = none
```

Create a compressed table in which one of the columns is not compressed

```
create table exemple (id int not compressed, prenom
char(50)) with compression = page
```

Create a table in which the LOBs are compressed

```
create table exemple (id int, descriptif text compressed
= 9) with lob_compression = 5
```

However, it should be noted that no syntax is used to compress existing data. These syntaxes only have an effect on future data. The only method to compress existing data is SELECT INTO.

Positive points

- Reduction of storage space
- Reduced disk accesses, thus speed gains
- Reduced RAM usage
- Possibility to compress LOB
- Possibility of not compressing certain columns for example if they are frequently consulted.

Negative points

- Compression is not recommended for in-memory databases.
- Replication of tables containing compressed LOBs not possible
- No compression syntax for existing data (you have to `select into`)
- Some types are not compressible: `float, double, real, smalldatetime ...`
- No full base compression mechanism

Comparative Experience #5

"Compression none, row and page

Let's create three tables compressed into `none`, `row` and `page` and fill them with 5200 rows of identical data then observe the size of the tables:

Compression	Number of rows	Number of pages
NONE	5200	153
ROW	5200	114
PAGE	5200	84

Figure 75 : Page-level compression is efficient

Maintenance

A Sybase DBA should consider implementing at least 4 regular maintenance tasks. Typically, off-peak hours.

- Backups
- Reorganizations
- The update statistics
- The DBCCs

NB.1: Always back up the system databases (except tempdb).

NB.2: Never reorg system tables.

The right sequence

There is a logical order to respect for these 4 operations:

Figure 76 : The right order to do maintenance is reorg then DBCC, then update stats then backup

Client tools

Client/server communication

Once you understand what the databases are for, you need to look at one key point: client/server communication. Sybase was the first software in the history of computing to provide a relational database in client/server mode.

In its simplest definition, a client is a binary + an interface file.

Sybase has invented its own protocol for communication between clients and servers: The **Tabular Data Stream protocol (TDS)**.

As clients are required to exchange data with servers, it is strongly recommended to update all clients after each dataserver update.

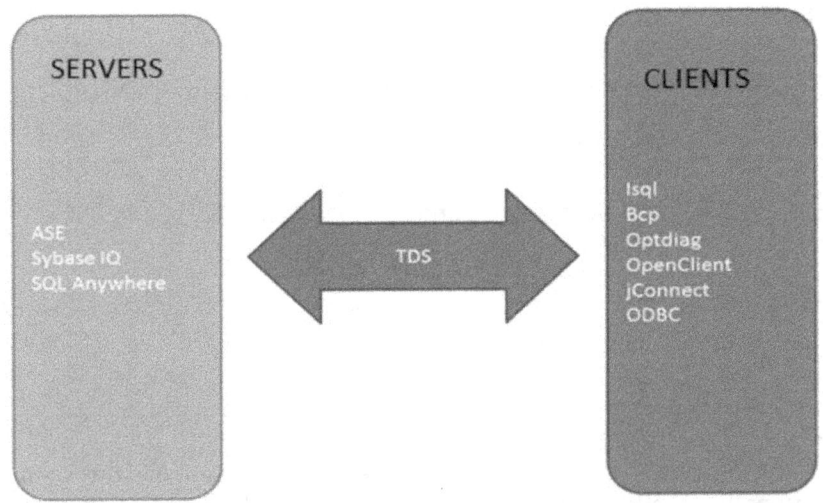

Figure 77 : TDS is the protocol for supporting communications between servers and clients

isql

`isql` is the traditional Sybase ASE customer. It is the simplest and most widespread. It allows you to connect to local or remote instances (as long as the sql.ini or interface file is properly filled in).

Usual syntax:

```
isql -U <login> -P <password> -S <instance> -w 1000
```

Under Unix, by writing "`vi`", isql allows you to edit a command line before launching a query.

By default, it does not log requests, except on Windows. To activate the history, it must be specified when calling isql.

```
isql --history 1024
```

Then the following commands help to navigate through the history.

h   see all the history.

h 2   see the 2 oldest orders.

h -2   see the 2 most recent orders.

??   recall the last order.

Diagnose connection difficulties

A DBA or even a simple user should be able to determine the various reasons why they cannot connect to a Sybase ASE instance. There are 3.

- **Dataserver unknown**: this is a message produced by isql when it is unable to find the requested dataserver in its interface file.

```
CT-LIBRARY error:
        ct_connect(): directory service layer:
internal directory control layer error:
Requested server name not found.
```

- **Dataserver unreachable**: this is a message produced by isql when the dataserver does not respond because it is stopped or does not exist where the interface file says it does.

```
CT-LIBRARY error:
        ct_connect(): network packet layer: internal
net library error: Net-Lib protocol driver call to
connect two endpoints failed
```

- **Incorrect login or password or locked account**: this is a message produced by the dataserver when the login does not exist or exists but the password is not the one mentioned or is locked.

```
Msg 4002, Level 14, State 1:
Server 'TACTILOU':
Login failed.
CT-LIBRARY error:
        ct_connect(): protocol specific layer:
external error: The attempt to connect to the server
failed.
```

bcp

It is a data import/export tool. It allows you to transfer a table to a text file or vice versa.

Export syntax

```
bcp base..table out file -U xx -P xx -S instance -c
```

Import syntax

```
bcp base..table in file -U xx -P xx -S instance -c
```

bcp in fast mode

In its import functionality, the tool can act very quickly (in "fast bcp" mode) provided that 2 rules are respected:

- `Select into` option enabled. The fast-BCP is an unlogged operation so it is recommended to make a dump database afterwards.
- No `clustered index` on the table. It is therefore advisable to drop any index before importing and to recreate it afterwards.

The other interest of the "fast bcp" mode is the fact that it is less likely to provoke full logs (transaction log filling).

We can summarize the best practices of bcp in in fast mode:

1. Dropping all the indexes of the table
2. Activate the select into on the base.
3. Run the bcp in.
4. Recreate all the indexes on the table.
5. Make a dump database.
6. Eventually, remove the `select into` option.

Default + null

It should be noted that one must be careful with columns that combine the two following characteristics: accept NULL + have a DEFAULT value. The bcp-in will tend to apply the default value wherever it should put null. To avoid this, it is advisable to remove the default from the column before running bcp in.

Triggers

It is useless to touch the triggers before a bcp-in because they are totally ignored by this kind of treatment.

Foreign keys

Foreign keys never disrupt a bcp-in. On the other hand, they sometimes prevent a table from being emptied before the bcp-in. To get out of it, you have to drop all the foreign key constraints that prevent the truncate of the table and then recreate them after the bcp-in.

Identities

With respect to columns with an identity, bcp-in can behave in two ways. With the "-E" option, it will insert all the rows as they are with the identifier that is in the file. While without the "-E" option, bcp will abandon the identities contained in the file to let the table number the new rows itself.

The separators

When the following error message appears, it is necessary to change the separator with the -t option, both in bcp-out and in bcp-in because the default separator (the tab) is already used in the data.

```
CSLIB Message: - L0/O0/S0/N24/1/0:
cs_convert: cslib user api layer: common library error:
The conversion/operation was stopped due to a syntax
error in the source field.
```

The 32K limit

By default, the bcp carries only 32768 characters maximum for each column. Any extra characters are simply truncated.

To overcome this problem, use the "-T" option followed by the desired number of characters.

The 2-billion-row limit

The bcp exports a maximum of 2,147,483,647 rows from a table. This limit is rarely met.

The isolation level of the bcp out

The bcp out isolation level is "1: read committed".

This means that if the table is being modified when the bcp starts, the bcp remains pending until the end of the transaction because it doesn't want to peddle values that could be rolled back. It does not mean that the whole result set is from the same moment. The content of the bcp is not atomic:

if there are a lot of rows, the first rows may not be the same age as the last ones because the table continues to "live" during bcp.

If there is already an exclusive lock on the table, the bcp remains suspended from the beginning:

```
C:\Users\Lionel>bcp example..momo out sorti.txt -Usa -S
TACTILOU -P lionel -c

Starting copy...
```

The bcp out is therefore not without impact on users and vice versa.

From an access concurrency point of view this level of isolation is an advantage: the table remains available most of the time! From an ACID point of view, it is bad: the table is not fixed and therefore the bcp may return temporally varied results.

In "repeatable read" or "serializable", it would be a completely different story. Access concurrency would fall sharply in favor of greater bcp consistency. During the whole bcp, no modification would be allowed on the table: they would all be suspended until the end of bcp. In production, this could be dramatic!

ddlgen

DDLGEN is the tool offered by Sybase to extract the syntax for creating objects from a dataserver. For example, a base, a table or a stored procedure. Its syntax is:

```
ddlgen -U<login> -S<dataserver> -P<password> -D<base> -
T<object type> -N<object name>
```

Example of use:

```
ddlgen -Usa -STACTILOU -Plionel -Example -TU -Nyellow
```

```
--------------------------------------------------------------------
-------------
DDL for Table 'example.dbo.yellow' -- DDL for Table
'example.dbo.yellow' -- DDL for Table 'example.dbo.yellow
--------------------------------------------------------------------
-------------
print '<<<<< CREATING Table - "example.dbo.yellow" >>>>>'
go
use example
go
setuser 'dbo' setuser
go

IF EXISTS (SELECT 1 FROM sysobjects o, sysusers u WHERE
o.uid=u.uid AND o.name = 'jaune' AND u.name = 'dbo' AND o.type =
'U')
        drop yellow table

IF (@@error != 0)
BEGIN
        PRINT 'Error CREATING table "example.dbo.yellow"''.
        SELECT syb_quit()
END
go

create yellow table (
        id                              int
not null,
        name                            varchar(40)
not null
)
lock datapages
with dml_logging = full
 on 'default
go
setuser
go
```

Limits

It is not possible to extract the DDL from a system table with ddlgen.

It is not possible to extract all the indexes from a database.

optdiag

It is the tool that allows you to extract a statistics report for an entire database, a table, its indexes, its columns.

Syntax:

```
optdiag statistics pubtune -Usa -Ppasswd -o pubtune.opt
```

Example of output (it's very verbose):

```
OptDiag/15.7/EBF 21339 SMP SP101 /P/X64/Windows
Server/ase157sp101/3439/64-bit/OPT/Thu Jun 06 12:33:02 2013
Adaptive Server Enterprise/15.7/EBF 21339 SMP SP101 /P/X64/Windows
Server/ase157sp101/3439/64-bit/OPT/Thu Jun 06 12:11:05 2013

Server name:
"TACTILOU

Specified database:
"example
Specified table owner:
not specified
Specified table:
not specified
Specified column:
not specified

Table owner:
"dbo
Table name:
"age

Statistics for table:
"age

      Data page count:
1
      Empty data page count:
0
      Data row count:
3.0000000000000000000000000000000
      Forwarded row count:
0.0000000000000000
      Deleted row count:
0.0000000000000000000000000000000
      Data page CR count:
0.0000000000000000000000000000000
```

```
        OAM + page count allocation:
2
        First extent data pages:
0
        Data row size:
20.0000000000000000000000000000000
        Parallel join degree:
0.0000000000000000000000000000000
        Unused page count:
6
        OAM page count:
1

  Derived statistics:
        Data page cluster ratio:
1.0000000000000000000000000000000
        Space utilization:
0.0299700299700300
        Large I/O efficiency:
1.0000000000000000000000000000000

No statistics for remaining columns:
"annee"
(default values used)
"prenom"

Table owner:
"dbo
Table name:
"articles

Statistics for table:
"articles
...

Optdiag succeeded.
```

Ribo

Ribo is a tool that allows to read TDS data frames circulating between an ASE and its customers (jConnect, Sybase Central, isql, bcp, optdiag...).

Configuring Ribo

Ribo is included in the jConnect driver so if JDBC is installed, Ribo is also installed.

Ribo requires that the Java JRE is already installed on the machine used for the following steps.

It needs the two environment variables JAVA_HOME and RIBO_HOME.

- The first one must point to a directory of the JDK recognizable by its content: "Welcome.html, lib, LICENSE, Copyright...".
- The second must point to the directory that contains Ribo. Generally, jutils-3_0\ribo

Integrate Ribo in the client/server connection

Next, you need to understand how Ribo intercepts the frames:

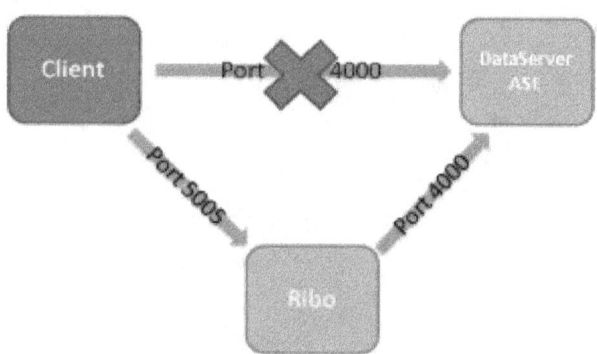

Figure 78 : Network installation of Ribo

Ribo must be interposed between the dataserver and the client. There are two methods for this:

a) Modify the dataserver port in sql.ini: the dataserver port must be replaced by the Ribo listening port.

b) Add a server [RIBO] in the sql.ini by specifying its server and its listening port. Then launch the client by directing it towards the RIBO server.

340

In both cases, Ribo will intercept the data, write it into a log file and then transmit it to the dataserver.

Launch Ribo

The most common command looks like:

```
Ribo -l port -s hostname -p port -c prefix -t
```

-l port: this is the listening port of Ribo. It is necessary to choose a free port. In general, for Ribo it is 5005 but it is not mandatory.

-s hostname: this is the name of the machine that hosts the dataserver.

-p port: this is the port of the ASE dataserver.

-c prefix: can be anything because it's just a prefix to name the log.

-t: do not write anything afterwards. This is an option to say that you want to translate the data frames into readable language.

-d: log displayed but not saved

Read the log file

Ribo writes to the log file while it is running. It does not render the hand spontaneously unless the user does CTRL-C. When you want to read the log, you need to go to %RIBO_HOME% and open a file with a name starting with the prefix chosen with the argument -c and ending with txt. This file contains a chronological trace of the data that circulated in Ribo. One of the dangers that Ribo exposes DBAs to is to fill a whole disk space with its verbose log, especially if it gets the error *"Error processing TDS. Attempting to skip"*.

sybmigrate

It is an essential tool for performing data migrations between very different instances: different versions, different page sizes, different platforms. It is a data converter.

The sybmigrate tool comes in the form of a client binary (like isql for example). It connects to two instances and circulates data from one to the other.

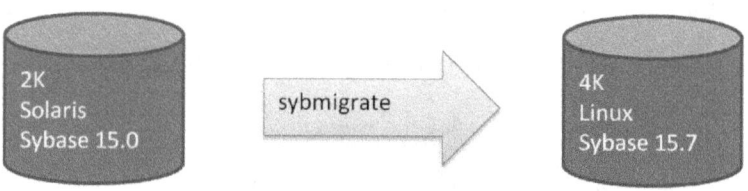

Figure 79 : Sybmigrate usages

It is launched with a few options including a resource filename. The resource file is simply a text file containing information about the source instance and database and the target instance and database.

For example:

```
[server]
source_ase=paris:5002
source_ase_login=sa
source_ase_password= FGVdf4
target_ase=tokyo:6002
target_ase_login=sa
target_ase_password= TPdJD7
```

```
[database]
source_database_name=pubs2
target_database_name=pubs2
```

First of all, sybmigrate must install a migration base to carry out the operation. This installation is done with the syntax:

```
sybmigrate -m setup -r resource.txt -l installation.log
```

Next, here is the syntax for triggering the migration itself:

```
sybmigrate -m migrate -r resource.txt -l migration.log
```

Precautions to be taken:

- It is necessary to provide as many worker processes on the source instance as in the data_copy_thread parameter of the resource file.
- The target database must exist, be empty and not created in for load.
- The sybmigrate needs to create temporary bases on the source instance.
- It is advisable to enable the select into option on the source database.
- There is no need to modify the interface files. The resource file can be filled with server names and port numbers.

There are various disadvantages with the sybmigrate. One of them is the loss of time induced by the fact that the target database must be created entirely without the "for load" option.

There is also the problem of stored procedures containing "#" tables. Sybmigrate does not like to create stored procedures when they evoke temporary " # " table names. To work around this, you need to enable the "deferred name resolution" option in the target instance. Syntax:

343

```
sp_configure "deferred name resolution" , 1
```

Quizz: questions

A/ What is ASE's most fundamental database?

B/ Which tool allows to extract rows from a table to put them in a file?

C/ What are the 4 maintenance acts that a DBA must put in place?

D/ Which stored procedure allows you to see the size of the bases?

E/ What are the two index architectures?

F/ Is it possible to change the page size of a dataserver?

G/ How do I know where the errorlog is?

H/ What should be done after each low logging operation?

I/ How many partitions can there be in a table at least?

J/ How to see the list of people connected to an instance?

Quizz: correct answers

A/ The master.

B/ bcp.

C/ Update statistics, reorg, backups and DBCC.

D/ sp_helpdb.

E/ Clustered and non-clustered.

F/ No.

G/ select @@errorlog.

H/ A dump database.

I/ One.

J/ sp_who.

What future for ASE?

SAP

The future of **Adaptive Server Enterprise** is in the hands of the German company, SAP, which acquired Sybase Inc. in July 2010. The successor version to ASE 15.7 is the first to be free of the word "Sybase".

SAP ASE 16.0 is unveiled in November 2013.

On the menu, several major innovations and increased compatibility with ... SAP.

- The support of the HANA product (DBMS both relational and decisional, operating entirely in RAM)
- Full-text audit
- New syntax "`create or replace`" (except for tables)
- Index compression (sheet pages only)
- Encryption of entire databases
- Multiple triggers: successive triggering
- Data cleaning after `drop table` (to ensure confidentiality of what is deleted)
- Configuration history
- Checking the dumps

Popularity

On the scale of "popularity of DBMS" published by the specialized site http://db-engines.com, SAP ASE remains in **11th position*** far behind the top three: Oracle, MySQL and Microsoft SQL Server. This confirms ASE's status as a niche DBMS, but does not reflect a decline.

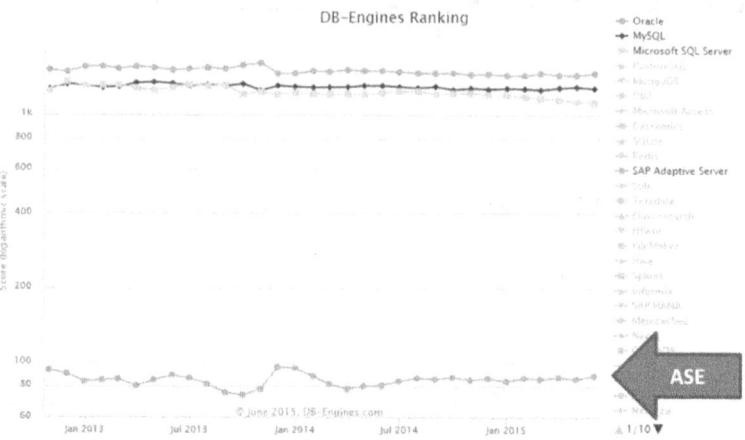

Figure 80 : Database systems popularity

*This graph is obtained by a popularity calculation including the number of mentions of the DBMS on Google and Bing, the general interest in the system in Google Trends, the frequency of technical discussions on the Stack Overflow and DBA Stack Exchange forums, the number of job postings on Indeed and Simply Hired, the number of CVs mentioning the DBMS on LinkedIn and the relevance of the DBMS name on the Twitter network. It therefore does not take into account market share or the number of instances installed worldwide.

Appendices

Online access

All of the following stored procedures are downloadable and updated on the internet.

URL: http://lionel.bolnet.free.fr/procs

User: ASE

Password: Sydney_2012

sp_activity

```
-- Display the activity rate of the instance

use sybsystemprocs
go

drop procedure sp_activite
go

create procedure sp_activite
as
        -- AUTHOR: LIONEL BOLNET
        -- ROLE: Display the activity rate of the instance

        select floor(100 * convert(float,@@cpu_busy) /
convert(float,@@idle)) as "CPU",
                floor(100 * convert(float,@@io_busy) /
convert(float,@@idle))) as "IO".
                        into #temporary

        exec sp_autoformat #temporary
go
```

sp_addlogin2

```
-- Create a login with an encrypted password
use sybsystemprocs
go

drop procedure sp_addlogin2
go

create procedure sp_addlogin2 @loginame varchar(255), @passwd
varbinary(128), @defdb varchar(255) = "master"
as
        -- AUTHOR: LIONEL BOLNET
        -- ROLE: Create a login with an encrypted password

        -- Create
        declare @command varchar(255)
        select @order = "sp_addlogin " + @loginame + " , password
, " + @defdb
        exec (@order)

        -- Allow
        exec ("sp_configure 'allow up', 1")

        -- Modify
        update master..syslogins set password = @passwd where
name = @loginame

        -- Prohibit
        exec ("sp_configure 'allow up', 0")

        -- Confirm
        select name, password from master..syslogins where name =
@loginame
go
```

sp_addlogin3

```
-- Create a login by specifying the encrypted password and the
suid
use sybsystemprocs
go

drop procedure sp_addlogin3
go
```

```
create procedure sp_addlogin3 @loginame varchar(255), @passwd
varbinary(128), @defdb varchar(255), @suid int
as
        -- AUTHOR: LIONEL BOLNET
        -- ROLE: Create a login by specifying the encrypted
password and the suid

        -- Create
        declare @command varchar(255)
        select @order = "sp_addlogin " + @loginame + " , password
, " + @defdb
        exec (@order)

        -- Allow
        exec ("sp_configure 'allow up', 1")

        -- Modify
        update master..syslogins set password = @passwd, suid =
@suid where name = @loginame

        -- Prohibit
        exec ("sp_configure 'allow up', 0")

        -- Confirm
        select name, password from master..syslogins where name =
@loginame
go
```

sp_bcp

```
-- Generate BCP out commands to extract all system tables
use sybsystemprocs
go

drop procedure sp_bcp
go

create procedure sp_bcp @password varchar(20) = """.
as
        -- AUTHOR: LIONEL BOLNET
        -- ROLE: Generate BCP out commands to extract all system
tables
```

351

```
        select "bcp " + db_name() + ".." + name + " out " +
@@servername + "." + db_name() + "." + name + ".txt -c -S " +
@@servername + " -U sa -P " + @password
        from sysobjects where type='S' and name not
in('sysdams','sysgams','syslogs')
        order by name
go
```

sp_datachange

```
-- Display the datachange of each column of a table
use sybsystemprocs
go

drop procedure sp_datachange
go

create procedure sp_datachange @nomtable varchar(200) = """.
as
        -- AUTHOR: LIONEL BOLNET
        -- ROLE: Display the datachange of each column of a table

        if @nomtable = """".
                select convert(char(50),o.name) as "Table",
convert(char(50),c.name) as "Colonne",
datachange(o.name,null,c.name) as "Datachange"
                from syscolumns c, sysobjects o
                where c.id=o.id and o.type= 'U'
                order by o.name, c.name
        else
                select convert(char(50),o.name) as "Table",
convert(char(50),c.name) as "Colonne",
datachange(o.name,null,c.name) as "Datachange"
                from syscolumns c, sysobjects o
                where c.id=o.id and o.type= 'U'
                and o.name = @nomtable
                order by o.name, c.name
go
```

sp_db

```
-- Display several information related to the current database
use sybsystemprocs
go
```

```
drop procedure sp_db
go

create procedure sp_db
as
        -- AUTHOR: LIONEL BOLNET
        -- ROLE: Display several information related to the
current base

        set nocount on

        select db_name() as "Name
        print ""
        select count(1) as "Objets" from sysobjects
        print ""
        select count(1) as "Process" from master..sysprocesses
where dbid = db_id()
        print ""
        select count(1) as "Users"    from sysusers where suid >
-2
        print ""
        select count(1) as "Alias"    from sysalternates

        set nocount off
go
```

sp_dbsize

```
-- Display the size of the logs and data of each database
use sybsystemprocs
go

drop procedure sp_dbsize
go

create procedure sp_dbsize
as
        -- AUTHOR: LIONEL BOLNET
        -- ROLE: Display the size of the logs and data of each
base

        -- Calculation of the number of pages in a megabyte
        declare @coef int
        select @coef = 1024*1024/@@maxpagesize
```

```
        -- Extraction and conversion to Mega
        select DB.name dbname, DV.name devname, size/@coef size,
        case
                when segmap      = 4 then "LOG"
                when segmap & 4 = 0 then "DATA
                else                        "MIXED"
        end contents
        into #TEMP1
        from master..sysdevices DV, master..sysdatabases DB,
master..sysusages US
        where DB.dbid = US.dbid and DV.vdevno = US.vdevno

        -- Transposition and Approval
        select dbname, sum(LOG) log, sum(DATA) data, sum(MIXED)
mixed from
        (
                select dbname, 0     as LOG, 0     as DATA, size
as MIXED from #TEMP1 where contents = "MIXED"
                union all
                select dbname, 0     as LOG, size as DATA, 0
as MIXED from #TEMP1 where contents = "DATA"
                union all
                select dbname, size as LOG, 0     as DATA, 0
as MIXED from #TEMP1 where contents = "LOG"
        )
        AGR group by dbname order by dbname
go
```

sp_dump_all

```
-- Save all the bases
use sybsystemprocs
go

drop procedure sp_dump_all
go

create procedure sp_dump_all @path varchar(50)
as
        -- AUTHOR: LIONEL BOLNET
        -- ROLE: Save all the bases

        print "Dump of all non-temporary bases".

        declare @order varchar(200)
```

```
        select "dump database " + name + " to '" + @path +
@@servername + "_" + name + "_" +

str_replace(str_replace(str_replace(convert(varchar(30),getdate(
),21),":",null),"/","."),"  ","_") + ".dmp' with compression=1"
as commande
                into #TMP1 from master..sysdatabases
                where status3 & 256 <> 256 and name <>
"tempdb"

        declare c cursor for select commande from #TMP1 for read
only
        open c
        fetch c into @order
        while (@@sqlstatus <> 2)
        begin
                print @order
                exec(@order)
                fetch c into @order
        end
        close c
        deallocate cursor c
go
```

sp_evolrows

```
-- Determine if a table is gaining or losing rows
use sybsystemprocs
go

drop procedure sp_evolrows
go

create procedure sp_evolrows @nomtable varchar(50)
as
        -- AUTHOR: LIONEL BOLNET
        -- ROLE: Determine if a table is winning or losing rows

        -- Declarations
        declare @prem int
        declare @two int

        -- First statement
        select @prem = row_count(db_id(),object_id(@nomtable))

        -- Waiting
```

```
        waitfor delay '00:00:10'.

        -- Second statement
        select @two = row_count(db_id(),object_id(@nomtable))

        -- Display
        select @prem
        select @two
        select @two - @prem as "Trend
go
```

sp_fixusers

```
-- Fixed all users attached to NULL login
use sybsystemprocs
go

drop procedure sp_fixusers
go

create procedure sp_fixusers
as
        -- AUTHOR: LIONEL BOLNET
        -- ROLE: Fixed all users attached to NULL login

        -- List of users to be corrected
        select a.name, a.suid into #TEMP1 from sysusers a left
join master..syslogins b on a.suid = b.suid where b.name is null
and a.suid > 0

        -- List of patches
        select a.name, "update sysusers set suid = " +
convert(varchar(10),b.suid) + " where suid = " +
convert(varchar(10),a.suid) correction from #TEMP1 a,
master..syslogins b where a.name = b.name
go
```

sp_fragmentation

```
-- Voluntarily create a fragmented table
drop table fragmentee
go

create table fragmentee (id int, nom char(50))
```

356

```
go

drop procedure sp_fragmentation
go

create procedure sp_fragmentation
as
        -- AUTHOR: LIONEL BOLNET
        -- ROLE: Create a fragmented table

        declare @i int
        declare @r real

        select @i = 0
        while @i < 5000
        begin
                select @r = rand()
                insert fragmented values (@i,
convert(char(50),@i))
                insert fragmentee values (10000 - @i,
convert(char(50),@i))
                insert fragmentee values (10000 - @i,
convert(char(50),@r))
                select @i = 1 + @i
        end

        select @i = 0
        while @i < 4000
        begin
                select @r = convert(int,floor(10000 * rand()))
                delete from fragmentee where id = @r + 17
                delete from fragmentee where id = @r + 9
                delete from fragmentee where id = @r + 3
                delete from fragmentee where id = @r + 1
                select @i = 1 + @i
        end
go
```

sp_help_frag

```
-- Assessing the fragmentation rate of a table
use sybsystemprocs
go

drop procedure sp_help_frag
go
```

```
create procedure sp_help_frag @nomtable varchar(50), @sample int
= 1000
as
        -- AUTHOR: LIONEL BOLNET
        -- ROLE: Evaluate the fragmentation rate of a table

        declare @requeter char(300)
        declare @tbltempo char(50)

        -- Creating a temporary sample table
        select @tbltempo = 'tempdb..T' + newid()
        select @requeter = 'select top ' +
convert(char(10),@echantillon) + ' * into ' + @tbltempo + ' lock
' + lockscheme(@nomtable) + ' from ' + @nomtable
        exec(@requeter)

        -- Play statistics on the sample table
        select @requeter = "update statistics" + @tbltempo
        exec(@requeter)

        -- Display analysis
        select convert(char(30),@nomtable) as "Table".
              ,
convert(float,row_count(db_id(),object_id(@nomtable))))) /
convert(float,data_pages(db_id(),object_id(@nomtable),0))) as
"Rows/page currently".
               , convert(float,row_count(2
,object_id(@tbltempo))))) / convert(float,data_pages(2
,object_id(@tbltempo),0))) as "Rows/page possible".

        -- Deletion of the temporary sample table
        exec('drop table '+@tbltempo)
go
```

sp_helpalias

```
-- Display all the aliases of a database
use sybsystemprocs
go

drop procedure sp_helpalias
go

create procedure sp_helpalias
as
```

```
-- AUTHOR: LIONEL BOLNET
-- ROLE: Display all the aliases of a database

select a.name as "Login", c.name as "User"
from master..syslogins a, sysalternates b, sysusers c
where a.suid=b.suid and b.altsuid=c.suid
order by a.name
go
```

sp_helpdevice2

```
-- Display devices as sp_helpdevice but less verbose
use sybsystemprocs
go

drop procedure sp_helpdevice2
go

create procedure sp_helpdevice2
as
        -- AUTHOR: LIONEL BOLNET
        -- ROLE: Display devices as sp_helpdevice but less
verbose

        declare @coef int
        select @coef = 1024*1024/@@maxpagesize

        select    d.name, min(d.high + 1)/@coef total,
sum(isnull(u.size,0))/@coef used, min(d.high + 1)/@coef -
sum(isnull(u.size,0))/@coef free
        from      master..sysdevices d left join
master..sysusages u
        on        u.vdevno = d.vdevno
        group by d.name
        order by d.name
go
```

sp_helplogin

```
-- Show all logins or the password of a login
use sybsystemprocs
go

drop procedure sp_helplogin
```

```
go

create procedure sp_helplogin @name char(100) = """.
as
        -- AUTHOR: LIONEL BOLNET
        -- ROLE: Display all logins or the password of a login

        if @name = """
                select suid, name from master..syslogins order by
suid
        else
                select suid, name, password, dbname from
master..syslogins where name = @name
go
```

sp_io

```
-- Determine if a session is doing physical I/O
use sybsystemprocs
go

drop procedure sp_io
go

create procedure sp_io @spid int = 0
as
        -- AUTHOR: LIONEL BOLNET
        -- ROLE: Determine if a session is doing physical I/O

        -- First statement
        select spid, physical_io into #PREM from
master..sysprocesses

        -- Waiting
        waitfor delay '00:00:10'.

        -- Second statement
        select spid, physical_io into #DEUX from
master..sysprocesses

        -- Joint
        if @spid = 0
                select A.spid, abs(6*(A.physical_io -
B.physical_io)) as IO_par_minute from #PREM A, #DEUX B where
A.spid = B.spid order by IO_par_minute
        else
```

```
          select A.spid, abs(6*(A.physical_io -
B.physical_io)) as IO_par_minute from #PREM A, #DEUX B where
A.spid = B.spid and B.spid = @spid
go
```

sp_kill

```
-- Display all the information about a spid and then the killer
use sybsystemprocs
go

drop procedure sp_kill
go

create procedure sp_kill @spid int
as
        -- AUTHOR: LIONEL BOLNET
        -- ROLE    killer

        declare @spid2 varchar(10)
        declare @spid3 varchar(30)
        select @spid2 = convert(varchar(10),@spid)
        select @spid3 = "kill" + @spid2
        dbcc traceon(3604)
        dbcc sqltext(@spid)
        dbcc traceoff(3604)
        select * from master..sysprocesses where spid = @spid
        exec sp_showplan @spid
        exec sp_who @spid2
        exec(@spid3)
        select @spid3 = @spid3 + " with statusonly
        exec(@spid3)
go
```

sp_kill_all

```
-- Kill all the users of a database
use sybsystemprocs
go

drop procedure sp_kill_all
go

create procedure sp_kill_all @database varchar(50)
```

361

```
as
        -- AUTHOR: LIONEL BOLNET
        -- ROLE    Kill all users of a database

        print "Massive Kill of the users of the base %1!",
@database

        declare @order varchar(200)
        select "kill " + convert(varchar(10),spid) as commande
                        into #TMP1
                        from master..sysprocesses
                        where spid<>@@spid and
dbid=db_id(@database)

        declare c cursor for select commande from #TMP1 for read
only
        open c
        fetch c into @order
        while (@@sqlstatus <> 2)
        begin
                print @order
                exec(@order)
                fetch c into @order
        end
        close c
        deallocate cursor c
go
```

sp_list_indexes

```
-- Display the list of indexes in the database
use sybsystemprocs
go

drop procedure sp_list_indexes
go

create procedure sp_list_indexes
as
        -- AUTHOR: LIONEL BOLNET
        -- ROLE: Display the list of indexes in the
database
```

362

```
      select a.name as "tablename", b.name as
"indexname"
      into    #temporary
      from    sysobjects a, sysindexes b
      where a.id = b.id and a.type = 'U' and b.indid
<> 0 and b.indid <> 255
      order by a.name, b.name

      exec sp_autoformat "#temporary
go
```

sp_purge

```
-- Purge a table without risking to fill the
logsegment
use sybsystemprocs
go

drop procedure sp_purge
go

create procedure sp_purge @table varchar(100),
@size int = 100
as
      -- AUTHOR: LIONEL BOLNET
      -- ROLE: Purge a table without risking to fill
the logsegment

      set nocount on
      declare @rowco int
      declare @total int
      select @rowco = 1
      select @total = 0
      set rowcount @size
      while (@rowco <> 0)
      begin
```

```
            select
convert(char(25),getdate())+convert(varchar(10),@to
tal)+' deleted rows.'
            exec("delete from " + @table)
            select @rowco = @@rowcount
            select @total = @total + @rowco
        end
        set nocount off
        set rowcount 0
go
```

sp_query

```
-- Display the text of a query
use sybsystemprocs
go

drop procedure sp_query
go

create procedure sp_query @spid int
as
        -- AUTHOR: LIONEL BOLNET
        -- ROLE: Display the text of a query

        dbcc traceon(3604)
        dbcc sqltext(@spid)
        dbcc traceoff(3604)
go
```

sp_rowmove

```
-- Moving some rows from one table to another
without filling the log or data segments
use sybsystemprocs
go
```

```
drop procedure sp_rowmove
go

create procedure sp_rowmove @table_source
varchar(50), @table_destination varchar(50),
@cleprimaire varchar(50), @where varchar(50) =
"1=1", @taillepaquet varchar(7) = "100"
as
      -- AUTHOR: LIONEL BOLNET
      -- ROLE: Move some rows from one table to
another without filling the log or data segments

      -- Declaration

      declare @nbligns int
      declare @nbtotal int
      declare @progres varchar(100)
      select @nbligns = 1
      select @nbtotal = 0

      -- Loop
      while(@nbligns <> 0)
      begin

            -- Explain
            select @progres =
convert(varchar(20),getdate(),16) + ": " +
convert(varchar(20),@nbtotal) + " lignes
deplacees."
            print @progress

            -- Copy
            exec("INSERT INTO " + @table_destination
+ " SELECT TOP " + @sizepackage + " * FROM " +
@table_source + " WHERE " + @where)

            -- Delete
```

```
            exec("DELETE FROM " + @table_source + "
WHERE " + @primary + " IN (SELECT " + @primary + "
FROM " + @table_destination + ")")

            -- Counting
            select @nbligns = @@rowcount
            select @nbtotal = @nbligns + @nbtotal

      -- End of loop
      end
go
```

sp_stats_date

```
-- Display the date of the table statistics
use sybsystemprocs
go

drop procedure sp_stats_date
go

create procedur sp_stats_date @tablename
varchar(255) = """.
as
      -- AUTHOR: LIONEL BOLNET
      -- ROLE: Display the date of the table
statistics

      if @tablename = """.
            begin
            select name, statmoddate into
#temporaire1 from systabstats a, sysobjects b where
a.id=b.id and b.type='U' order by 2
            exec sp_autoformat "#temporary1
            end
      else
            begin
```

```
          select name, statmoddate into
#temporaire2 from systabstats a, sysobjects b where
a.id=b.id and b.name=@tablename
          exec sp_autoformat "#temporary2".
          select moddate into #temporaire3 from
sysstatistics where id = object_id( @tablename )
order by 1
          exec sp_autoformat "#temporary3
          end
go
```

sp_status

```
-- Display 23 essential information about the
instance
use sybsystemprocs
go

drop procedure sp_status
go

create procedure sp_status
as
      -- AUTHOR: LIONEL BOLNET
      -- ROLE: Display 23 essential information
about the instance

      -- Introduction
      set nocount on
      create table #temporary (COL1 char(20), COL2
char(60))

      -- Writing
      insert into #temporaire values
("Login/User/Spid",suser_name()+" / "+user_name()+"
/ "+convert(varchar(5),@@spid))

      -- Display
```

```
select COL1 as YOU, COL2 as "" from #temporary
truncate table #temporary
print ""

-- Writing
insert into #temporary values
("Name",@@servername)
insert into #temporary values
("Version",@@version)
insert into #temporary values
("Errorlog",@@errorlog)
insert into #temporary values ("Page
size",convert(char(60),@@maxpagesize))
if @@version_number >= 15700
  exec('insert into #temporary values ("Kernel
mode",@@kernelmode)')
else
  insert into #temporary values ("Kernel mode",
"No kernel mode for this version")

-- Display
select COL1 as INSTANCE, COL2 as "" from
#temporaire
truncate table #temporary
print ""

-- Writing
insert into #temporaire select "Creation",
convert(char(60),crdate) from master..sysdatabases
where name = "master"
insert into #temporaire select "Upgrade" ,
convert(char(60),crdate) from master..sysobjects
where name = "sp_dboption"
insert into #temporary values
("Startup",convert(char(60),@@boottime))

-- Display
```

```
      select COL1 as EVENTS, COL2 as "" from
#temporary
      truncate table #temporary
      print ""

      -- Writing
      insert into #temporaire select "Max memory",
convert(varchar(60),value) + " (" +
convert(varchar(60),2*value/1024) + " Mo)" from
master..sysconfigures where comment = "max memory"
      insert into #temporary select "Number of
engines" , convert(char(60),count(1)) from
master..sysengines

      -- Display
      select COL1 as CONFIGURATION, COL2 as "" from
#temporary
      truncate table #temporary
      print ""

      -- Writing
      insert into #temporaire select "Total",
convert(char(60),count(1)) from
master..sysprocesses
      insert into #temporaire select "Utilisateurs",
convert(char(60),count(1)) from
master..sysprocesses where suid <> 0
      insert into #temporaire select "Bloquees",
convert(char(60),count(1)) from
master..sysprocesses where blocked <> 0
      insert into #temporaire select "Log suspend",
convert(char(60),count(1)) from
master..sysprocesses where cmd = 'LOG SUSPEND'
      insert into #temporaire select "Transactions",
convert(char(60),count(1)) from
master..systransactions where spid <> @@spid

      -- Display
```

```
      select COL1 as SESSIONS, COL2 as "" from
#temporary
      truncate table #temporary
      print ""

      -- Writing
      insert into #temporaire select "Listener",
convert(char(60),address_info) from
master..syslisteners

      -- Display
      select COL1 as ECOUTE, COL2 as "" from
#temporaire
      truncate table #temporary
      print ""

      -- Writing
      insert into #temporary select
                              case when
name=db_name() then " Vous etes dans" else "" end+
                              case when
status&32<>0 or status&256<>0 or status2&16<>0 or
status2&32<>0 or status2&128<>0 then "Offline" else
"" end,

      convert(char(60),name)
                                         from
master..sysdatabases order by name

      -- Display
      select COL1 as DATABASES, COL2 as "" from
#temporaire
      truncate table #temporary
      print ""

      -- Writing
      insert into #temporaire select
convert(char(20),cmd), db_name(dbid) from
```

```
master..sysprocesses where cmd like 'DUMP%' or cmd
like 'LOAD%' or cmd like 'ONLI%'

        -- Display
        select COL1 as DUMP_OU_LOAD, COL2 as "" from
#temporaire
        truncate table #temporary
        print ""

        -- Conclusion
        drop table #temporary
        set nocount off
go
```

sp_sizeable

```
-- Display tables in order of size
use sybsystemprocs
go

drop procedure sp_sizes
go

create procedure sp_sizes
as
        -- AUTHOR: LIONEL BOLNET
        -- ROLE: Display tables in order of size

        select data_pages(db_id(),id) as "nb_pages",
data_pages(db_id(),id)*(@@maxpagesize/1024)/1024 as "Mo",
data_pages(db_id(),id)*(@@maxpagesize/1024)/1024/1024 as "Go",
name as "Table_name"
        into #temporaire from sysobjects where type='U' order by
1

        exec sp_autoformat "#temporary"
go
```

sp_thresholdaction

```
-- Empty the transaction log when the threshold is triggered
```

```
use sybsystemprocs
go

drop procedure sp_thresholdaction
go

create procedure sp_thresholdaction
as
        -- AUTHOR: LIONEL BOLNET
        -- ROLE: Empty the transaction log on threshold
triggering

        declare @order varchar(200)
        select @commande = "dump tran " + db_name() + " with
truncate_only"
        print @order
        exec(@order)
go
```

sp_who_group

```
-- Display the number of processes by grouping by various
criteria
use sybsystemprocs
go

drop procedure sp_who_group
go

create procedure sp_who_group @type int = 1
as
        -- AUTHOR: LIONEL BOLNET
        -- ROLE   by grouping by various criteria.

        if @type = 1
        begin
                select l.name as login, count(*) as nb_process
                from    master..sysprocesses p left join
master..syslogins l
                on      p.suid=l.suid
                group   by l.name
                order   by 2
                compute sum(count(*))
        end
        else if @type = 2
        begin
```

```
                select program_name as program, count(*) as
nb_process
                from    master..sysprocesses
                group by program_name
                order by 2
                compute sum(count(*))
        end
        else if @type = 3
        begin
                select cmd as command, count(*) as nb_process
                from    master..sysprocesses
                group by cmd order by 2
                compute sum(count(*))
        end
        else if @type = 4
        begin
                select hostname as host, count(*) as nb_process
                from    master..sysprocesses
                group by hostname
                order by 2
                compute sum(count(*))
        end
        else if @type = 5
        begin
                select db_name(dbid) as "database", count(*) as
nb_process
                from    master..sysprocesses
                group by db_name(dbid) order by 2
                compute sum(count(*))
        end
        else if @type = 6
        begin
                select convert(char(20),loggedindatetime,102) as
conndate, count(*) as nb_process
                from    master..sysprocesses
                group by convert(char(20),loggedindatetime,102)
order by 2
                compute sum(count(*))
        end
        else
        begin
                print "1 = group by login
                print "2 = group by program
                print "3 = group by command"
                print "4 = group by hostname
                print "5 = group by database
                print "6 = group by conndate
        end
```

```
go
```

sp_who_tempdb

```
-- Display the number of tempdb pages occupied by each session
use sybsystemprocs
go

drop procedure sp_who_tempdb
go

create procedure sp_who_tempdb
as
        -- AUTHOR: LIONEL BOLNET
        -- ROLE: Display the number of tempdb pages occupied by
each session

        select spid, convert(int,pssinfo(spid,"tempdb_pages"))
nb_pages_tempdb
        from    master..sysprocesses
        where convert(int,pssinfo(spid,"tempdb_pages")) > 0
        order by 2
go
```

sp_who2

```
-- Display the list of processes except mine and those of the
system
use sybsystemprocs
go

drop procedure sp_who2
go

create procedure sp_who2 @spid int = 0
as
        -- AUTHOR: LIONEL BOLNET
        -- ROLE: Display the list of processes except mine and
those of the system

        if @spid = 0
        begin
                select a.spid, suser_name(a.suid) loginame,
a.status, a.cmd, count(b.state) opentran, db_name(a.dbid)
```

```
        dbname, a.hostname, a.program_name programname, a.clientname,
        a.blocked blk_spid, a.loggedindatetime
                into #temporaryA
                from master..sysprocesses a left join
master..systransactions b
                on a.spid = b.spid
                where a.suid <> 0 and a.spid <> @@spid
                group by a.spid
                order by a.status, a.suid

                exec sp_autoformat "#temporaryA
        end
        else
        begin
                select a.spid, suser_name(a.suid) loginame,
a.status, a.cmd, count(b.state) opentran, db_name(a.dbid)
dbname, a.hostname, a.program_name programname, a.clientname,
        a.blocked blk_spid, a.loggedindatetime
                into #temporaryB
                from master..sysprocesses a left join
master..systransactions b
                on a.spid = b.spid
                where a.spid = @spid
                group by a.spid

                exec sp_autoformat "#temporaryB
        end
go
```

sp_who2_loop

```
-- Display a looped sp_who2
use sybsystemprocs
go

drop procedure sp_who2_loop
go

create procedure sp_who2_loop @spid int, @number_of_turns int =
5
as
        -- AUTHOR: LIONEL BOLNET
        -- ROLE: Display a sp_who2 in a loop

        declare @i int
        select @i = 0
```

375

```
        while @i < @number_of_turns
        begin

                select getdate() heure, a.spid, suser_name(a.suid)
loginame, a.status, a.cmd, count(b.state) opentran,
db_name(a.dbid) dbname, a.hostname, a.program_name programname,
a.clientname,  a.blocked blk_spid, a.loggedindatetime
                into #temporaire from master..sysprocesses a left
join master..systransactions b
                on a.spid = b.spid
                where a.spid = @spid
                group by a.spid

                exec sp_autoformat "#temporary

                drop table #temporary

                waitfor delay "00:00:05"

                select @i = @i + 1
        end
go
```

Thanks

Pascal Rougeaux, DBA Sybase

Silvère Massuet, DBA Sybase